How to Sell
to the Government

D1599952

How to Sell to the Government

The 30 Billion Dollar Market

**Your Complete Guide to Doing Business
with Canadian Government Departments, Agencies and
Crown Corporations, and Cracking the Provincial and
U.S. Government Markets**

Hawley Black

Macmillan of Canada
A Division of Canada Publishing Corporation
Toronto, Ontario, Canada

To Venere and Reta
Who Make It All Possible

Canadian Cataloguing in Publication Data

Black, Hawley L.
  How to sell to the government

Includes index.

ISBN 0-7715-9947-1/Casebound
ISBN 0-7715-9923-4/Paperback

1. Government purchasing—Canada. 2 Public contracts—Canada. 3. Government purchasing— United States. I. Title.

JL186.B53 1989   354.710071'2   C88-095204-0

Designed by Craig Allen

MACMILLAN OF CANADA
A Division of Canada Publishing Corporation
Toronto, Ontario, Canada

Printed in Canada

Acknowledgements

No book of this scope could have been written without a great deal of information and support from a number of individuals and organizations inside and outside of government.

Foremost, I would like to thank Jeanne Kaufman of the national accounting and management consulting firm Deloitte, Haskins and Sells/Samson Belair for her constant help, encouragement, and ideas on this book. My thanks, too, to Bert Kaufman for his input. Peggy Edwards deJourdan and Sharon Irven also deserve my appreciation for their support.

The idea for a book which looks at *all* federal procurement came from interviews for magazine articles I conducted a couple of years ago with then SSC minister and now minister of Consumer and Corporate Affairs, the Hon. Harvie Andre, and Raymond V. Hession, then deputy minister of Supply and Services. I would like to express my appreciation to a number of individuals and units at SSC. These include: deputy minister Georgina Wyman, Sami Sourani's fine statistical analyses, the headquarters directorates and regional offices who have helped me so much, and former assistant deputy ministers Robert Emond and Art Bailey.

Other key Canadian departments or agencies and some of the key individuals in them who deserve special thanks include: Max Reid and Al Kilpatrick at External Affairs Canada; at the Department of National Defence and the Canadian Armed Forces, the Hon. Perrin Beatty and the staff of its Directorate-General of Information; and the Department of Industry, Science and Technology, notably, its Small Business Office.

The effort and support of Richard Woods, formerly the SBO's director-general and now with the Western Diversification Office, and David Arenburg of the SBO Secretariat were vital to this project. Alex Alberani was also most supportive.

At the National Research Council, I would like to single out vice-presidents Keith Glegg and Dr. Clive Willis for their help.

I would like to thank the Treasury Board; the Privy Council Office; the Canadian Commercial Corporation, the Export Development Corporation and the Canadian International Development Agency, and a number of other departments, ministries, agencies and Crown corporations, and the U.S. departments of Commerce and Defense.

Among Canadian national associations which have provided assistance are: the Canadian Institute of Chartered Accountants, the Canadian Bar Association, the Aerospace Industries Association of Canada, Electrical and Electronic Manufacturers Association of Canada, Canadian Maritime Association, Canadian Industrial Benefits Association, Canadian Federation of Independent Business, Institute of Public Administration, Purchasing Management Association of Canada, Investment Dealers Association of Canada, Canadian Business Press Association, Canadian Public Relations Society, International Association of Business Communicators, Canadian Exporters Association, and the Canadian Manufacturers' Association.

Consultants I would like to acknowledge include: Bill Lee, Al O'Brien, Leonard Knott, and David Eisenstadt, and many others who must remain unidentified for the moment. An exceedingly well informed and supportive individual has been Mike O'Brien, publisher of Maclean Hunter's *Aerospace and Defence Technology* and *The Wednesday Report*.

When Linda McKnight, now of Macmillan of Canada, suggested a decade ago that I write a book for her, neither of us had any idea that it would be this one. Thanks for waiting so long.

I also was fortunate to have as my editor at Macmillan Sheldon Fischer, whose suggestions were most appropriate.

In completing this book, I was indeed blessed with an absolutely superb research and editorial assistant in Calgary, Diane Jennens. Earlier on, Luba Fillipoff served as research assistant. I also should thank Barbara Gardner of the Southern Alberta Institute of Technology of Calgary for her support, Cal Booth for his technical help with the computer part of this work, both in its Ottawa and its Calgary components, and Dr. Joel Birdwell for his help with software.

Contents

Introduction

We've all heard about the $600 toilet seats and the $300 screwdrivers that some governments buy. While these purchases may make us doubt that we've been getting fair value for our taxes, they also hint at the profitability of doing business with the government. In Canada, government is *very big business*.

Canadian governments together with all of their entities this year will spend some $90 billion just to buy goods and services, and that figure is going up. Indeed, just several years ago the total came to only $73 billion, according to a federal-provincial study.

In comparison, the 1983 procurement budget for General Motors came to $3.18 billion; for Imperial Oil $1.70 billion; for Zellers $1.28 billion; for Shell Canada $1.18 billion; and for Chrysler Canada $.80 billion, according to the June 1985 edition of *The Magazine That's All About Small Business.* In other words, Canadian governments deliver the purchasing clout of 22 GMs.

As a business journalist and a consultant to business, I find the most common problem in selling to government is just getting a handle on it. "It" in this case is composed of 23,000 federal, provincial, or municipal departments, agencies, commissions, boards, Crown corporations, universities, hospitals, and institutions.

Ottawa itself presents the outsider with a large, complex and intimidating procurement bureaucracy. So big is Ottawa's supply need that it spends $2 billion and 23,000 person-years annually simply to *run* the supply system. And although the Canadian procurement system is more centralized than in the U.S., there are still many confusing government organizations involved in the process.

This book demystifies the government world. It puts basic, and essential, non-secret information usually available only to civil servants and government consultants into your hands so that you can market your goods and services to the largest and the most centralized of these governmental entities: the Canadian federal government and its creatures. *How to Sell to the Government* is your roadmap to these markets, and to the lucrative provincial and U.S. government markets.

This book gives you a big jump on your competition, and can save you thousands of dollars in research and consulting expenses or in costly trial-and-error attempts to approach government buyers. It puts the essential information together, helps you to understand the rules of the procurement game and the players involved, and shows you how to develop a comprehensive marketing strategy. It's a book you will want to consult again and again.

I've concentrated on the federal government for several reasons. This year, that government (exclusive of its crown corporations) will pay some 80,000 suppliers $15 billion for goods and services just to keep its own operations going. In addition, some 147 Crown corporations will spend upwards of another $15 billion. Together, these two components account for one-third of the procurement budgets for the entire Canadian public sector.

However, those 80,000 suppliers referred to represent only a fraction of the 1.5 million businesses in Canada. A great many Canadian businesses are prevented from breaking into these markets, largely because of their lack of know-how. Despite the vast sums spent by federal agencies and departments, relatively few businessmen and -women know much about this immense market or how to sell to it, judging from repeated surveys of businesses, Members of Parliament, and the public. When government, somewhat sporadically, does talk to suppliers, its words sound like dull self-serving departmental propaganda, or a pretentious message from God. In both cases, they are usually ignored.

Rarely do government supply guides or officials use clear, simple English (or French, for that matter). Less often still does a publication or speaker tell you what products are bought across the entire expanse of government departments, who the important buyers are, or where to find them. Unfortunately for you, successfully selling to Ottawa means constantly learning and relearning how to win government contracts, who to approach, and where to collect basic data on the procurement system. Getting on the government "list" becomes a depressing, almost full-time job. It doesn't have to be.

Of course, all this reticence in some agencies is a boon to the consulting business. My years of experience have shown me that that's exactly what ninety per cent of new potential suppliers to government want: basic information on how the procurement system works, who the purchasing departments or agencies are, how to get listed with them, and who to contact in each agency or department. Some Ottawa consultants and newsletter publishers earn a very good living simply by providing clients with this routine information on a retainer or fee basis, much of it taken out of publications listed in this book.

In fact, my main aim in writing this book is to give you the same basic information that federal insiders have at their fingertips, so that you can make a "go" or "no go" decision quickly and move on rapidly to the important proposal, promotional or marketing strategies for your chosen targets, that mark you as a serious bidder or supplier. I believe you are your own best government-relations expert, and you can do the job well, given the facts, and perhaps some expert help at key stages. I also hope to give the better companies, individuals, and products, not just the better-connected ones, a fair chance at government procurement dollars.

While government financial support for this book was offered, I made a conscious decision not to accept any public funds. So I owe no debts to any government official, agency or politician. That makes this book and this advice uniquely impartial. It also makes my national seminars on how to sell to the government especially useful in keeping you up-to-date on the latest news in procurement plans, personnel changes, phone numbers and markets.

This book also means that if you talk to a government-relations or procurement consultant or an official or politician, you will be reasonably well-informed and working from the same knowledge base he or she is; in some cases your knowledge will be the greater of the two. So, using the insider material presented here, you can make a lot of important choices before approaching the government. That informed position of strength is essential when marketing to government.

In putting this book together, every effort was made to see that up-to-date names, addresses, and phone numbers were included. However, government staff and phone numbers change often, and the book publishing process takes several months. So be prepared to seek out new contacts in your targeted department or corporation and add them to your resource list. Whatever the minor changes, this book sets you squarely on the way to meeting what may become your newest and largest business client: the federal government.

CHAPTER ONE

The Buyers, The Sellers, and the Market – An Overview

Canada's Public Sector – A Giant Market

There's a very large and—according to some—spendthrift buyer out there. "It" spends more by far than even the largest corporation in the Canadian market purchasing goods and services, and some of its many subdivisions alone spend in excess of $10 billion a year. It prefers Canadian or North American suppliers, has an AAA credit rating, and pays on time. Once you're in the door, repeat customers are easy to maintain and quite profitable.

I am talking, of course, about the biggest business in Canada: the government. According to a 1988 federal-provincial study called *Canadian Public Sector Market,** Canadian federal, provincial, and municipal governments and the businesses they own spent $73 billion in 1983. They will spend around $90 this year.

Government expenditures cover a wide variety of products and services: office equipment, data-processing equipment, basketballs and hockey sticks, printing, photography, footwear, bulldozers, tractors, all-terrain vehicles, petroleum products, engineering, ships, planes, cleaning services, typing services,

---

* All government booklets, brochures, directories, and other publications mentioned throughout the text are listed in the subsection in Chapter 8 entitled "The Government As Publisher".

1

accounting services, carpentry, fine and performing arts, and a horde of other materials, supplies, machines and services.

In fact, there is virtually nothing offered in the marketplace that federal departments, Crown agencies or corporations do not buy, as you will see in the lists in Appendix I at the end of this chapter. Indeed,Ottawa's largest central purchasing agent, Supply and Services Canada (SSC), lists 17,000 goods and services that it buys for departments and agencies. These range from destroyers to rowboats and canoes; from advanced jet aircraft to bicycles and paper clips; from divots to divans.

Goods that the federal government require include all forms of food, drugs, and clothing and just about everything that is required to equip an office. Anything that you can conceive of in the mechanical, electrical, and electronic field is included: computers, generators, agricultural, and industrial machinery as well as nails, screws, nuts and bolts.

In the service area the government looks for movers, aerial surveys, snow removal, graphic arts, editing, cleaning services, security services, bus, ship, and air transportation. Almost every area of social, human, and physical scientific research and development falls within a federal department's or agency's area of responsibility for contracting.

The *Public Sector Market* study estimated that on any given day Canadian governmental agencies were spending $20 million on services and goods. Or to put it another way, that's around $10,000 for every one of Canada's 750,000 small businesses. In fact, in a very real way, SSC and departmental buying-agents represent a market which, successfully tapped, can assist Canadian firms to increase their business volume both domestically and abroad. However, in order to succeed in Ottawa, you must be highly competitive in terms of quality, price, delivery, and customer support. You will find some major opportunities, but you will also find eager and highly professional competitors.

Despite these golden opportunities, many ordinary individuals and small companies are wary of approaching this market. They cite their lack of inside knowledge and experience, or frustration with red tape, and small profit margins. Or they complain that it is just too difficult to get started in the immense Canadian public-sector market, that they don't have any "pull", or that it's just for the big corporations. And, despite the vast sums spent by federal agencies and departments to persuade businesses to offer their services or goods to the government, relatively few Canadian and U.S. businessmen and -women take advantage of this vast market.

Still, self-employed individuals and small- and medium-sized firms manage to win some business, despite a widely-held belief that only large corporations can do business with the government.

This book was written to remedy those problems. Its single purpose is to show *you* how to access this market. To sell to the federal government market you need to know who does the buying for Ottawa, how the government buys and the special language of public-sector procurement, and you need to look at the entire spectrum of government buying. I hope to show you that whatever your line of business, and whatever the size of your business, it is possible for you to get a piece of the action.

Governments buy goods and services for many of the same reasons that businesses do. Governments and their enterprises buy in order to serve their clients or "customers" (that is, the citizens of the land) and to survive and grow. In our society, governments provide citizens with hospitals, schools, roads, housing, food, defence, transportation, energy, and thousands of other items. In almost every case, governments are only the broker, and they rely on the private sector to directly provide the goods and services they need to deliver their programs.

Let's take a closer look at who spends all this money and where it goes. One-third of all domestic public-sector dollars are spent in Ontario; one in five goes to Québec firms; 13.5 per cent to Alberta; 10.4 per cent to British Columbia; and 7.9 per cent to Saskatchewan businesses, with the remainder spread across the country. Almost half the money spent (48.7 per cent) goes to the service industry, followed by manufacturing (37.0 per cent), while primary industry gets 14.3 per cent. Domestic sources accounted for 84 per cent of the government's total expenditures.

Public-sector purchases of manufactured goods are concentrated in seven industries which got a total of $12.4 billion in

1983. In descending order of expenditures, they are refined petroleum and coal products; printing and publishing; aircraft and parts; other machinery and equipment; other electrical and electronic products; office, store and business machines; and communications and other electronic equipment. In each of these categories, over $1 billion was spent.

In the services sector, communications and other utilities account for $7.2 billion; transportation and storage, $4.7 billion; health and social service industries, $6.0 billion; and nine other industries together received $16.7 billion.

Now, who gets all this money? To whom do the contracts go? You may be surprised to learn that many are given to companies with fewer than 100 employees and/or $2 million in sales, that is to small businesses, according to SSC deputy minister Georgina Wyman. Indeed, many contracts go to very small firms and self-employed individuals.

So far I've been talking about "the government", as if it were one single entity. In fact, it's a complex set of markets.

The federal government alone is comprised of a host of different departments, agencies, commissions and semi-independent corporations of varying size, each subject to common government-wide rules, but made unique by its tasks and its structure. There are 30 or so federal departments; 12 provincial and territorial governments and their departments and offices; almost 16,000 educational institutions; close to 5,000 municipalities; 1,124 hospitals; over 800 business establishments owned by the three levels of government and presently 423 federal and provincial special funds. Each of these more than 23,000 institutions is a distinct market that determines its own requirements for goods and services.

You can see from this brief overview that there is a very large market in the public sector. And that market is your opportunity, if you can get a handle on it. To sell your goods and services in this huge, sprawling arena, your first and biggest challenge will be to find and access the various public sector segments in Canada. You've got to find a way to overcome the numbers and distances involved. This book can be your major tool in achieving the expertise to research and target this market with confidence. Many businesses have penetrated this market and been rewarded with increased prestige from government sales, and a discipline and network that has allowed them to leapfrog into the international marketplace.

Your Marketing Strategy

Hitting all, or a large number, of these governmental purchasers, or even finding them, would be a major marketing challenge for IBM or General Motors with pots of money and large marketing, service and research-and-development resources. So it may seem quite impossible to a smaller business. Yet, right now, you are probably serving a number of them already, indirectly. But whether or not that's the case, you can borrow a leaf from the Big Business marketing book either to break into this immense source of dollars, or expand your share if you are already there. The key is careful *target marketing*.

Target marketing is not mass marketing: it is not going after every single governmental entity. Rather it means going after every potential customer in the particular kind or category of market to which you want to appeal. For example, you might direct your efforts specifically at all the purchasing agents who buy high-tech products, or who hire construction workers, or towards all the entities who buy fine art, or just those who purchase laboratory equipment.

You attempt to match your particular products and strengths to the needs of a particular target sector ("place") in the market, and do this at the right time. You facilitate this match by good promotion, which can include personal selling, media advertising or other sales techniques; and by pegging your product at the right price. These four elements in your strategy—product, place, promotion, and price—are called the *marketing mix*.

The sheer number of governmental entities requires you to segment your large target market into smaller sub-markets. You might, in fact, develop several different strategies, one to sell to a large department, and another for use with smaller ones. Perhaps you could use one strategy for departments that are spread out across the country, and another for those that are concentrated in the capital. Or you could concentrate only on agencies or departments with a strong interest in research and development rather than production; or on those who frame policies and purchase in just one industry, say farming.

For each sub-market, you develop an appropriate marketing strategy. The strategy encompasses your view of what your firm will do in that market, your sales goals and capabilities; it is based on an analysis of the market, your resources, and the related marketing mix. In other words, your strategy states how, when and where you plan to "win the game". Strategy guides you in directing and concentrating your efforts towards profitable markets, rather than going after all of them at once in a helter-skelter fashion. You can waste a lot of time, effort, and money writing or talking to officials, so you want to make sure you are dealing only with those who fit in with your particular plan.

Tactics are the short-term plans you develop to implement the long-term goals. Let's assume you've decided to sell $100,000 worth of goods this year to each of the dozen biggest-spending departments in Ottawa; that's your goal. That strategic decision cuts out the other 30 departments: this year, you won't spend any time going after them. Tactically, you could then start by finding out who the biggest twelve are, and how to get on their list of prospective suppliers. Or you might begin by going after the two departments where you already know someone, and approach one new one each month, and so on.

Overall, then, your aim is to reach and sell to a significant number of those 23,000 organizations, at a reasonable cost to yourself. Your goal is simply to sell enough of your product at a fair price with minimal effort to make a good profit. You get the idea: sell to the better prospects without spinning your wheels. (See Chapter 9 for more discussion of marketing strategy and tactics.)

But there are still more ways of getting new public-sector markets for your business.

The Provinces and the Feds

In Canada municipal governments are creatures of the provinces and territories. So, to simplify, we can divide all 23,000 of our potential governmental buying-entities into two classes: they are either provincial or federal. In fact, your sales strategy definitely should target provincial and territorial governments, and their related agencies, since together they account for some forty per cent of Canadian public-sector expenditure.

While provinces and territories are significant buyers in their own right for your services or goods, there are also other good reasons for developing business connections. Frequently, provincial and territorial governments have a lot of information and influence on the sources of goods and services bought by their junior institutions. For example, a province might require that the hospitals or schools in its jurisdiction give preference to provincially-based firms in their purchasing. Furthermore, sometimes the province controls all purchasing for its schools, hospitals or correctional institutions through central procurement agencies.

And, of course, provincial purchasing budgets are generally larger than those of the third-level governments or individual institutions. If you are regionally based, you might want to target your closest federal, provincial, and municipal markets first.

On the down side, though, just listing the various provincial governmental and semi-governmental entities in Canada could have made this book the size of an encyclopedia. Instead, I have chosen to concentrate here on the really big fish, the smaller number of large and more centrally located buyers in the Canadian public-sector procurement world: the federal government, its departments, agencies and Crown corporations, who together account for thirty-five per cent of Canadian government procurement, some $30 billion a year.

However, to help you establish or broaden your contacts with provincial and territorial governments, through whom you can research their own needs and those of their municipal entities, and hone your submission to Ottawa, you will find a list of key provincial procurement contacts in Appendix III of this chapter.

Many firms who sell a great deal to government cover themselves and minimize their chance of being "captured" by one governmental entity by selling to another level of government, or to foreign governments. Some companies also try to diversify across various government bodies at the same level of government. Whatever your strategy, you've got to start somewhere.

But you will probably find that if you are dealing with the provinces, you may be able to get them to help you sell to the feds, or at least get the paperwork done or contact the right individuals; and the opposite is equally true.

Just a few hundred federal entities spend about one-third of the public-sector total. Comparatively, then, the feds are relatively convenient targets and are well-off financially. And as already mentioned, building a base at the federal level is useful in another way. Your work there can make you more marketable to the provinces: it can be a sort of "Good Housekeeping Seal of Approval". If you know which ones these are and who to contact, you can be well on your way to selling to the feds, and to broadening your base through sales to the provinces.

Why You Should Deal with the Feds

By any standards, the 40 or so Canadian federal-government departments and the 150 or so federal Crown or government-owned corporations and various independent agencies, which employ some 800,000 individuals, are a very big market—worth a whopping $30 billion a year.

While the feds are very worthwhile customers themselves, that government's influence over public-sector procurement goes far beyond Ottawa. Ottawa's tremendous financial resources and its national legislative powers give it strong moral or political influence on provincial and, in turn, local government spending and purchasing.

In addition to subsidizing suppliers to government through various incentive programs such as the Western Diversification Office, the Atlantic Canada Opportunities Agency, or the Department of Regional Industrial Expansion (DRIE)*, Ottawa also lends the provinces a hand through bulk purchases. This is

---

*   As this book went to press, there were some indications that DRIE and the Ministry of State for Science and Technology (MOSST) might be merged to form a new department to be called either the Department of Industry, Science and Technology (DIST), or ISTC (Industry, Science, Technology Canada). Since this possible merging, and the name to be used, were not certain, however, the old names have been used here.

designed to reduce unit costs and to help Canadian industries achieve economy of scale in their production runs.

Recent examples of joint federal-provincial procurements include a purchase of 29 Canadair CL-215 waterbombers; bulk drug procurements for vaccines and high-dollar-value drugs for the provincial health programs; bulk buying of heating oil for the Ontario government; and bulk purchase of educational supplies.

Federal-provincial procurement likely will become even more significant in the future. Indeed, some provinces now share "sourcing information" or suppliers lists with the feds. The November 1987 *Report on Public Sector Procurement Initiatives* by the federal, provincial, and territorial procurement ministers called for "greater information sharing among jurisdictions on sources of supply", including the issue of a *Practical Guide to Government Procurement in Canada*. This book, it is hoped, will help this useful initiative.

As well, some provincial governments from time to time tend to follow federal policy and practices. Thus, the word "ministry" and the "minister of state" position in the Cabinet have spread from Ottawa to some provinces, and the idea of a department of "supply and services" reached provincial capitals. So, today's federal procurement structure, priorities, projects and methods of funding often signal the shape of provincial ones tomorrow.

To market really well at the provincial level in Canada, then, you need to know how the federal procurement bureaucracy operates, who runs it, how to access it, and what are its favourite buzzwords, alphabet soup, and panaceas. You also should realize that the federal public sector is still expanding, despite some strong efforts on the part of the Progressive Conservative government to cut spending. Indeed, there is some evidence to show that freezes in federal hiring and person-years simply result in greater use of and higher fees for outside firms, especially in the services sector.

Some of this increase in spending comes from new Tory perspectives on issues like Canadian defence. In that area, defence minister Perrin Beatty has even managed to table a *Defence White Paper*, some two decades after the last one. Beatty is determined to see that Canadian defence policy and procurement is "policy driven, not formula driven". His view implies that government will be making significant new purchases for the Canadian military in the future.

Part of this is a catch-up effort after years of neglect under preceding governments. According to a former senior procurement officer in the Department of National Defence (DND), DND should have been replacing about five per cent of its total capital inventory each year to maintain a constant level of capability. However, it has not been able to do this. So for fifteen years ships, planes, trucks, weapons, and other capital equipment have been deteriorating without being replaced. This has meant the Canadian Armed Forces (CAF) have had to cannibalize much of their equipment to keep some of it in operation.

For example, three of the Canadian navy's current twenty-three "active" destroyers have been stripped to keep the others afloat, and sixteen are antiques by naval standards. In essence, the much touted order of six new Canadian patrol frigates will simply replace six of these veterans still in service by 1990. Brand new Aurora long-range patrol aircraft have been confined to hangars for parts to keep their sister planes in the air.

Ottawa's penchant for using procurement to promote social and economic objectives through pet programs such as "industrial benefits" or "world product mandates" has increased the costs and delayed the delivery dates of the items. Thus Ottawa will pay $1,314 (Can.) to buy a Canadian-made copy of the U.S. M-16 automatic rifle which it could have bought from the Americans at $660 per weapon—only to find that its specified ammunition does not work. Similarly, Canada could easily have bought six frigates at much lower unit costs and with an earlier delivery date from foreign suppliers than would have been possible from Canadian suppliers and then spent the savings on job creation, military pay, other weapons, or elsewhere.

Overall, though, Supply and Services Canada (SSC) officials argue that the "buy Canadian" policies mean Canadian tax dollars that otherwise would have gone offshore are kept at home. Federal spending mounts, and Ottawa never seems to move far from the bedrooms and the boardrooms of the nation. As

William Stanbury, a University of British Columbia professor of regulatory studies, notes, Canadian business is still greatly over-regulated. As well, he points out, the federal government has its own enterprises, such as Air Canada and the CNR, which compete within the private sector. Quite aside from the favouritism that this sometimes leads to, it also means that Ottawa must often subsidize these operations; and, overall, Crown-enterprise bureaucrats usually manage to expand their empires. So the federal purchasing pot is likely to remain healthy. We will look at some of these big spenders in detail in Chapter 6.

Another reason for cultivating the feds is that the existing General Agreement of Tariffs and Trade (GATT) opens up a potential $40-billion-a-year international public-sector market to Canadian firms. GATT countries include the U.S., the United Kingdom, most West European and Scandinavian countries, Japan, Hong Kong, and Singapore. As you will see in Chapter 5, the feds are your gateway to these markets.

Needless to say, the PC's proposed free-trade deal with the United States would also open up vast U.S. public-sector markets to Canadian businesses. At present, one defence analyst estimates Canadian firms are treated as domestic U.S. firms only on some $15- to $20-billion-worth of United States defence contracts—less than the size of the Canadian federal purchasing budget, or about the size of the Province of Québec's budget. In practice, Canadian firms get about ten to twenty per cent of this.

Finally, as you will see in Chapter 5, other governmental markets are opened by the Crown-controlled Canadian International Development Agency (CIDA), the Canadian Commercial Corporation (CCC), and the Export Development Corporation (EDC).

From a strategic point of view, perhaps the most important reason for cultivating the federal government is that compared to some provinces, and to the U.S. government which has 4,500 purchasing offices, the federal purchasing bureaucracy is much more centralized into two super agencies: Supply and Services Canada (SSC) and its construction and building sister, Public

Works Canada (PWC). This makes Ottawa an attractive, easy target for private-sector suppliers.

Even then, getting on SSC's or PWC's lists is only one path to Ottawa's dollars. You also could do an end-run around the SSC system. Indeed, in March 1986 various individual departments spent $12 million on their own on personal service contracts which do not come under SSC. That's $150 million a year for opinion-giving, typing, translation, cooking, and other services, on a departmental official's signature.

Before looking at the details of federal procurement practices which will take up the next few chapters, I'd like to dispel a few myths about the arena of government-business interaction.

Old Wives' Tales About Federal Procurement

The System Favours Big Firms

As many small businesses see it, the federal procurement system is skewed in favour of large companies. SSC officials deny this. They quickly point out that overall, some thirty per cent of all contracts by value administered by SSC are let to small businesses or to individuals: that comes to $2 billion a year. Generally, Ottawa counts as small businesses those enterprises with fewer than 100 employees in the manufacturing sector, and fewer than 50 employees in other sectors, usually with sales of less than $2 million a year.

To look at it in another way: 80.6 per cent of all contractual documents went through regional offices, though these account for only 19.4 per cent of value. What this means, says Eric Shelton, vice-president of Nova and the chairman of the $3.7 million federal task force on government procurement, is that sometimes "it seems that everyone gets a bit of the pie but no one is very viable."

The SSC report *Contracting Statistics* reveals that in 1986-87 nearly two-thirds of SSC contracts were worth less than $2,500 each. These accounted for only 4.71 per cent of dollars spent. Only one-fifth of one per cent of the 294,000 contracts signed by SSC were individually worth more than $2 million, though this

small number of contracts accounted for 54.6 per cent of the
$8.7 billion in goods and services bought through SSC that year.

As the federal government's main purchasing agent, SSC
handles most of its contracts. An internal SSC study, entitled
"Small Business Share of Supply Program, Prime Contracts in
Canada, Fiscal Year 1985-86", looked at SSC's small-business
record over several years. Its findings are reported in the following chart:

Small Business Share of SSC Contracts (by dollar value)				
1981-82	1982-83	1983-84	1984-85	1985-86
37%	33%	30%	31%	28%

The 1986-87 figure has risen to thirty-three per cent, according to SSC. Yet, as you will see in later chapters, there are ways
for small businesses to improve their chances of getting a fair
hunk of the enormous federal procurement pie.

Big Contracts Are Handled Differently

Contracts worth over $2 million require Treasury Board ap-
proval. So this level marks the point at which paid lobbyists and
technical experts who work to have their clients' products
bought are called in to sell to the government. In Chapter 9, you
will see how you can get in on these buys too and on Major
Crown Projects or MCPs, costing $100 million plus.

While SSC exercises considerable discretion in awarding contracts up to $10,000, MCPs are subject to special rules, and highly
formal, detailed reviews by several federal agencies, usually the
departments of National Defence, Transport, DRIE and the
Treasury Board. Here socio-economic benefits to the country
are important factors, and a series of approvals is needed for
each buy.

In 1985, Shelton's task force identified 49 Major Crown
Projects. They included:

Department of Defence	26 procurements
Transport Canada	7 procurements
Other departments	4 procurements
Transport Canada	6 projects
Public Works	4 projects
Other departments	2 projects

Probably fewer than fifty per cent of the value of these very large ventures will be bought in Canada. However, with a round figure of around $27 billion to be spent, MCPs should not be ignored. As you will see, it is here you can form alliances with other firms interested in part of a larger whole.

There Is No Real Competition for Contracts

Most small businesspeople seem to know that a great deal of federal buying is done without any competition. That sentiment is accurate. Thus the federal task force on program review found that only forty-three per cent of services and forty-five per cent of goods had been awarded by competition.

This overall perception also leads many small businesses to feel that they have no chance to win such *sole-source* or directed buys. As you will see in Chapters 7 and 9, that does not have to be the case. Small firms and individuals can get a good share of prime contracts if they follow my guidelines. And you can win your fair share of competed contracts.

You Need Political Pull

The recent contest between Canadian-owned Canadair and U.K.-controlled Bristol Aerospace of Winnipeg over maintenance contracts on the new CF-18 fighters shows how big contracts can be politicized. Indeed, many federal suppliers are very concerned that federal purchasing rules have been changed, in light of the Cabinet's overruling a civil service recommendation to award the maintenance contract to Bristol, in favour of Montréal-area Canadair. Bristol had been given the top technical evaluation and had submitted the lowest cost estimate, two items that traditionally should have meant they would be awarded the job. Instead, regional and political factors were given the most weight, after a strong lobby of PC ministers and MPs by Canadair. Since there were many more MPs in Québec than in the West, the results were predictable. (I should point out that, shortly after the first contract had been awarded, Ottawa gave Bristol another large maintenance contract.)

However, as Ken Rowe, president of the Aerospace Industries Association at the time of the Canadair decision, put it, once uncertainty creeps in, bidding is untenable for executives wishing to enter a competition. Allegations of influence-peddling in Ottawa by lobbyist friends of the Progressive Conservative government, allegations of kickbacks, and suggestions of conflicts of interest among some federal ministers deepened this uncertainty. Senior SSC officials, on the other hand, today insist that this interference is an exception.

Much government procurement, especially for locally bought goods or for price-sensitive items, like paperclips, that are bought repeatedly, probably is non-partisan. So you usually do not need a government-relations expert or a lobbyist. Indeed, political favouritism is probably less prevalent in federal procurement now than in earlier years, or than it still is in some other industrial countries.

You Can't Get Through the "Red Tape"

There's no denying it, there is a lot of red tape involved in selling to Ottawa; and it's hard to find out what Ottawa wants to buy but you can cut down on the runaround by realizing that there is a hidden agenda behind some buys; by judicious requests for information; by carefully targeting your efforts; and by getting one group of officials to help you with another. If you monitor the buying departments and the purchasing agencies regularly so that you are familiar with their practices, you can avoid spending a lot of work on a bid or proposal that is not right for you.

If you do want to bid or approach an official, ask yourself what factors you can control or what assets you have that might be critical to your chances. Are you being asked to provide your expertise, provide some special resource, or maybe solve a problem? Decide just what are they asking and build your approach and proposals around that essential need.

Why Do We Have an SSC and PWC?

In earlier days, the great federal patronage plums in contracting were for transportation, notably canals and railways. Given Canada's minimal armed forces in the last century, military procurements were not a major component. This changed during and since the World Wars.

Indeed, a 1930s inquiry into Defence Department purchasing, prompted by the infamous Bren-gun scandal, helped bring Supply and Services into being. With the coming of the Second World War, a Department of Munitions and Supply was established in order to separate those who purchased weapons from those who used them. The first head of this department was the legendary C. D. Howe. The Department of Munitions and Supply became the Department of Reconstruction and Supply in 1945. Later, as a result of the recommendations of the Diefenbaker-appointed Glassco Commission on government efficiency, Ottawa broadened the mandate of the Defence Production Department to include non-defence items. From these two bodies Supply and Services (SSC) was born.

Today, SSC buys everything from a specially constructed washroom for the Queen to emergency air charters. At one point, the department became owners of 540 miles of gas pipeline while Inter-Provincial Pipeline awaited a licence for the Sarnia-Montréal line. As Keith Glegg, now vice-president of the National Research Council of Canada (NRC), sees it, the relatively centralized federal procurement system "has made it possible for full-time professional buyers to do the buying. This also means that selling to the Canadian government is much easier than selling to other governments. The system facilitates seller and buying-agency expertise."

PWC has become a building, property management and construction version of SSC, for similar reasons. In fact, Glegg notes, the federal procurement system has been "remarkably free of corruption and kickbacks. It is a curious mix of helpfulness and toughness. SSC is the exception in government procurement in Canada and in North America in terms of its size, nature, and scope."

SSC and PWC buy for federal departments and for some federal agencies. As a rule, the departments decide on their needs, on the specifications, schedule, and budget. SSC or PWC does the tendering and pricing and manages the buy. In SSC's case, there are now 15 acts, statutes, and orders-in-council, through which ministers, including the minister of Supply and Services, have procurement responsibility to Parliament. In making their decisions, purchasing officers must consider the traditional broad federal socio-economic goals such as industrial development, regional development, international environment, federal/provincial relations, and job creation.

When looking at bids, SSC, PWC, and their client departments are supposed to consider technical acceptability of the bid, price, delivery, Canadian industrial benefits, suppliers' subcontracting programs showing small-business plans and regional distribution of work, and assumption of risks. In practice, there are problems with all of these.

In principle, PWC's and SSC's first job is deciding who the possible suppliers are, and at what price the goods or services can be provided. If it is a larger procurement, the agency may do a price-and-availability (P & A) survey first. The client department then either abandons its query, or, if it decides to go ahead, writes a detailed Statement of Work (SOW) or specification for the item. SSC or PWC then may issue a Request for Proposals (RFP) for "hard bids". For example, for a large military purchase this request may be nothing more than a letter, or may comprise a 10-volume report for a big-ticket, once-in-a-lifetime buy, like ships. Together with the amount of money the department is going to spend, this RFP is the key documentary information you need in order to bid on that purchase.

As you will see in Chapter 6, how Crown corporations or independent federal agencies buy is sometimes a little harder to fathom. The National Research Council, for example, is designated as an independent Schedule-B agency under the Financial

Administration Act, the statute which governs all federal contracting; yet it still purchases supplies through SSC.

On the other hand, the Canadian National Railways (CN) and Air Canada also are independent Crown-owned entities, but they are not allowed to buy through SSC. They are subject to normal business economics and political pressures in their buying. Chapter 6 shows you how to access these targets, too.

Appendix I

Categories of Goods Bought through SSC

(excerpted from SSC's Suppliers Guide)

Abrasive
Adhesives
Agricultural Machinery
Agricultural Supplies
Agricultural Equipment
Air-Circulating Equipment
Air-Conditioning Equipment
Aircraft Accessories
Aircraft Components
Aircraft Ground-Handling
  Equipment
Aircraft Landing Equipment
Aircraft Launching Equipment
Airframe, Structural Components
Alarm Systems
Ammunition
Animals, Live
Apparel
Athletic Equipment
Automatic Data-Processing
  Equipment (including Firmware)
Automatic Data-Processing Software
Automatic Data-Processing
  Supplies and Support (General
  Purposes)
Bearings
Books
Brushes
Building Materials
Cable and Cable Fittings
Chain and Chain Fittings
Chemical Products
Chemicals
Cleaning Equipment
Cleaning Supplies
Clothing
Coherent Radiation Equipment
Commercial Appliances
Commercial Furnishings
Communication Equipment

Compressors
Construction Equipment
Construction Materials
Containers
Cycles
Dental Equipment
Dental Supplies
Detection Equipment
Docks, Floating
Drying Equipment
Electrical-Equipment
  Components
Electric Wire
Electronic-Equipment
  Components
Engine Accessories
Engine Components
Engines
Excavating Equipment
Explosives
Fibre Optics Accessories
Fibre Optics Assemblies
Fibre Optics Components
Fibre Optics Materials
Fire Control Equipment
Fire-Fighting Equipment
Fixtures, Lighting
Flags
Food-Preparation Equipment
Food-Serving Equipment
Fuels
Furnace
Furniture
Furs
Ground-Effect Vehicles
Guided Missiles
Hand Tools
Hardware
Heating Equipment
Highway-Maintenance
  Equipment

Hose and Hose Fittings
Household Appliances
Household Furnishings
Insignia
Instruments
Laboratory Equipment
Lamps
Leather
Lighting Fixtures
Lubricants
Lumber
Maintenance and Repair-Shop
  Equipment
Maps
Marine Equipment
Materials-Handling Equipment
Measuring Tools
Mechanical Power Transmission
  Equipment
Medical Equipment
Medical Supplies
Metal Bars
Metal Sheets
Metalworking Machinery
Millwork
Minerals and their Primary
  Products
Mining Equipment
Motor Vehicles
Musical Instruments
Nonmetallic Crude Material
Nonmetallic Fabricated
  Materials
Nuclear Reactors
Office Devices
Office Machines
Office Supplies
Oils
Ores and their Primary Products
Packaging Material
Packing Supplies
Paints
Phonographs
Photographic Equipment
Pipe and Pipe Fitting
Plumbing Equipment
Plywood
Pontoons
Power and Power-Distribution
  Equipment

Prefabricated Structures
Publications
Pumps
Radios
Railway Equipment
Recreational Equipment
Refrigeration Equipment
Repair Shop Equipment
Rescue Equipment
Rope and Rope Fittings
Safety Equipment
Sanitation Equipment
Scaffolding
Sealers
Security-Detection System
Service Equipment
Sewage-Treatment Equipment
Ship Equipment
Ships
Shoe Findings
Signal Systems
Small Craft
Space Vehicles
Special-Industry Machinery
Steam Plant
Tents
Text-Processing Systems
Textiles
Tires and Tubes
Toiletries
Tractors
Trade Equipment
Trailers
Training Aids
Training Devices
Tubing and Tubing Fittings
Turbine Components
Turbines
Valves
Vehicular-Equipment
  Components
Veneer
Veterinary Equipment
Veterinary Supplies
Visible-Record Equipment
Water-Purification Equipment
Weapons
Woodworking Equipment
Woodworking Machinery
Waxes

Categories of Services
Bought through SSC

Accommodation and Food
Agricultural Services
Audio-Visual and Photographic Services
Building/Installation Special-Trade Services
Business Services
Commercial-Air Services
Communications Services
Construction
Consulting/Professional Services
Educational Services
Financial, Insurance and Real Estate Services
Health and Welfare Services
Personal Services
Printing Services
Science and Technology
Surveying and Mapping Services
Transportation and Charters
Utilities (Electricity, Water, Gas, and Sanitary Services)

Appendix II

Key Provincial Government Procurement Contacts

Newfoundland

Department of Public Works and Services
St. John's A1C 5T7
Telex: 016-4197
General Inquiries
(709) 576-3439

Minister, Hon. Dr. Hugh Twomey
(709) 576-3678

Deputy Minister, Wayne Mitchell
(709) 576-3676

Queen's Printer, D. Dawe
(709) 576-3649

Government Purchasing Agency
5th Floor, Atlantic Place
St. John's A1C 5T7
Executive Director, E. E. Rowe
(709) 576-3343

Prince Edward Island

Department of Industry
Shaw Bldg., P.O. Box 2000
Charlottetown C1A 7N8
General Inquiries
(902) 368-4240

Minister, Hon. Leonce Bernard
(902) 368-4230

Deputy Minister,
Michael S. Kelly
(902) 368-4250

Department of Finance
95 Rochford Street, Shaw Bldg.
P.O. Box 2000
Charlottetown C1A 7N8

General Inquiries
(902) 368-4070

Minister,
Hon. Gilbert R.Clements
(902) 368-4050

Deputy Minister,
W. Philip MacDougall
(902) 368-4051

Purchasing Division
Director, John E. MacRae
(902) 368-4045

New Brunswick

Department of Supply and Services
Centennial Bldg., P.O. Box 6000
Fredericton E3B 5H1
General Inquiries
(506) 453-2525

Minister, Hon. Bruce Smith
(506) 453-2591

Executive Asst., Gary Lenehan
(506) 453-2591

Deputy Minister's Office
Deputy Minister, Max C. Lewis
(506) 453-2504

Administration and Services
Asst. Deputy Minister, J.H. Fowler
(506) 453-3707

Supply Director, Kevin Burns
(506) 453-2914

Buildings Division
Asst. Deputy Minister, Neil Coy
(506) 453-2228

Nova Scotia

**Department of Government
Services**
1505 Barrington Street
P.O. Box 54
Halifax B3J 2L4

Minister,
Hon. Michael A. Laffin
(902) 424-2900

Deputy Minister,
Michael Zareski
(902) 424-2901

Queen's Printer, B. Hamm
(902) 424-4480

Property and Services Division
Executive Director, D. Hiltz
(902) 424-2904

Design and Construction Services
Executive Director,
Brian Stonehouse
(902) 424-2950

Nova Scotia Government
  Purchasing Agency
Director, Allan Timmins
(902) 424-5522

Québec

Department of Supply and Services
(Ministère des Approvisionne-
  ments et Services)
Complexe G
1045, rue de la Chevrotière
Québec G1R 5L4

General Inquiries
(418) 643-3360

Minister (ministre),
Gilles Rocheleau
(418) 643-3360

Deputy Minister (Sous-ministre),
Jean-Marc Bard

Sous-ministre adj., directeur
général de la gestion des contrats
  et services,
Germain Halley
(418) 643-2993

Direction général des services immobiliers
  et des relations avec les organismes
Sous-ministre adj.,
  directeur général, Jacques Privé
(418) 643-2993

Direction générale des
  approvisionnements
150, boul. St.-Cyrille est, 8e ét.
Québec G1R 5K4

Directeur général,
Jean-Claude Careau
(418) 643-3395

Société Immobilière du Québec
475, rue St.-Amable, 7e ét.
Québec G1R 4X9
Telex: 051-3535

Président directeur général,
Miville Vachon
(418) 643-1259

Ontario

Ministry of Housing
777 Bay Street
Toronto M5G 2E5

General Inquiries
(416) 585-7041

Minister,
The Hon. Chaviva Hosek
(416) 585-7111

Deputy Minister,
Gardner Church
(416) 585-7100

Ministry of Industry, Trade and Technology
Hearst Blk., 900 Bay Street
Toronto M7A 2E1
Telex: 06-219786

General Inquiries
(416) 965-1586

Minister,
The Hon. Monte Kwinter
(416) 965-1617

Small Business, Services and
  Capital Projects
Asst. Deputy Minister,
J. D. Girvin
(416) 965-4036

**Ministry of Government
  Services**
Ferguson Blk.,
77 Wellesley Street W.
Toronto M7A 1N3

General Inquiries
(416) 965-3535

Minister,
The Hon. Richard Patten
(416) 965-1101

Deputy Minister,
Dennis Caplice
(416) 965-1104

Supply and Services Division
12th Floor, Ferguson Blk.
77 Wellesley Street West
Toronto M7A 1N3

Executive Director,
Anne Beaumont
(416) 965-1206

Realty Group
12th Floor, Ferguson Blk.
77 Wellesley Street W.
Toronto M7A 1N3

Asst. Deputy Minister,
Robert W. Riggs
(416) 965-7757

Design and Construction Division
13th Floor, Ferguson Blk.
77 Wellesley Street W.
Toronto M7A 1N3

Executive Director,
Robert Lowry
(416) 963-1553

Manitoba

**Department of Government
  Services**
Legislative Building
Winnipeg R3C 0V8

Minister, Hon. Albert Driedger
(204) 945-3723

Deputy Minister, Eric Harbottle
(204) 945-4414

Property Management
1700 Portage Avenue
Winnipeg R3J 0E1

Executive Director, S. Ursel
(204) 945-7535

Purchasing
530 Century Street
Winnipeg R3H 0L8

Director, E. F. Baranet
(204) 945-6380

Saskatchewan

**Saskatchewan Property
  Management Corporation**
2045 Broad St.
Regina S4P 3V7

Minister, Hon. Graham Taylor
(306) 787-2833

President, Otto Cutts
(306) 787-6520

Realty Division
Vice-President, Ken Rankin
(306) 787-6565

Supply Division
Asst. Vice-President, Al Moffat
(306) 787-6873

Queen's Printer, Bill Matthew
(306) 787-6892

Alberta

**Department of Public Works,
  Supply and Services**
6950—113th Street
Edmonton T6H 5V7

Minister, Hon. Ernie Isley
(403) 427-3666

Deputy Minister,
Edward R. McLellan
(403) 427-3921

Capital Development
8215—112th Street
Edmonton T6G 5A9

Asst. Deputy Minister,
A. (Tony) Hargreaves
(403) 427-3835

Property Management
8215—112th Street
Edmonton T6G 5A9
Asst. Deputy Minister,
Dan Bader
(403) 427-3875

Information Services
Asst. Deputy Minister,
Bob Gehmlich
(403) 427-7756

Supply Management
Asst. Deputy Minister,
S. A. Pepper
(403) 427-8894

Procurement Division
Executive Director, Bob Peyton
(403) 422-2654

Supply Operations Division
Executive Director,
Murray Tyreman
(493) 422-2657

British Columbia
**Ministry of Economic
  Development**
1405 Douglas Street
Victoria V8W 3C1
Telex: 049-7368 (Victoria)
Telex: 04-55459 (Vancouver)
Facsimile: 387-5741 (Victoria)
Facsimile: 660-2457 (Vancouver)

Minister, Hon. Elwood Veitch
(604) 387-1241

Assistant Deputy Minister,
R. A. Food
(604) 387-6700

Purchasing Commission
200, 4000 Seymour Place
Victoria V8X 4Y3
Chairman, R. A. Food
(604) 387-6700

Chief Executive Officer,
C. S. Hutchings
(604) 389-3305

Supplier Development and
  Policy Branch
Director, F. Leonard
(604) 389-3306

Purchasing
Director, P. Sloan
(604) 389-3307

Yukon
**Department of Government
  Services**
P.O. Box 2703
Whitehorse Y1A 2C6

Minister, Hon. Roger Kimmerly
(403) 667-5877

Deputy Minister, Frank Fingland
(403) 667-5744

Asst. Deputy Minister,
George Salmins
(403) 667-3418

Supply and Services
Director, Sam Cawley
(403) 667-5289

Queen's Printer and Printing
Services Manager, Trevor Sellars
(403) 667-3585

Property Manager, Mike Bartsch
(403) 667-5104

Public Works Director,
Doug Campbell
(403) 667-5150

Northwest Territories
**Department of Government
  Services**
P.O. Box 1320
Yellowknife X1A 2L9
Telex: 034-45531

Minister, Hon. Nick Sibbeston
(403) 873-7123

Deputy Minister, John Quirke
(403) 873-7622

Asst. Deputy Minister
Don Johnston
(403) 920-8749

Supply and Services
Director, Norm Phillpot
(403) 920-8663

Department of Public Works and Highways
P.O. Box 1320
Yellowknife X1A 2L9
Telex: 034-45536

Minister,
Hon. Nellie Cournoyea
(403) 873-7962

Deputy Minister,
Larry Elkin
(403) 873-7114

Contracts and Capital Planning
Director, Joe Auge
(403) 873-7256

Architectural Division
Director, Nicholas Marach
(403) 873-7535

Operations Division
Director, Les Clegg
(403) 873-7397

Transportation Engineering Division
Director, Andrew Gamble
(403) 873-7800

CHAPTER TWO

Playing the Procurement Game

Some Basic Rules for Federal Contracts

Half of the federal government's total purchasing dollars is spent without any competition. Yet its purchasing policies and regulations are rationalized around certain uniform principles, especially the notion of competition, and even procurements from sole sources also pay at least lip service to those principles. So it's worth your while to become familiar with them, either to learn to live with them, or to get around them when you go after a job. Both competitive contracts and many non-competitive ones are influenced by considerations other than price, quality, or quantity.

Foreign versus Canadian Sourcing

Ottawa has a long-standing policy to restrict the solicitation of tenders to Canadian-based firms, providing there is sufficient competition. Deciding who counts as competition and how sufficient "sufficient" is, is of course up to federal officials .

Determining what a "Canadian-base" is or is not is no easy task in these days of relatively free trade and freedom of companies from one country to do business in another. In fact, many measures that would otherwise be preferentially applied to Canadian companies are circumscribed because of commitments under the General Agreement on Tariffs and Trades. The proposed Canada-U.S. free trade arrangement would go further in limiting preferential treatment.

27

The GATT Agreement on Government Procurement which binds the signatory countries is, according to an SSC statement, "designed to open a substantial portion of government procurement to international competition on a non-discriminatory basis." GATT stipulates that each signatory's laws, regulations, procedures, and practices regarding government procurement of certain goods and related services must not discriminate between products or suppliers from other signatory countries.

In other words, Canada and other GATT countries must treat foreign suppliers for those goods covered by the agreement in the same way that they treat domestic suppliers. On the other hand, GATT does not cover research and development, marine transportation, defence and services not related to goods, and the Canadian government freely uses its procurement in these sectors to promote domestic over foreign firms. The governments of the U.S. and those of all other GATT countries do the same in their own countries.

The preference Supply and Services Canada gives domestic over foreign firms shows up in its suppliers lists which categorize or tag firms according to four priority groups. In theory, this grouping is supposed to be used as a guide in making an initial selection of bidders, with Canadian firms receiving preference over foreign ones and manufacturers having precedence over distributors. In practice, however, according to one SSC director-general, there really isn't much difference between the four priority groups. As he puts it, "if a foreign firm listed with us, or about which we are aware, is at all qualified, we consider it anyway. I can't recall any time we cut out a firm just because it was not Canadian. We really are more concerned with what the company does in Canada or for Canada than whether or not it has Canadian owners or directors."

Since there are very few large Canadian-owned firms in key sectors such as aerospace or defence, SSC has deemed many foreign firms to be "Canadianized" in order to get them onto the list. SSC also has a "rationalization policy which permits foreign multi-nationals to be treated as Canadian-based manufacturers for particular products," notes an SSC Aerospace Marine and Electronics Systems (AMES) Directorate official.

So, many large contracts, such as the purchase of naval helicopters, go to foreign suppliers. But as a manufacturer in Canada, you need to remember that the principle works both ways. That is, if *you* can provide better prices or better quality to a foreign government-purchaser, then your business too can pick up international sales and, as you will see in Chapter 7, you can earn big dollars as a subcontractor for a major Canadian or foreign firm. As in any business, it's a matter of finding out where and when you can compete best and focussing on those specific situations.

National Developmental Goals

If no truly Canadian-based supplier can be found, the government can still choose between foreign-based suppliers according to whether or not *some* percentage or some components of the product are originally produced in Canada. This is an example of the application of a preference policy or what the feds call *premiums*—in this case, "the Canadian content premium"— which is a calculation of the difference in foreign content value between competing bids.

Another criterion used to distinguish between prospective suppliers has the unmemorable designation "Contribution to Canadian Value Added" (CVA). This term refers to wider issues than the strictly economic ones, and asks which potential supplier's product does more to address the somewhat subjective issues of promotion of research-and-development, regional development, and self-sufficiency in certain sectors.

These days, too, Ottawa is particularly concerned about employment equity. Thus, suppliers who have 100 or more employees and who are bidding on federal contracts worth $200,000 or more are asked to make a formal commitment to ensure that a certain number of women, aboriginal people, visible minorities, and disabled persons are hired if no people from these categories are already on that company's staff. This provision is administered by Employment and Immigration Canada. However, government suppliers are not singled out by this requirement: all companies in the federal jurisdiction with more than 100 workers have to follow this regulation, too.

Other federal procurement goals include general industrial development, "international environment" (whatever that is), federal/provincial relations, the encouragement of Canadian-based multi-national enterprises, and employment creation. Lesser goals are assistance to small business, or improved supplier relations. All of these are good buzzwords to stick into your proposals in any case.

While we do not always know how those inside government weigh these criteria individually, one senior SSC official has stated that a 5 per cent bonus is allowed for "superior Canadian industrial benefits". In another field, SSC's all-purpose listing publication, *Suppliers Guide,* indicates that contracts awarded under the SSC's "Contracting-out Policy in Science and Technology" give highest priority (at least in theory) to Canadian industrial performers. Where a Canadian industrial performer cannot be found, the procurement is to be contracted to other organizations such as universities and provincial-government research operations. (Bear in mind that most Canadian federal R & D is carried out "in-house" in government laboratories.)

The North American Defence Common Market

Another important fact to keep in mind is that, as Canada's Auditor General has pointed out, Canada really has two parallel purchasing operations for military goods. The routine SSC one, which favours the higher priority groups (i.e., Canadian-based manufacturers), and the U.S. Defense Department's Cooperative Logistics program, accessed in Canada through DND. This means that a Canadian or a U.S. company can have two separate direct channels to sell their goods or services to the military in the other country, one through SSC and one through DND. And both already are part of a long-standing Canada-U.S. free trade agreement. For information on marketing security and other aspects of the U.S.-Canada defence-sharing agreements and selling to the U.S. government, see Chapter 5.

The Subcontracting Option

It does not take long to notice that the few medium- to large-sized firms in Canada seem to take turns as the prime or main contractor for Ottawa. No matter which one is "in" with Ottawa at the moment, though, rarely do these *primes* handle servicing or make all their components in-house. This can present some excellent chances for you to get a part of Ottawa's money through subcontracting. Frequently, red tape and requirements for sales are reduced, too. You let the large firm do the legwork and take the risks and then you join the action by subcontracting for your specialty to the larger firm. You will find a contact list for a number of larger Canadian firms in Chapter 7.

Profit Limits

Because of the dogma of competitive tenders, bureaucrats always say they want to let the competitive bid process set the price when calling for federal goods and services. However, in many cases the Canadian feds will still try to negotiate a price when there is only a single source. When there is only one known supplier for a particular commodity, SSC tries to limit profit to about 10 per cent, although it will readily accept 20 per cent of total contract costs on contracts of over $50,000.

The Major Types of Contracts

1. Goods Contracts

Federal purchases of goods are supposed to go through Supply and Services Canada, say government policy directives and the Treasury Board (TB) of Canada, its general management agency. The Board has given SSC the authority to contract for goods without TB approval if the contract amount does not exceed $1 million, or $2 million if at least two valid tenders have been received and the lowest tender has been accepted. These dollar-thresholds for contracts generally are far above those of other departments.

Astute marketers, therefore, often price their package or products to keep within these threshold limits to maximize sales income and minimize the approval process.

However, other departments can buy up to $40,000 worth of goods from a supplier on their own or up to $100,000 where two valid tenders have been received. And they can buy again from the same buyer, or can go directly to the Board for approval on larger buys.

Like SSC, Public Works Canada (PWC) can enter into contracts without TB approval or public-tender call for construction items under $30,000. At TB's discretion, this can rise to $200,000, or even to $5,000,000, when at least two valid tenders have been received, the lowest tender accepted and the contract price is firm.

2. Services Contracts

The contract approval process is different with service contracts, contracts to provide continuing services like engineering or typing. Departments and agencies do not have to go through SSC except for specified items like electronic data-processing. Many of the contracts not needing approval are rent-a-body contracts, which do not involve creation of an employer-employee relationship between the business supplying the service and the feds.

When TB approval is not an issue, all you may have to do in most cases is convince a single contracting authority in one department to issue you with a Letter of Intent, a purchase order or a contract. (Many individuals are hired into the public service every year after coming to a bureaucrat's attention when working on a service contract.)

Ottawa's general manager, TB, divides service contracts into two categories: non-consulting-services contracts and consulting-services contracts. A non-consulting services contract is one for the provision of services other than consulting services, and includes the rental of personal property. For example, non-consulting services might include the repair and servicing of computers. A contract to set up a new system or evaluate the existing system would likely be a consulting contract. SSC may enter such contracts without TB approval when the amount payable does not exceed $1 million, or does not exceed $2 million and at least two valid tenders have been received.

PWC is given similar authority to contract without TB approval when the contract does not exceed $100,000, or is under

$400,000 if at least two valid tenders have been received and the lowest tender accepted.

There are no threshold restrictions on daily or other time-rate fees for services contracts with established firms of professionals which are competitively selected through tenders, provided the proposed contract amount is within the approved authority of the department or agency.

Without competitive tendering, departments can issue service contracts to established firms of professionals for under $500 a day, as long as the total cost of the contract remains within the departmental approval. For new or not-yet-established firms of professionals, departments are supposed to go to Treasury Board for prior approval of fees that exceed $350 a day. Fees for services of individuals engaged by Cabinet decision or order-in-council for more than $350 a day also are allowed only with prior Treasury Board approval. Daily fees are expected to reflect task requirements, individual qualifications, market conditions, honoraria or fees paid to those outside the firm, composition of fees, and Treasury Board fee guidelines or circulars.

Contracts of this sort tie in with a third area where SSC has less control.

3. Consulting and Professional Services

SSC can sign a "consulting services contract" for a qualified individual or firm without TB's approval for less than $75,000, or for $150,000 when at least three proposals have been considered. However, any contracting authority, that is, any agency or departmental head or deputy minister and a few other officials, can individually contract for up to $25,000 for consulting services. This is raised to $50,000 when at least three proposals have been considered.

In principle, Ottawa would like consulting services to be awarded competitively. In the government's eyes, ideally, this would include at least three proposals; an evaluation of proposals based on criteria published in the invitations for proposals; and evaluation carried out by individuals qualified to judge the competing proposals against the statement of work and evaluation criteria. Federal policy stipulates that whether or not a formal competition is held, the consultant's qualifications must always be a factor in any decision.

Prior to buying consulting or professional services, client departments are required to prepare a Statement of Work (SOW). The SOW is an internal government document which is supposed to detail the work to be carried out, and its quantity and quality, but is not to be so stiff that it discourages initiative or innovation on the part of the supplier. It should identify the specific stages of the work, their sequence, and their relationship to the overall work. Thus, the type, magnitude, and complexity of the work determines the degree of detail required in the Statement of Work. SOWs, which are sometimes but not always part of the tender documents, can provide you with valuable information on the requirements to be met. Ask the buying department for a copy.

There are four alternative methods of selecting consultants, according to the competitive norm. One involves price alone, and is rarely used. The second involves evaluation of competitive proposals, that is, officially judging one proposed approach better than another. The third is based entirely on the qualifications of the competitors, and is frequently applied in contracts under $25,000. And the fourth involves "directing" a contract to a particular firm without any form of competition. In this case, departments are supposed to fully document the circumstances.

For contracts over $25,000, competitive proposals are commonly solicited through a Request for Proposal (RFP). Here a relatively few firms, or a rotated list of firms, are asked to suggest an answer to a problem. Inclusion on the list of invitees is supposed to be based on the firm's track record in the relevant field; its qualified personnel; its access to supporting resources; its capacity to complete the work within the required time; its past performance on federal government contracts; the location of the consultant's office in relation to work area; and, especially for defence-related tasks, the security-level clearance or "sensitivity" required by the assignment.

Proposals are evaluated to see whether the consultant or individual is capable of carrying out the work; whether the company's suggested approach to the problem will produce the desired results; whether the estimated costs are realistic; and whether the proposed fees are reasonable.

Fuzzy Federal Frontiers

If you've gathered by now that you could drive a Mack truck through the lines separating consulting services and non-consulting services contracts, and goods contracts, you get a perfect score of 100 on our quick test of federal rules. And the line between which section or centre in SSC handles some of these contracts is a bit vague too.

Sometimes these uncertainties can work for you. As my late father used to put it, "Sometimes in chaos there can be profit." You may be able to shop around within SSC or in departments until you find someone who will buy your goods or services. *Then* you decide what to call it.

For example, let's say you run a small marketing company, and you feel that the feds should benefit from your expertise. You could sell your skills as a consultant through SSC's Science and Professional Services Directorate, through the Bureau of Management Consulting, or maybe through its Communications Services Directorate, on behalf of a client. (Of course, you could also go directly to the client department itself.)

However, if the sums you are discussing are relatively small or if consulting contracts are undergoing stiff examination by Treasury Board or Parliament, presto, you may find yourself providing research services, or writing and editing services. Or your work might even become a book or pamphlet, magically making it a good, not a service. That's where some legwork inside the government, a friendly fed, or a good consultant can help you too.

The Tendering Process

According to an SSC spokesman, "any individual or firm, no matter how large, how small or where it is located in Canada, has the right to apply to do business with the federal government." That is the second regulation on which SSC operates. Guided by Treasury Board and its Government Contract Regulations which govern all contracts, this means that government contracts are supposed to show fairness in spending public money, while still providing, of course, the "best value" to the taxpayer. (You can buy a copy of the Government Contract Regulations at your local federal bookstore, or check your nearest federal government office. Be warned, though; it isn't light reading.)

Agencies also are to provide qualified firms with equal access to government business. Yet, small businesses often do not perceive the government as very amiable. Indeed, a January 1987 preliminary report by DRIE's Small Business Consultation Committee on Government Procurement for the Minister of State for Small Business found that communication between SSC and industry was a one-way street; it was all from SSC to industry. Study chairperson Alex Alberani wrote that "manufacturers or suppliers and client or user departments rarely exchange information on products/services . . . . Weak relations also exist between procurement officer [in SSC] and client department in regard to correlating specific purchases." In other words, don't be surprised if you sense some confusion when talking to an SSC procurement officer about your project. And don't be too astonished if a departmental procurement officer doesn't know about it or what its status is.

Ottawa's main purchasing agents, Supply and Services Canada and Public Works Canada, recruit contractors or suppliers in a number of ways. Perhaps the best known of these is the *source listing*. SSC, PWC, client departments, and other common-service agencies amass lists of possible suppliers for various items. Sometimes, however, these lists are less than what they seem to be. For example, SSC's much-touted National Automated Sourcing Information System (NASIS) "is not structured to give buyers access to cross-referenced product, manufacturers, or cost comparisons for different regions across Canada," the Small Business study found. Instead data are collected based on existing products that fit into the government's shopping list and generally these findings are not available to MPs, the press, or buyers.

Knowing how to get on these lists and how the lists are used by SSC purchasing officers is a crucial step in your overall plan to become a government supplier.

But first a word to the wise. The government often pre-selects or *pre-qualifies* bidders. To get on the short list for work, your firm or your products may have to be tested or screened by pur - chasing officers. While there is a lot of pressure from the Department of Regional Industrial Expansion (DRIE) and from business to change to a post-qualification system, when only likely bidders would be subjected to the full red tape-treatment, this has not come about so far.

Pre-qualification is most apt to occur when goods and services which are not in common commercial supply are involved and special government specifications have to be met, such as in the provision of military vehicles or special scientific equipment. It might happen when the cost of bidding is significant to the ex- tent that it "would be unfair to firms of unknown capability to present them with the hazard of disqualification after the ex- pense of tendering has been incurred"; when the competence of the low bidder must normally be specially verified by product testing or on-site visit, both common for defence purchases; or when there are simply too many firms on the bidders' lists and SSC wishes to trim its list of prospective suppliers.

The government can ask for bids, proposals, or prices in a variety of ways. For large construction competitions, it some- times holds design competitions as a first step towards picking a contractor for a project. This means that non-essential con- siderations such as esthetics can sometimes be used to eliminate bidders before bids are asked from the short list based on essen- tial criteria. This two-step procedure is being used more frequently in the U.S. and Canada. Phase one involves a num- ber of firms making proposals. In phase two, prices determine the competition from a short list of acceptable proposers.

However, the majority of federal government and SSC pur- chases use three methods to solicit bids. We will look at each one in turn.

How Does the Government Get Suppliers?

(A) Invitation To Tender

Invitations To Tender (ITTs) are generally used for easily defined, non-construction goods that are commercially available "off the shelf", where the total price is more than $25,000 and the items are to be bought competitively. (The $25,000 limit is an SSC one. The TB-imposed threshold is $30,000.) ITTs are used when the goods required can be defined by clear criteria; when prices can be easily compared; when the government wants a low bidder to get the job; and when it does not intend to negotiate a contract. As a rule, two or more "qualified" sources are asked to bid.

Usually, responding tenders to unclassified ITTs are publicly opened and anyone can attend. The contract is awarded to the supplier with the lowest-priced *responsive bid,* that is the bid which fully meets the defined requirements, essential elements, and terms and conditions of the ITT, including factors like price, quality, Canadian content, delivery, and performance. SSC considers bids that deviate from the ITT's terms, conditions, and elements as *non-responsive* and, therefore, disqualified. Senior management, sometimes including TB officials, usually must approve any rejection of the lowest bid.

Contact an SSC or PWC contracting office or headquarters, listed at the end of Chapter 3, or the issuing department, to get details on tender notices, distribution of tender documents, on the receipt and opening of tenders, security, and other procedural matters.

(B) Request For Quotation

Requests for Quotation (RFQs) are often used for requirements valued at less than $25,000, and cases where the cost in resources or time to solicit tenders by ITT would be relatively high. Requirements that exceed $25,000 are not supposed to be broken down into a number of separate purchases to get around this dollar threshold, but they frequently are.

Responses to RFQs are not opened in public. The contract is awarded to the supplier with the lowest-priced responsive bid or to the supplier whose quotation most effectively meets identified factors requested in the solicitation.

A derivative of the RFQ which you may be involved in is the Telephone Buy or T-Buy. This is a method of purchasing lower-dollar values (LDVs) or inexpensive items. These include items which can easily be identified over the telephone for competitive requirements with a value up to $2,500, and non-competitive requirements up to $5,000.

Low Dollar Value Purchases

You will recall from Chapter 1 that small businesses account for some thirty per cent of the value of all purchases made by SSC. In 1983-84, this came to $1.6 billion in purchases. However, $1.4 billion of these purchases was for items that individually had a value of $10,000 or less. The $10,000 threshold then marked the limit of what SSC called low-dollar-value (LDV) procurements. That limit now has been raised to $25,000.

Using the old ceiling, the task force on program review found LDVs accounted for ninety per cent of the total *number* of government annual purchases, but only twenty per cent of the *dollar value* of procurements. Administratively, these purchases cost $150 million a year to handle. In the absence of solid data, the task-force report *Spending Smarter* speculated that "the vast majority of these purchases are from small businesses. SSC alone annually issues $6.8 million worth of goods under $250 per unit, and it is estimated that departments directly purchase some $500 million themselves."

T-Buy contracts are awarded verbally with supporting documents following the award. The process is relatively simple, efficient for all involved, and SSC feels it is quite as effective as the traditional methods. It involves minimal paperwork on both sides of the transaction.

Bid Rotation

Bid rotation is another basic SSC mechanism for smaller buys nationally or regionally. It is an automated process applied on small dollar requirements (usually less than $10,000) when a large number of suppliers are available. The number of bidders will be restricted based on the value of previous bid opportunities that they have had over time, to ensure that every eligible supplier will have the opportunity to bid on an equivalent value of business. This policy, too, is designed to reduce the government's administrative costs for low-dollar-value requirements.

You should note, though, that the federal Department of Regional Industrial Expansion's Small Business Consultative Committee on Government Procurement has concluded that rotation source-lists "do not equate fairness to suppliers in its procedural applications . . . they should be abolished", and also cautions that "registration on a source-list does not guarantee the supplier an invitation to bid."

(C) Request For Proposal

For non-competitive requirements valued at more than $25,000 and for items that are to be bought competitively but for which selection cannot be made based solely on the lowest price, SSC may issue a Request for Proposal (RFP). PWC and other departments can issue them too.

An RFP outlines a problem or need which suppliers are asked to solve. The successful contractor is chosen based on the effectiveness of the proposed solution instead of the price alone. Suppliers are expected to submit detailed technical, managerial, and cost proposals. Usually the government will provide the necessary designs and specifications to the final bidder and sometimes to all bidders. Sometimes, though, in contract definition phases of an MCP (such as the recent purchase of frigates), you may be hired to prepare the "specs" for the government to use in issuing the RFPs or in awarding the work.

Frequently, RFPs are issued for goods contracts in which all terms but the price and a few specifications are subject to negotiation. The winner must have met all of the specifications and other mandatory requirements set out in the request, and have suggested the best solution to the problem at the best possible price. An RFP also may be issued for a service contract, usually where the service required can be well defined. Suppliers usually where the service required can be well defined. Suppliers show how they can provide the service for a specified budget. Again, the "best" proposal, at "lowest" cost, or the best techni-cal/managerial proposal, is supposed to win, but both of those calls are somewhat subjective.

Other government departments or agencies often initiate the request to SSC for an RFP and assist in evaluating bidders, there-by adding to the impression that contracts go to inside favourites or to whomever can please SSC, PWC, or the particular pur-chaser in the case. In most cases, in fact, contracts go to companies who are listed because SSC or someone in the sys-tem considers them qualified to do the task, or because they are firms SSC wants to test. Sometimes, though, a firm gets on the list because it asked to be put on that particular list or because it has complained that it had not been given a chance to prove itself. I suspect that it would rarely win or get later offers.

Before evaluation of the proposals has been completed, one or more proponents may be asked to submit additional support-ing data, provided it will not prejudice other applicants or affect price, cost, quantity, quality, or delivery of the items or service proposed. But if negotiations are permitted at all, they are sup-posed to include all firms submitting valid proposals. In theory, negotiations with a single firm are allowed only if it has sub-mitted the only valid proposal; or if it has been selected after SSC has evaluated more than one valid proposal and negotia-tions would not have changed the winner.

The Crown can also negotiate with the potential supplier *after* making its choice, to obtain fair value. Then it will be rep-resented by SSC or, if of a technical nature, by the contracting officer of SSC with representatives of the department.

RFPs are much less price-centred than ITTs or RFQs. Other factors considered in awarding the contract include the supplier's past performance, technical capability, management abilities, quality, life-cycle costs, and follow-up services. The contract is awarded to the supplier who makes a proposal the government feels would most effectively satisfy this wide range of requirements identified in the solicitation. In very technical matters, the purchaser might have to evaluate in great detail a researcher's past experience, curriculum vitae, publications, etc.

In very large dollar purchases, like the new navy helicopters, army tanks, or airport radar systems, oil sands projects, or even the National Art Gallery, the government may short-list the number of bidders to a half-dozen companies or so. Since there are not many companies of this size in Canada, whoever does not win a big contract today may get one tomorrow. The winner becomes the main or "prime" contractor on the particular project or purchase.

Again, I advise you to keep on eye on these prime contractors who get government work in Canada or the U.S. Go after the primes, many of whom are mentioned in Chapter 7, in much the same way you go after the feds. Get on their lists, and show them you can do a job or provide a product. As well, you can show them how to integrate your ideas or products into their marketing strategies, for the Canadian, U.S., or other governments, and for other, still larger, firms.

(D) Standing Offer (SO)

The Standing Offer is, fundamentally, an effective means of ensuring stable prices for certain items required on a continuing basis over a long period of time. Both regions and SSC headquarter's product-directorates use standing offers.

It's simple; but there are some widespread misunderstandings about it. First, this is not a contract specifying that a certain amount must be purchased. Rather, it is an agreement in which government departments and agencies deal on an as-and-when required basis, at a pre-arranged price, under certain fixed terms and conditions, during a specific time period. From the time an SO is established, there is no obligation until the user department or agency places a "call-up" or order with the supplier.

SOs are used regularly to buy plumbing supplies, pharmaceutical supplies, repair and maintenance of equipment, professional services and data-processing supplies and services. As a rule, they are in place for one year and are normally restricted to items and services available through outlets near the user department or agency location.

There are four different types of SOs. They are: (1) National Master Standing Offers (NMSO), usable by many departments or agencies; (2) National Individual Standing Offers (NISO), used by one department or agency; (3) Regional Master Standing Offers (RMSO), used by many departments or agencies within an SSC regional supply area; and (4) Regional Individual Standing Offers (RISO), regional in scope, usable by only one customer department or agency.

There are no special source lists for SOs. Bids are sought in the usual manner. Contracts may be terminated for non-performance, failure to comply with terms and conditions of the contract, if the contract is wrongly awarded or if the good or service is no longer needed.

While there is no legal obligation for the Crown to contract for any or all of the estimated buy, it is certainly worthwhile for you to negotiate this type of agreement with a federal department. Aside from what you may sell, it keeps you on Ottawa's active list of supply sources; and it shows your bank and other governments that you have the federal "Seal of Approval". And if you are able to set a handsome price with the government in one SO, you will find that other buyers also frequently accept the same rate without a question.

(E) Selling Directly to Departments and Agencies

It is worth stressing again that you must hit individual departments and agencies which fund SSC's and PWC's procurement activities, or which buy goods and services directly. Pay special attention to the big buying departments like National Defence and Transport, and to common-service agencies and departments with a special interest in your type of products or services. (See especially Chapters 4 and 5.)

As well, you should go after the major Crown corporations like CN, Air Canada, or Canada Post. You are given contact points for these corporations in Chapter 6.

(F) Unsolicited Proposals

The Unsolicited Proposals (UP) Program, run through SSC's Science and Professional Services Directorate, allows firms to submit proposals for scientific work, in theory without having a sponsor in government. In fact, says Keith Glegg, a National Research Council vice-president, to make the UP Program work for you, you really have to find a particular agency and some one person in that agency in a position of responsibility to take you under his or her wing: in short, you usually have to find a sponsor first.

Proposals containing unique ideas or opportunities are written and submissions are made without government solicitation. They come from individuals, private organizations and businesses, non-profit organizations, universities, public-research organizations and industrial-research institutes. And sometimes they are accepted.

(G) Letter of Intent

Letters of Intent, to be used only in exceptional cases, are very common contractual documents used to buy goods or services. These Letters are commitments on behalf of a minister to pay you for your effort, or to place a contract with you to do some work or supply a product. Since you can be paid against the Letter, in effect it often signifies a go-ahead on service contracts, and provides some initial capital. It also is a document around which SSC or the Treasury Board can approve some form of more formal contract.

A Letter states the work authorized, the maximum liability of the Crown in dollars, and how payment will be made. In theory, a Letter cannot constitute contractual commitment in cases where the project requires Treasury Board approval. Letters of Intent cannot be signed by an SSC procurement officer without prior approval of the Deputy Minister or of the Treasury Board.

Although it is not supposed to be done, larger projects are often broken down into small bites so that a departmental contract or a Letter of Intent can be used for each part.

(H) Sole-Sourcing

About half of all federally-bought goods and services are bought by dollar value without competition or are sole-sourced. In a sole-source buy, only one source is approached for a particular procurement. Sometimes such a buy involves a specified good the government needs, nationally or regionally, or a firm may have a monopoly of the technology essential to the procurement. Possibly, too, the scope or volume needed is beyond the normal capability of the industry; or, in contrast, it is a very small buy that might be relatively expensive to award competitively. Other situations in which sole-servicing occurs are when there is a need to conserve some resource; or, most frequently, the work is of pressing urgency. Again, you should try to develop a strategy to get at this large pot of dollars by developing unique products or by teaming up with other firms who already have them or have the government's ear.

(I) Purchase Orders

For some very small purchases, a contracting officer may do nothing more than issue a Purchase Order (PO) of a conventional type in order to buy what he or she needs.

Sending in Bids

Responses to ITTs, RFPs, or other solicitations may be submitted by mail, facsimile, telex or telegram, unless instructed otherwise in the solicitation. Always make sure you have included the bid number, closing date and hour, item number, price, delivery date, FOB point, federal sales tax, and any deviations from the original tender document. For RFPs, be sure to contact the officer who sent out the proposal to find out the minimum information required, and to let him or her know you are interested.

There is one basic requirement that SSC insists overrides any other. Bids must be delivered to the proper contracting office location, not the regular departmental offices, and by the specified time and date. SSC does not accept late bids. However, to cope with the vagaries of the Canada Post, it has a delayed-bid policy.

In essence, this policy assumes a time period of forty-eight hours for delivering a piece of mail in Canada, which may be rather short if you live in Newfoundland or B.C.—or even maybe Toronto. In any event, SSC checks to see if the Canada Post Corporation cancellation time-stamp or the receipt issued by Canada Post Corporation shows the bid was mailed at least forty-eight hours prior to the closing time and date for the invitation. If so, it concedes the bid is not late but has been delayed by Canada Post Corporation and you cannot be held responsible for the delay.

Nonetheless, you should protect yourself if you mail a bid to the feds, even if you think there is plenty of time. Get it registered as proof of timely mailing. Use Priority Post, courier, or registered mail. Remember, SSC is usually inflexible when it comes to accepting late bids, so be smart and business-like: get your bid in on time.

SSC Headquarters will accept bids twenty-four hours a day. During office hours, deliver them to the designated office. After hours, deliver them to the commissionaire's desk in the headquarters-building lobby in Hull. Regions accept bids only during office hours. Bids are deposited in double-locked boxes. You should confirm a telegraphic bid submitted before closing time in the manner outlined in the solicitation.

Evaluation of Bids

The evaluation of bids involves reviewing each bid submitted and assessing it to ensure it responds fully to each requirement defined in the bid document. SSC handles or is involved in this aspect for goods or services buys, and PWC handles construction items. The departments who pay the bills are also involved.

SSC regularly complains that most bidders do not seem to have read the requirements before bidding. So be warned, and don't waste the government's or your own time tendering or going after contracts where you will automatically be disqualified. Read the requirements carefully, and answer them all precisely. If you have trouble, ask SSC or the client department, or consult an outside expert.

The requirements in the bid document form the basis on which the bids are evaluated. Prominent among them are technical acceptability —if you don't have it, you are ninety per cent sure of being rejected—and price, which is almost as important.

Other considerations include quantity; delivery schedule; Canadian industrial benefits; a subcontracting program showing the small-business plan; regional distribution; and assumption of risks.

Small firms are not expected to file subcontracting plans and many large ones who are supposed to haven't had to do so, or the plans are never really monitored by government, although this is changing as a result of a new SSC-DRIE/DIST initiative (discussed in Chapter 7). So which of the above factors matter and how much they matter is largely up to the public servants and politicians.

Never send in a bid, proposal quotation, or tender that does not answer *all* of the requirements sought, or that suggests a different product than the one being sought. Otherwise, SSC likely will treat your reply as non-responsive. You really may have a good new product to sell to Ottawa, but usually this just is not the time or place to sell it.

Non-Responsive Bids

The government takes the lowest-priced responsive tender if it represents best or at least fair value to the government. The next higher SSC management level, and sometimes the Treasury Board, have to approve decisions to turn down a low bid.

One major exception to the practice of awarding to the lowest bidder is a Request for Proposal where other factors may influence the decision. RFPs are problem- rather than price-oriented, argues SSC. However, in these cases and in the case of a Request for Quotation (RFQ), such factors usually will be identified in the bid document.

As a rule, non-responsiveness is the only reason for rejecting a low tender. However, SSC has a broad definition of non-responsiveness. For example, a bid might not meet the specified technical requirements; Ottawa might be buying snowploughs, and a supplier might be selling snowblowers. Or maybe the feds want 500-ml tins but a supplier only makes 1,000-ml ones.

Another common problem that can lead to instant rejection is suggesting some pricing or basis of payment different from the one stated in the ITT. If the feds propose to pay for work on an hourly rate, do not confuse them with daily rates, even if they would be a better deal for the government. Make their job easy for them. Fill in the blanks according to what *they* want.

In principle, then, all responsive tenders are eligible for the contract. Sometimes, though, Ottawa finds there are no accept-able tenders, and cancels the ITT. It then may reinvite tenders or may issue an RFQ to get an acceptable price.

When there is only one responsive tender, the government may give the firm the job, and follow the rule for non-competi-tive tendering with this sole potential supplier. Like any sharp businessperson, SSC frequently will try to negotiate a better price on such a deal. However, its practical leverage is severely limited if it really needs the work, or if the firm has some unique product or expertise. In fact, SSC is *obligated* to negotiate a price when there is only one responsive tender, or two or more respon-sive tenders are received but the prices do not represent fair value to the government. SSC then can seek a best and final offer. Note that any change to the original tender must be made in writing and must be specifically referred to in the body of the bid documents as part of the supplier's tender.

Fine-Tuning Your Bid

You should think ahead about how to handle some of Ottawa's motherhood causes, like Canadian content. For instance, SSC permits a premium of up to ten per cent of the difference in foreign content on competing bids in favour of sources with the greater Canadian content. "Canadian content" is defined brief-ly as that portion of the selling price of a product or service as-sociated with work and consequent job creation in Canada.

However, this ten per cent premium does not apply to: Major Crown Projects (over $100 million); procurement subject to the GATT agreement on government procurement; procurements for foreign governments on behalf of the Canadian Commercial Corporation; or usually to procurements under $25,000. Generally, however, Canadian content is a good feature to push in any application or sale.

After a contract is awarded by SSC, you should request the name of the successful bidder and the contract price paid so you

can analyze where you went wrong. Awards over $50,000 are
published in SSC's *Bulletin of Business Opportunities*; R & D contracts are published in its *R & D Bulletin*. (See Chapter 8.)

In years past, the department would also tell you the unit
prices as well, a practice that still exists in the U.S. government.
However, since the passage of the Canadian federal Access to
Information Act, which is supposed to give citizens access to
routine government information, SSC refuses to do this any
longer. It argues that this is commercially confidential information which it cannot by law divulge. Similarly, other departments
are refusing to release details of Memoranda of Understanding
(MOUs) between major prime contractors and the Department
of Regional Industrial Expansion calling for subcontracting to
small businesses.

To put it mildly, as it stands now, this policy seriously under-
mines SSC's official position that it "de-briefs" unsuccessful
applicants, and it is a major hindrance to opening up subcontracting opportunities. When and if free trade with the U.S.
comes, this likely will be a major point of contention, since the
U.S. government does provide unit prices.

Meanwhile, information-access experts tell me, if this con-
fidentiality issue is pushed with the government, the information
probably would be released because taxpayer funding is involved. Certainly, too, there are many in the department who
would welcome releasing the information since it would likely
mean some lower prices for federal buys.

In the meantime, if you really want to find out what your
competitor's bid was, contact the federal Information Commissioner at 1-800-267-0441.

Finally, you should remind yourself that roughly half the time
the government will be awarding a non-competitive contract. In
these cases, the government tries to determine the "best value"
for money spent. The elements in those decisions are product,
resource, operating, and contingent costs. Product cost is the
price for the widget to the government and includes transportation and installation. Resource prices include departmental
costs like specification writing, quality assurance, and contract
administration. Operating costs include repair, maintenance,
and recovery costs. Contingent costs include the cost to the user

department of not having the service or item at the time or place it is needed.

Thus, when composing your bid documents, you should keep these factors in mind in tailoring your bid to win the jobs you are going after.

Ending or Changing the Contract

Contracts can be terminated for the convenience of the Crown, on default of the contractor, or by mutual consent.

Default frequently results when a contractor goes into bankruptcy, or breaches the agreement, for example, by not delivering on time or on specification. "For convenience" usually occurs when funds have been cut, or a program has been discontinued. It also can be used when a technical breakthrough renders the requirements obsolete and a default termination cannot be considered because the contractor is not in default; or when it would not be to the advantage of the government to agree to termination by mutual consent.

As a recent *Commentary* from the Ontario law firm of Osler, Hoskin and Harcourt puts it: "Termination by mutual consent may be instituted by the contracting officer only after a written legal opinion has been obtained from the Department of Justice. . . . Termination by mutual consent will not be used by the Crown where it is in the interest of the Crown to issue a default termination." Where a part of the contract is being reduced, an amendment to the contract may do.

A department must make a written submission or a request for approval to Treasury Board before a contractor can be compensated for extra costs. Extra payments will not normally be approved, notes the Osler *Commentary*, "if they are due solely" to "increases in labour or material costs; changes in freight rates; revisions in exchange rates; increases in taxes and duties; delays caused by the contractor; errors on the part of the contractor; other difficulties which the contractor overlooked but should have foreseen." The government *can* be tightfisted when it wants to be.

CHAPTER THREE

Getting on the List

Only when you succeed in getting your name into the government's procurement system do you finally exist—so to speak—and become a candidate for a government job or project. This chapter deals with the most common question, "How do I get on the list?", that is, the main rosters from which SSC and PWC draw the business firms they invite to submit bids.

As already stated, in principle, any individual or firm, no matter how large or small, wherever located, has the right to apply to do business with the federal government and SSC. But SSC and other departments, agencies, or Crown corporations do not advertise all their bids widely, and in many cases do not advertise them at all. SSC keeps records of thousands of commodity groupings that it purchases. Matched against these, officials tell us, are the names of all the companies that have informed the department that they wish to be considered as suppliers as well as those that are considered capable of carrying out the terms and conditions of a contract.

Quite often, SSC solicits bids directly from vendors named in its source-lists without further advertising its needs for a specific commodity or service. That's why it is so important that you not only keep a lookout for advertised projects, but that you get the advantage of being on the list of the select few.

"Do Not Write In This Space. . ."

The number of government source-lists and the complexity of some registration procedures can be troublesome. According to one SSC official, SSC's lists contain over 28,000 names at headquarters alone and a total of over 60,000 at the regional level. As you will see, there are other lists as well, and there is no single place in the federal government where you can go to get "on the list". No one really is sure how many lists there are .

Indeed, many of the 30 purchasing departments and dozens and dozens of federal agencies maintain multiple source-lists. That's equally true for the 150 Crown corporations, and for the prime contractors who hire "subs" or outside experts or contractors. That means more selling and paperwork for you—but it also means many more sales opportunities.

Nor is the procedure or paperwork the same from one list to another. So, just getting the forms can be hard enough, and filling them all out can be mind-warping. And don't forget all the updates and interim reports yet to come.

Like anything else, though, adding your name to the government's roster is very much a matter of starting at the beginning and doing things one at a time, in some sort of priority that you have determined.

The beginning for most firms is SSC, or PWC for construction contracts, since together they process about two-thirds of total buys for the government proper. This chapter is about getting on the source lists in SSC and PWC, which fortunately are both regulated by the government-wide Government Contract Regulations (GCR), which spell out the procedures and forms to be used. They also are governed by similar though not quite identical internal departmental regulations, have comparable policies and procedures and present relatively centralized marketing targets. Let's look at how you get on the main SSC list first, then on the ones at PWC. In the next chapter, we will look some at other common-service or procurement agencies, and at some of the departmental and branch lists in SSC and elsewhere.

Sometimes SSC or a buying department may suggest to a known firm that it apply to be put on the lists, but most commonly, the first step is for an interested firm simply to ask to be registered as a supplier. Secondly, in many cases the firm must provide some proof of its ability to carry out a contract. In PWC cases, this sometimes involves a performance or "security" bond or deposit. In SSC cases, inspections of premises or testing of products is more common, especially for defence or high-technology buys.

Until recently, SSC required a firm to fill out at least one elaborate questionnaire at the outset for each *commodity*—that is what SSC calls goods or services—it wanted to sell to the government at the national level. The seller faced equally complex forms to get on a regional source-list.

Happily, for most small firms, the listing process is now divided into two distinct steps, reducing a firm's initial paperwork a lot at the start, and increasing SSC's. Unfortunately, though, while SSC has allocated extensive resources to persuade more firms to list (including, they say, 70,000 *Suppliers Guides* sent out with the forms inside), it may not have prepared itself internally to process all the new applications. So it could take some time to get your first (Part I) listing-form processed, or to handle your second (Part II) or follow-up form, which is even more detailed.

To add to the delays, SSC local and regional offices do not seem to have the *Guides* in any quantity for some reason, so you will have to contact SSC in Ottawa. You do this by contacting:

Supervisor
Supplier Registration Services
Statistical Information and Data Management Services
Supply and Services Canada
11 Laurier Street
Hull, Québec K1A 0S5
(819) 956-3444

Now let's look at the listing form itself.

The Forms

Inside the *Suppliers Guide*, you will find the forms which make up step one of the current national listing process: form DSS-MAS 10550, the National Application for Source Listing (a green form). You will also find DSS-MAS 10550, the Regional Operations Application for Source Listing (a white form).

Each of these two forms is actually quite short by federal standards—two pages only—although their bilingual format probably makes them seem longer. If the forms are handled correctly, you can get listed quickly and cheaply. Assuming that you want to sell only a couple of products, you can probably get through the first part of the listing phase in an evening.

Fill out the national application if you can supply goods beyond a single provincial boundary or offer services other than those prefixed with an "R" in the services listings of the *Suppliers Guide*. Otherwise, complete the regional application.

SSC's *Guide* says you should complete just one regional application: "'Regional' applicants will be considered for source listing by the appropriate regional office(s) only. 'National' applicants will be considered by both Headquarters and the appropriate regional office(s). In this manner, you or your firm are considered for inclusion in all applicable source lists at one request." In practice, most astute buyers fill out a separate white form to each regional office where they want to sell.

Later, in step two, after SSC has reviewed the initial information, you will be asked for further details about the types and prices of services or goods you can offer, and your ability to deliver them on time, on price, and on specification.

Before filling in the papers in their final form, many suppliers take their drafts to the nearest local SSC office or to a provincial procurement or federal or provincial small-business office, since these often have staff to help you with the details or check your draft answers over for free. In Vancouver, for example, SSC is housed with the province in the B.C. Enterprise Centre. Or you can get help with your application by calling (819) 956-3444 and asking for a Sourcing Coordinator.

The SSC regional offices, in addition to being physically closer to you than Ottawa, in some cases are also closer to you psychologically. In Ottawa, public servants deal with other public servants most of the time. In the regions, though, they frequently deal with "real people"—private companies like yours—and are more likely to talk your language. Of course, like their headquarters counterparts, regional officers are very busy individuals, and you should be fully prepared before you go to see them. First impressions are important.

Filling Out the Forms

Remember, you have to fill out *both* forms if you want to sell at both national and regional levels, and a *separate* white form for each branch office where you want to be listed. While you may choose to register only in the region in which your head office or main plant is located, says SSC, if your company has more than one branch or franchise in different cities or areas, indicate their location for potential listing in the nearest SSC branch office.

Next, you are asked to tell SSC which products you want to supply, nationally and regionally. You do this by referring to the list of "Goods Categories" or the list of "Services Categories", provided in Section II of the *Suppliers Guide* (and included as appendices in Chapter 1 of this book). You are asked to list them by SSC title and GSIN (pronounce *Gee-Sin*), standing for "Goods and Services Identification Numbers". Most suppliers find this list to be the most intimidating part of all.

GSIN are broad descriptions of goods or services, but not of "services related to goods", that is, services sold or wrapped into a purchase that includes goods, such as a weapons purchase. Each definition has a numeric or alphanumeric code which designates the commodity grouping in which SSC places the product or service. As the *Suppliers Guide* puts it: "The association of qualified firms to applicable GSINs result in source lists". You might notice, by the way, that this process makes it hard to sell a totally new product. (If SSC hasn't got it on its list, it's as if it doesn't really exist!)

You use the lists of commodities and services in Section II with their codes and descriptions to complete block 8 on the regional form, and block 20 on the national form. "If you cannot make an association between your products/services and Section II, provide a brief description," says the *Guide,* but SSC likely hopes you don't provide one.

On both forms, SSC asks you to complete all blocks. In civil service terms, this means that if you do not know or if the section does not apply, write "N.A.", for Non-Applicable or Not Available. *Never* leave it empty.

The term "Industrial Sector" means the sector which SSC thinks best denotes your type of business. It does not refer to the clientele you serve. For example, if you make farm machinery, the correct sector would be "Manufacturing Industries," not "Agricultural and Related Service Industries".

It would help if you had a crystal ball or a consultant around, but there are other ways to answer this one. Just make a stab at it. Go to SSC, DRIE, or your province for help, or call on other federal agencies like Statistics Canada, Labour Canada, or the Canadian Employment and Immigration Commission to help pick the applicable sectors. When your form is complete, run it past an official at your nearest SSC office.

"Size of Business" means your average employment, and includes your corporate affiliates in Canada. It is based on the number of persons employed on any basis for the past twelve months. If your firm has not been in existence for twelve months, use the average employment of your business and its corporate affiliates during the period it has been in existence.

Continuing, SSC's *Guide* says: "Your consent is required for the release of certain information held in the SSC automated sourcing system to third parties for sourcing purposes." Third parties are identified as other levels of governments, i.e. provincial or municipal governments. Data subject to this consent, requested in block 19 of the national and block 10 of the regional form, would include:

> Name and address (bid-solicitation points)
> Language of preference
> Expressed export interest
> Business size
> Industrial sector
> Commodities for which you are registered as a potential
>   supplier and associated data
> Ownership (country)

This is intended to allow SSC to provide basic data on your firm and your products to other federal agencies, and to provincial or foreign departments or agencies who may take part in joint procurements or sourcing with Ottawa. It promises that "all financial and sales data would be excluded." As a rule, public servants are careful with such information. However, it is possible that this information eventually will become public and therefore available to your competitors. Of course, SSC reminds you, "Provision of the information requested is voluntary. It is necessary, however, so that SSC can make a fair decision." Admittedly, there is some duress involved because if you do not provide it, you probably will not get bid requests.

Suppliers of services related to goods are asked to put the following codes before the commodities they handle.

X—"Repair, overhaul, modification, maintenance, calibration".

R—"Rental", includes short-term leasing of goods or equipment for temporary requirements, which may be extended. Maintenance is usually included in the rental. Typical rentals are garden-and-lawn equipment, construction equipment, office equipment and vehicles. Rental does not include services such as charters of ships and aircraft.

L—"Leasing" covers the rental of goods and equipment for long-term or continuing requirements. It is an alternative to purchase. Maintenance terms are normally specified in the lease.

D—"Production Design" is used to mean separate design services related to the acquisition of specific goods, but not scientific research and development.

I—"Installation" includes installation of government-furnished equipment such as aircraft engines, equipment in ships and other separately identified installation requirements. It excludes installation work covered in acquisition costs and building-related installation, and it is not the same as acquisition.

Question 17 on the national form asks if you have an export interest. I strongly suggest that even if you don't and don't expect to have one, you always answer "yes". I propose this because you may change your mind or be tempted to do so if you learn of good opportunities, and it is always a good idea to get on every federal list you can. Moreover, you will find that officials in agencies like the Canadian Commercial Corporation, External Affairs Canada, or the Export Development Corporation sometimes are better informed, less busy, or more helpful than some SSC staff. Frequently they know of other federal sales possibilities.

When you have completed filling out the forms, send the regional form to your nearest SSC office. (See Appendices I and II.) National forms can be delivered in person to:

Supply and Services Canada
Sourcing and Materials Priorities Group
Place du Portage, Phase III
11 Laurier Avenue
Hull, Québec K1A 0S5

or be mailed to:

Supply and Services Canada
Ottawa, Canada
K1A 0S5

Follow-up Forms

In some cases, your GSIN selections in Part I may be enough to enable SSC to determine your source-list registration. In other cases, after your Part I national form arrives in Ottawa, SSC will send you a more detailed listing of GSINs within your selected broad commodity grouping(s) and the commodity-related questionnaire(s) (Part II). This is to let you more precisely provide GSIN listings for those products/services purchased on a national basis which you feel you can supply. "Indiscriminate selection must be avoided to preclude the listing of your firm for goods or services it is unable to furnish," warns the *Guide*. SSC may also request more detailed documentation to support your requested listings.

When Part II is received by the Sourcing and Materials Priorities Group, the two parts will be "brought together", as SSC officials tend to express it, and forwarded to product managers for a decision on whether or not to accept your request to be listed. Some federal buys, especially high-technology or defence ones, also require quality-assurance programs. Block 18 of the national form asks for this information. Third-party certification programs such as the Canadian Standards Association (CSA), Z-299 and Allied Quality Assurance Publications (AQAP) are common and widely recognized. (The former DND

1015 form is now AQAP No.1, DND 1016 is now AQAP No.4 and DND 1017 is now AQAP No.9.)

If you undertake research-and-development projects or perform related scientific activities, refer to the Science and Technology listing in the Services part of Section II of the *Guide*.

The *Guide* has one further warning: "Applicants, however, should be aware that the federal government has a Conflict of Interest and Post-Employment Code. If you or any employee of your company is an employee of the federal government, or was an employee of the government at the Senior Management level or higher within the last year, this code applies. If this situation exists, you or your company should declare a potential conflict of interest at the time of your application. Failure to do so may have a significant effect on your potential listings."

This prohibition does not seem to have stopped a number of former senior civil servants and generals from being hired lately by suppliers. In practice, military personnel below the rank of general usually are not included, nor are most public servants.

You can get your copy of the Code, Catalogue No. BT 53-3/1985, from:

> Canadian Government Publishing Centre
> Supply and Services Canada
> Ottawa, Canada K1A 0S9

Frequently Asked Questions About Sourcing

How Do You Show You Are Interested?

The onus is on you to write, telephone, or visit a local SSC office or headquarters. As one SSC officer puts it, "SSC feels that in the buyer-seller relationship, you, the seller, have the obligation to tell SSC, the buyer, what you want to sell." In addition, he says, since SSC and departments are spending the taxpayers' dollars, "the government tries to establish that the firms it may be dealing with are competent." That's the rationale behind the follow-up forms SSC asks you to fill out, and the SSC pre-qualification policy.

Again, remember that since SSC lists are maintained on a commodity or service basis, the precision of your answers may mean the difference between receiving a bid or not. "Our inventory contains about 20,000 commodities or services, so you have to be precise. In most cases the information we get on the application is sufficient," says John Corr, director-general in charge of audit in SSC.

Always keep an ear and eye out to find out who the key individuals are who make the decisions to buy your products in SSC and in line departments. Then show them you can produce.

Are There Specialized Source-Lists?

SSC maintains specialized source-lists in science and technology, publishing, and many other sectors. Write to the appropriate directorate (see Appendices I and II) to inquire about them.

Am I on the List, and Am I Listed for the Right Thing?

When you have been fully registered, the HQ Sourcing and Materials Priorities Group or the appropriate regional office is supposed to notify you of the overall listing decision. If they do not or you are not happy with your listing, write to or visit them.

How Much Does It Cost to Get Listed?

Like other potential suppliers, you may fear that you will never be paid for the time and effort you put into filling out the forms to get yourself on a federal source-list, or for the large amount of work involved in writing proposals.

But you can be compensated either directly or indirectly for this work. Ultimately, of course, the payoff is in the profits on sales you make after putting in your bid. Lately, though, many large federal buys have an initial "contract definition stage" so that the prime contractors, subcontractors, and consultants get paid up-front for the R & D and paperwork. Another option is to add that time as a general and administration (G & A) expense to your contract.

How Does Ottawa Keep Your Sourcing Information Current?

Keeping your sourcing data up to date is a shared responsibility between you and the government. You should regularly review your application and notify SSC of any changes so you don't miss opportunities. It is your responsibility to keep SSC informed of changes that affect your capabilities, such as change of plant location, new research capabilities, expanded production facilities, or new product lines.

SSC also conducts regular reviews of its source-lists on a three-year cycle, so you will be receiving periodic requests for updates. Respond to these requests made by SSC to update the information held on your firm, even if there is nothing new, so they know you are alive. If you need help or feel that your file needs updating, contact the nearest SSC office and request updating.

When Is a Firm Removed from Source-Lists?

Names of suppliers are removed from source-lists as a matter of course when SSC receives evidence of a supplier's request for removal; supplier's bankruptcy or business failure, permanent shutdown, fire or other disasters which render the enterprise inoperable for an extended period; or when mail is returned to the department.

SSC may also take your name off when you frequently fail to bid without adequate reason, or you do not meet the terms and conditions of contracts. In these cases, an SSC official says, you would be informed before your name is removed and the reason for the decision would be given to you.

Can Suppliers Be Reinstated after Removal from Source-Lists?

SSC says that in principle a decision to remove a supplier from source-lists for cause is not irrevocable. If a supplier can furnish satisfactory evidence to support the claim that the circumstances leading to the removal have been rectified, the firm's name will again be added to the applicable source-lists.

What Does SSC Do When It Does Not Have a Commodity-List or Source-List?

When SSC does not have listings for a particular commodity, it may seek suppliers or develop lists of possible suppliers from relevant professional, business, or trade magazines, like *Aerospace and Defence Technology*, *Cable Communication Magazine*, *Materials Management and Distribution*, *Canadian Research*, *Modern Purchasing*, or *Canadian Building*, the Yellow Pages, industry directories, trade shows, newspapers, or trade indexes. Making your products and name known in business magazine articles or advertisements can be a very effective way to become listed for government subcontract work.

What is NASIS?

All sourcing-lists are currently in the process of being recorded on-line on SSC's National Automated Sourcing Information System—NASIS. NASIS eventually will provide information on registered suppliers which can be accessed through SSC or buying-department terminals. It will be national in scope, and it currently has sourcing-information on approximately 90,000 potential suppliers across the country.

It is important to note that you, the supplier, must ensure that you are properly listed in the system and with all the appropriate SSC regional offices. Many suppliers seem to think that if a firm lists itself at a regional level, it is automatically listed at a national level, or if listed at a national level it is automatically given a regional listing. This is not so. These are separate listings.

So when you see a NASIS terminal at a SSC booth in a trade show, or next time you are at one of SSC's purchasing offices ask for a printout on your company and check that you're properly listed for everything you can or might supply, and for the geographical markets that interest you. Specifically ask for a printout of your regional and your national listing.

You also should remember that SSC has a policy of "area buying", that is, of requiring regional-supply centres to solicit bids within the geographic area closest to the end-user, provided there is adequate competition. When competition for a particular requirement may extend beyond the immediate area, existing source-lists are obtained from the other regional offices and/or from headquarters.

Ottawa's Other Big Sourcing System: Public Works Canada

In fiscal year 1985-86, while SSC placed $4.9 billion in contracts for federal departments and agencies, Ottawa's other big central-purchasing agency, Public Works Canada (PWC) was spending another $1.28 billion.

As Canada's biggest property manager, PWC handles 3.5 million square metres in government-owned assets, 2.1 million square metres in leased premises, and 0.4 million square metres in lease-purchase properties, totalling some 2,500 owned and 3,200 leased properties. Since PWC has a total staff of only 7,600, that means a lot of contracts or orders have to be given to the private sector for goods, services, and space. Defence Construction Canada, which reports to PWC's minister, also handles construction and major property maintenance for DND.

To cope, PWC hires everything from architectural, engineering, and heavy construction to building-cleaning services from the private sector, and sets general office standards for the government. Since it is hard to apply a civil-service test when hiring an elevator operator, such blue-collar government jobs are frequently handled by PWC through the local government MP or minister. Yet many PWC contracts and jobs are very white-collar, and very impressive in dollars paid.

PWC is a big builder by North American standards. Last year, for example, it spent $450 million to design and contract for its federal clients and provided $4.57 million for applied research, development, and demonstration. In addition to spending $507.5 million on behalf of federal departments on long-term contracts, PWC, like SSC, has some big clients. Its biggies in 1986-87 were:

Client	$ million
Canada Post Corporation	160.7
Transport Canada	82.8
Fisheries and Oceans	56.1
Correctional Services Canada	53.5
Royal Canadian Mounted Police	53.3
Indian and Northern Affairs Canada	46.8
Agriculture Canada	43.1
Environment Canada	33.7
Health and Welfare Canada	25.3
Other federal clients	131.9

This year, the minister of Public Works and his PWC officials will hand out some $600 million for construction, architecture, and engineering to some of the 15,000 contractors and 5,000 consultants on PWC source-lists.

It remains something of a mystery why PWC and SSC both buy similar items such as engineering and architectural services, although this overlap may stem from ancient departmental histories or competing political empires. Clearly, the trick here is to get on one or more of its source-lists, and then let your price, selling ability, track record, merits, and personality, help you.

Recent PWC advertising asserts that "You Want to Do Business with PWC." It boasts: "At PWC we ensure: competitive tendering; equal opportunity to tender; identical information to all bidders; best value and fairness in spending public funds." Get a copy of the department's convenient booklet *Doing Business with PWC: A Directory of PWC Contacts*, which gives the names, titles, and phone numbers of key PWC personnel.

Regrettably, SSC does not have a similar department-wide guide for SSC suppliers, although SSC's Aerospace, Marine and Electronics Systems (AMES) Directorate does have one of its own, and its July 1988 edition of the *R & D Bulletin* also listed key Science and Professional Service Directorate staff. Chapter 8 tells you how to get these and other useful government publications free.

PWC's tendering process is laid out in the government-wide Government Contracting Regulations already referred to, and in internal PWC policy and procedural guidelines. Internal directives deal with advertising tender calls, distributing tender documents, receiving and opening tenders, bid security, and other procedural matters. Tenders are to be used for repair and construction work where possible.

Overall, GCRs let PWC award a contract up to $30,000 without a public tender call, if the need is one of pressing urgency in which delay would be injurious to the public interest; if the nature of the work is such that it would not be in the public interest to invite tenders; or if only one firm is capable of completing the contract. In very special circumstances, PWC can award a construction contract valued in excess of $30,000 without public tender call; sometimes as high as $200,000.

Although you may be working for PWC as a contractor, a consultant, or as a leaser of property, let's talk about the contractor part first.

Becoming a PWC Contractor

Construction and Technical Services, including construction, repair, renovation and restoration, are part of the ACCORD (Administration and Control of Contracts and Regional Data) system. This regionally-based "Contractors Index" is a computerized inventory of qualified contractors, both individuals and firms, who are invited on a rotating basis to bid for PWC contracts under $30,000. Public tenders are usually called for contracts over this limit.

Between $10,000 and $30,000 wide tenders are also the preferred route. Between $1,000 and $10,000 tenders are normally invited from at least three contractors on the index. Below $1,000, the regional offices get a quotation from the next contractor on the index rotation. The index is categorized into particular trades and specialties.

The PWC listing-forms seem delightfully simple. Since they are flip-forms with English on one side and French on the other, they are much less cluttered-looking than the bilingual SSC sourcing-forms.

Starting with the names of your principal partners and officers, the value of contracts for which you wish to be considered, your largest prime-contracting job to date, the largest contracts to date, a recent banking and work reference, and whether or not you are incorporated, the form provides a handy checklist for you to list your trade/specialty: something SSC would have a hard time doing with 20,000 different products.

The list covers general contracting, site work, concrete, masonry, carpentry/woodwork, thermal and moisture protection, doors and windows, finishes, specialty work, equipment, furnishings, special construction, conveying systems, mechanical work, and electrical work, with subcategories provided for each. You also are asked if you are interested in repair or servicing/cleaning, construction/installation. Some suppliers have found that just filling out the form suggests new types of work.

The department says "the performance of all contractors is monitored for quality of work and delivery date." Two or more branches of the same firm can apply.

For larger construction contracts, public tenders are advertised through newspapers, but "the notice normally appears only once in each paper." You can see the tender documents at a PWC office, your construction association, or local post office.

Becoming a Consultant to PWC

The real goodies at PWC are for architectural and engineering (A & E) consulting. PWC invites proposals from Canadian and sometimes foreign firms or individuals listed in its consultants inventory. These include the building sciences, behavioural science, and fine arts. You register by filling in a very simple questionnaire, which is obtained from that branch (see Appendix IV), Architectural and Engineering Services Branch, Public Works Canada, Ottawa K1A 0M2, or from a PWC regional office listed at the end of this chapter (Appendix I).

A & E consulting contracts are selected from the PWC consultants sourcing-list, where fees are under $15,000. Between $15,000 and $200,000, "consultants are selected on a non-competitive basis under ministerial authority"—in other words, through political patronage. The department short-lists commissions over $100,000, with the minister making the decision under $400,000, and Treasury Board over that figure.

Leasing to PWC

PWC leases by open tendering for large office accommodation. These opportunities are advertised publicly, and are based on detailed PWC specifications. For office space of less than 250 square metres, it invites tenders from selected suppliers. Its guidelines say that "all bids are reviewed publicly and analyzed by a team of technical specialists."

Like SSC, and other common-service agencies to be covered in Chapter 4, PWC disqualifies tenders for several reasons, including incomplete forms, a bid not in accord with the requirements of the tender documents or a bid without a proper performance bond. The successful bidder also has to be judged able to guarantee the necessary equipment, capable of carrying out the task, have a satisfactory record and have balanced unit prices.

Bids have to be on the PWC-provided forms. "The low bidder will be awarded the contract if . . . the contractor is judged to be competent and capable of carrying out the full scope of the work," say PWC guidelines.

If the lowest tender is still too high, PWC may negotiate with the low bidder for a reduced price, provided the changes in the nature of the work are minor and the reduction sought is less than ten per cent of the value of the tender. Otherwise, tenders will usually be reinvited from at least the three low tenderers. In some cases, all tenderers on the original tender call may be reinvited.

In the next chapter, we will look in more detail at SSC and its many sourcing-systems, and at some other common-service purchasing agencies, where you might be able to sell at one stop.

Appendix I

Contact List
for Supply and Services Canada

Senior Officials

Minister and Receiver General for
Canada
Hon. Otto Jelinek
(819) 997-5421

Deputy Minister and Deputy
Receiver General for Canada
Georgina Wyman
(819) 956-1707

Corporate Policy and Planning
Sector
Assistant Deputy Minister
R. D. Weese
(819) 956-1711

Management and Operational
Services Sector
Assistant Deputy Minister
A. G. Ross
(819) 956-1738

Finance and Administration
Sector
Assistant Deputy Minister
S. E. Whiteley
(819) 956-1715

Supply Operations Sector
Assistant Deputy Minister
B. T. Boyd
(819) 956-1727

Supplier Contact Points at Headquarters

To Become Registered or to Contact SSC's Main Sourcing-List:

Statistical Information and Data Management Branch
Corporate Supplier Services Group
4th Floor, Core B3
Place du Portage, Phase III
11 Laurier Street
Hull, Québec
Tel: (819) 956-3400
Telex: DSS HULL 053-3703

Mailing Address:
Statistical Information and Data
Management Branch
Corporate Supplier Services Group
Ottawa, Canada K1A 0S5

Supplier and Registration and
Data Management Section
Tel: (819) 956-3444
Telex: DSS HULL 053-3703

Supplier Relations Section
Tel: (819) 956-3400
Telex: DSS HULL 053-3703

Bid Receiving Unit
Core OA1 (Main Lobby)
Place du Portage, Phase III
11 Laurier Street
Hull, Québec
Tel: (819) 997-9776
Telex: DSS HULL 053-3703
DEX: 3200 (819) 956-3370
Rapicom 6200: (819) 994-0080

To Be Listed with and to Consult Headquarters Directorates:

Supply and Services Canada
Place du Portage, Phase III
11 Laurier Street
Hull, Québec
Telex: DSS HULL 053-3703

Mailing Address:
Supply and Services Canada
Ottawa, Canada K1A 0S5

Aerospace, Marine and Electronics Systems Directorate(AMES)
Director General
H. T. Webster
(819) 956-0010

Aerospace and Electronics
  Procurement Branch
8th Floor, Core C1
Tel: (819) 956-0236

Marine and Armament
  Procurement Branch
6th Floor, Core C1
Tel: (819) 956-6684

Communications Service Directorate (CSD)
Director General
N. Manchevsky
(819) 997-5321
Communications Services
  Procurement Branch
1st Floor, Core C2
Tel: (819) 997-7266

Canadian Government Printing
  Services
3rd Floor, National Printing Bureau
  Bldg.
45 Sacré-Coeur Blvd.
Hull, Québec K1A 0S7
Tel: (819) 997-7261

Canadian Government
  Expositions/Audio-Visual Centre
Expositions Group
440 Coventry Road
Ottawa, Ontario K1A 0T1
Tel: (613) 993-1848

Sponsor Program Group
150 Kent Street
Ottawa, Ontario K1A 0M9
Tel: (613) 996-7722

Photo Centre Group
Tunney's Pasture
No. 18 Goldenrod Street
National Personnel Records Centre
Ottawa, Ontario K1A 0M9
Tel: (613) 990-8245

Canadian Government Publishing
  Centre
2nd Floor, National Printing Bureau
  Bldg.
45 Sacré-Coeur Blvd.
Hull, Québec K1A 0S9
Tel: (819) 997-4962

Industrial and Commercial Products Directorate
Director General
G. J. Brown
(819) 997-7052

Transportation and Energy Products
  Branch
7th Floor, Core B3
Tel: (819) 994-3343

Scientific, Electrical, Mechanical &
  Construction Products Branch
7th Floor, Core A2
Tel: (819) 994-4211

Consumer Products and Traffic
  Management Branch
9th Floor, Core B3
Tel: (819) 997-5219

Office Automation, Services & Information Systems Directorate
Director General
B. H. E. Maynard
(819) 956-1181

Procurement Operations Branch
2nd Floor, Core C2
Tel: (819) 956-1184

Product Technology and
  Account Management Branch
3rd Floor, Core C2
Tel: (819) 956-1001

Science and Professional
  Services Directorate
Director General
N. Bhumgara
(819) 956-1782

Science Programs Branch
12th Floor, Core C1
Tel: (819) 956-1784

Science Branch
12th Floor, Core C1
Tel: (819) 956-1788

Professional Services Branch
10th Floor, Core C1
Tel: (819) 956-1412

**Bureau of Management
Consulting**
Director General
Seymour Isenberg
(819) 992-3574

Audit Services Bureau
Director General
E. R. Salmon
(819) 995-6341

**Canadian General Standards
Board**
Executive Director
P. C. Cameron
(819) 956-0432

Security Branch
Director
E. J. Snyder
(819) 953-3623

**Statistical Information and
Data Management Branch**
Director
C. Donnelly
(819) 956-3410

Address:
Supply and Services Canada
Place du Portage, Phase III
11 Laurier Street
Hull, Québec K1A 0S5

Publishing Centre:
Supply and Services Canada
Canadian Government
  Publishing Centre
Ottawa, Ontario K1A 0S9

Supplier Contact Points in Your Community

Atlantic Directorate

Director General:
S. J. Hammond

Supply and Services Canada
6th Floor, Ralston Bldg.
1557 Hollis Street
Halifax, Nova Scotia B3J 1V5
Tel: (902) 426-9333
Telex: DSS HDD HFX 019-22513
Rapicom 3100: (902) 426-8444

Mailing Address:
Supply and Services Canada
P.O. Box 2252
Halifax, Nova Scotia B3J 3C8

Nova Scotia Region
Supply and Services Canada
2 Morris Drive
Burnside Industrial Park
Dartmouth, Nova Scotia B3B 1S6
Tel: (902) 426-3881
Telex: DSS REGSUP DRT
  019-31554
Rapicom 3100: (902) 426-8808

Halifax Office, CFB Halifax
Supply and Services Canada
Building D 155, 3rd Floor
Halifax, Nova Scotia B3K 2X0
Tel: (902) 426-4889
Telex: BASESUPPLYHFX
  019-23541

New Brunswick Region
Saint John District
Supply and Services Canada
Room 229, Customs Bldg.
189 Prince William Street
Saint John, New Brunswick
E2L 2B9
Tel: (506) 648-4895
Telex: DSS REGSUP SNB
014-47293
Rapicom 3100: (506) 648-4376

Moncton Purchasing Office
Supply and Services Canada
P.O. Box 746
310-H Baig Blvd.
Moncton, New Brunswick
E1E 1C8
Tel: (506) 857-6020
Telex: DSS SUP MCTN
016-2663
Rapicom 3100: (506) 857-6759

Newfoundland Region
St. John's District
Supply and Services Canada
Building 205, Mitchell Place
Pleasantville
St. John's, Newfoundland
A1A 1S8
Tel: (709) 772-5396
Telex: DSS REGSUP SNF
016-4672
Rapicom 3100: (709) 772-4603

Goose Bay Purchasing Office
Supply and Services Canada
Building 271
P.O. Box 7001, Station A
Goose Bay, Labrador A0P 1C0
Tel: (709) 896-5911
Telex: DSS SUPCEN GBAY
016-2240

Prince Edward Island Region
Charlottetown Purchasing Office
Supply and Services Canada
17 Queen Street, Lowden Bldg.
Charlottetown, P.E.I. C1A 4A2
Tel: (902) 566-7386
Telex: DSS SUPCHTN
014-44233

Québec Directorate

Director General: P. Comeau

Supply and Services Canada
3rd Floor, East Tower
Guy Favreau Complex
200 Dorchester Blvd. W.
Montréal, Québec H2Z 1X4
Tel: (514) 283-1310
Telex: DSS MDO MTL 05-267472
Rapicom 3100: (514) 283-5504

Western Québec Region
Supply and Services Canada
800 Golf Road
Nun's Island
Montréal, Québec H3E 1G9
Tel: (514) 283-4863
Telex: DSS REGSUP MTL 05-25425
Rapicom 3100: (514) 283-5708

Laval Purchasing Office
Supply and Services Canada
250 Montée St.-François,
Room F 32
Laval, Québec H7C 1S5
Tel: (514) 661-5987
Telex: SOLGENMAS VOL
05-268866

Longue-Pointe Purchasing Office
Supply and Services Canada
6769 Notre-Dame Street East
Montréal, Québec H1N 2E9
Tel: (514) 283-8097
Telex: DSSMASMLP MTL
05-828670

Mailing Address:
Longue-Pointe Purchasing Office
Supply and Services Canada
P.O. Box 6109
Montréal, Québec H3C 3H7

Eastern Québec Region
Supply and Services Canada
Room 301,
1040 Belvedere Avenue
Québec, Québec G1S 4N1
Tel: (418) 648-3151
Telex: DSS REGSUP QBC 051-3559
Rapicom 3100: (418) 648-2209

Rimouski District
Supply and Services Canada
140 St. Germain St. W.
Rimouski, Québec G5L 4B5
Tel: (418) 722-3382
Telex: DSS MAS MJLI 051-86402
Rapicom 3100: (418) 722-3396

Alma Purchasing Office
Saguenay, Lac St. Jean Region
Supply and Services Canada
170 St. Joseph Blvd. South
Alma, Québec G8B 3E8
Tel: (418) 662-6613
Telex: DSS PUR ALMA 051-36348
Rapicom 3100: (418) 662-3398

Central Directorate

Director General
D. G. Fournier

Supply and Services Canada
Place du Portage
Phase III, 7A1
11 Laurier Street
Hull, Québec K1A 0S5
Tel: (819) 997-5757
Telex: DSS 3029-5011032
Rapicom 5000: (819) 953-1068

Mailing Address:
Supply and Services Canada
Ottawa, Ontario K1A 0S5

Central District/Ontario Region
Supply and Services Canada
6205 Kestrel Road
Mississauga, Ontario L5T 2A1
Tel: (416) 670-6200
Telex: DSS REGSUP TOR
  06-217616
Facsimile: (416) 676-3375

South-Western District Office
Supply and Services Branch
Dominion Public Bldg.,
Room 504
457 Richmond Street
London, Ontario N6A 3E3
Tel: (519) 679-4035
Telex: IAND LDN 064-7127

Thunder Bay Purchasing Office
Supply and Services Canada
Government of Canada Bldg.,
Room 322
33 Court South
Thunder Bay, Ontario P7B 2W6
Tel: (807) 345-8252
Telex: DSS PUR THB 07-34257

Pembroke Purchasing Office
Supply and Services Canada
215 Pembroke Street East
Pembroke, Ontario K8A 3J8
Tel: (613) 735-4158
Telex: DSS SUP PEM 053-34528
Rapicom 3100: (613) 735-4521

South-Eastern District Office
Supply and Services Canada
407 Counter Street
Kingston, Ontario K7K 6A9
Tel: (613) 545-8058
Telex: DSS KDO KGTN 066-3379
Rapicom 3100: (613) 545-8067

Mailing Address:
South-Eastern District Office
Supply and Services Canada
P.O. Bag 6400
Kingston, Ontario K7L 5J5

Downsview Purchasing Office
Supply and Services Canada
c/o CFB Toronto
Bldg. 151
Downsview, Ontario M3K 1Y7
Tel: (416) 635-4731
Telex: DSS DNVW TOR 065-24081

Burlington Purchasing Office
Supply and Services Canada
867 Lakeshore Road
Burlington, Ontario L7S 1A1
Tel: (416) 336-4974
Telex: CCIW BUR 061-8296

Mailing Address:
Burlington Purchasing Office
Supply and Services Canada
P.O. Box 846
Burlington, Ontario L7R 3Y7

North York Purchasing Office
Supply and Services Canada
c/o Atmospheric Environment
 Services
4905 Dufferin Street
Downsview, Ontario M3H 5T4
Tel: (416) 667-4929
Telex: DOE HQAES TOR
 06-964582

North District Office
Supply and Services Canada
147 McIntyre Street West
North Bay, Ontario P1B 2Y5
Tel: (705) 476-4340

(National) Capital Region
Capital Region Supply Centre
Supply and Services Canada
1010 Somerset Street West
Ottawa, Ontario K1A 0T4
Tel: (613) 995-1121
Telex: DSS ISC OTT 053-3983
Rapicom 3100: (613) 995-6512

Western Directorate

Director General: R. Neville

Supply and Services Canada
Harry Hayes Bldg., Room 584
220 – 4th Avenue S.E.
Calgary, Alberta T2G 4X3
Tel: (403) 292-4582
Rapicom 120: (403) 292-4586

Mailing Address:
Supply and Services Canada
P.O. Box 2950, Station M
Calgary, Alberta T2P 4C3

Manitoba Region
Supply and Services Canada
100 Otter Street
Winnipeg, Manitoba R3T 0M8
Tel: (204) 949-6100
Telex: DSS REGSUP WPG
 07-57734
Rapicom 3100: (204) 949-7796

Shilo Purchasing Office
Supply and Services Canada
P.O. Box 160
Shilo, Manitoba R0K 2A0

Tel: (204) 765-4779
Telex: DSS SHILO 07-50297

**Alberta and Northwest
Territories Region**
Supply and Services Canada
15508 – 114 Avenue
Edmonton, Alberta T5M 3S8
Tel: (403) 495-3704
Telex: DSS REGSUP EDM
 037-3960
Facsimile: (403) 495-3399

Calgary District
Supply and Services Canada
220 – 4th Avenue S.E.
Room 620
Calgary, Alberta T2G 4X3
Tel: (403) 292-5701
Telex: DSS REGSUP CGY
 038-21884
Rapicom 3100: (403) 292-4421

Saskatchewan Region
Saskatchewan Regional Supply Office
1783 Hamilton Street
Regina, Saskatchewan S4P 4H3
Tel: (306) 780-7332
Telex: DSS REGSUP REG 071-2731
Rapicom 3100: (306) 780-6845

Pacific Directorate

Director General:
George Suffidy (Acting)

Supply and Services Canada
1133 Melville Street, 8th Floor
Vancouver, British Columbia
V6E 4E5
Tel: (604) 666-6983

British Columbia and Yukon Region
Supply and Services Canada
12171 Horseshoe Way
Richmond, British Columbia
V7A 4Z6
Tel: (604) 272-9015
Telex: DSS REGSUP VCR
 043-55731
Rapicom 3100: (604) 272-9007

Vancouver Island District
Supply and Services Canada
Room 318
Canadian Customs House
816 Government Street
Victoria, British Columbia
V8W 1X2
Tel: (604) 388-3160
Telex: DSS DISSUP VIC
049-7380
Rapicom 3100: (604) 388-3344

Abbotsford Purchasing Office
Supply and Services Canada
33344 King Road
Abbotsford, British Columbia
V2S 6E3
Tel: (604) 854-2516
Telex: DSS REGSUP VCR
043-55731

Marine and Industrial Machinery
  Procurement Division
120 Lonsdale Avenue
North Vancouver,
British Columbia
V7M 2E8
Tel: (604) 666-3216
Telex: DSS MARINE VCR
043-52735

Whitehorse Purchasing Office
Supply and Services Canada
102 – 307 Jarvis Street
Whitehorse, Yukon Territory
Y1A 2H3
Tel: (403) 668-5808
Telex: DSS PUR WHSE
036-8-297
Rapicom 3100: (403) 668-6012

European Region

England
European Region
Canadian Dept. of Supply and
  Services
Macdonald House
No.1 Grosvenor Square
London, England W1X 0AB
Tel: 011-44-1-629-9429-437-612
Telex: DSS LDN
  (via External Affairs)
Rapicom 3100: 011-44-1-491-3968

Germany
Canadian Government – Lahr
Supply and Services Canada
c/o HQ CF Europe
CFPO 5000
7630 Lahr/Schew, West Germany
Tel: 011-49-7821-37864

Canadian Government –
  Koblenz
Supply and Services Canada
Mainzer Strasse 39
Post fach 566
5400 Koblenz
Federal Republic of Germany
Tel: 011-49-261-1-7054
Telex: 0862661 BWB KOBLENZ

Washington Region
Director
Washington Region
Supply and Services Canada
Canadian Embassy
2450 Massachussetts Ave. N.W.
Washington, D.C.
U.S.A. 20008
Tel: (202) 483-5505
Telex: 008-9532
  (CAN DSS ITC WSH)
Rapicom 3100: (202) 485-5520

Appendix II

ORGANIZATION CHART, SUPPLY AND SERVICES CANADA

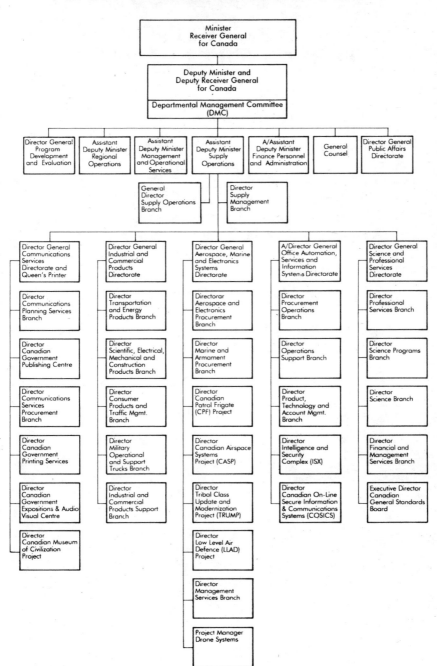

Minister
Receiver General
for Canada

Deputy Minister and
Deputy Receiver General
for Canada

Departmental Management Committee
(DMC)

Director General Program Development and Evaluation

Assistant Deputy Minister Regional Operations

Assistant Deputy Minister Management and Operational Services

Assistant Deputy Minister Supply Operations

A/Assistant Deputy Minister Finance Personnel and Administration

General Counsel

Director General Public Affairs Directorate

General Director Supply Operations Branch

Director Supply Management Branch

Director General Communications Services Directorate and Queen's Printer

Director General Industrial and Commercial Products Directorate

Director General Aerospace, Marine and Electronics Systems Directorate

A/Director General Office Automation, Services and Information Systems Directorate

Director General Science and Professional Services Directorate

Director Communications Planning Services Branch

Director Transportation and Energy Products Branch

Directorar Aerospace and Electronics Procurement Branch

Director Procurement Operations Branch

Director Professional Services Branch

Director Canadian Government Publishing Centre

Director Scientific, Electrical, Mechanical and Construction Products Branch

Director Marine and Armament Procurement Branch

Director Operations Support Branch

Director Science Programs Branch

Director Communications Services Procurement Branch

Director Consumer Products and Traffic Mgmt. Branch

Director Canadian Patrol Frigate (CPF) Project

Director Product, Technology and Account Mgmt. Branch

Director Science Branch

Director Canadian Government Printing Services

Director Military Operational and Support Trucks Branch

Director Canadian Airspace Systems Project (CASP)

Director Intelligence and Security Complex (ISX)

Director Financial and Management Services Branch

Director Canadian Government Expositions & Audio Visual Centre

Director Industrial and Commercial Products Support Branch

Director Tribal Class Update and Modernization Project (TRUMP)

Director Canadian On-Line Secure Information & Communications Systems (COSICS)

Executive Director Canadian General Standards Board

Director Canadian Museum of Civilization Project

Director Low Level Air Defence (LLAD) Project

Director Management Services Branch

Project Manager Drone Systems

Appendix III

CONTACTS FOR PUBLIC WORKS CANADA

Minister
The Hon. Stewart McInnes
(613) 998-0948

Deputy Minister
Robert Giroux
(613) 998-8118

Director, Materiel and Facilities Planning
O. Hartwick
(613) 998-2020

Address:
Sir Charles Tupper Bldg.
Riverside Drive
Ottawa, Ontario K1A 0M2

Regional Offices

Atlantic Region
Director General: G. Westland
P.O. Box 2247,
Postal Station M
Halifax, Nova Scotia B3J 3C9
Tel: (902) 426-2341

Québec Region
Director General: G. Wolfe
Guy Favreau Complex
6th Floor, East Tower
200 Dorchester Blvd. W.
Montréal, Québec H2Z 1X4
Tel: (514) 283-4850 or 283-4906

National Capital Region
Director General: P. Letellier
Place du Portage
Phase IV
Ottawa, Ontario K1A 0M3
Tel: (819) 997-7475

Ontario Region
Director General:
Suzanne Borup
4900 Yonge Street
Willowdale, Ontario M2N 6A6
Tel: (416) 224-4100

Western Region
Director General:
E. Bauckman
9925 – 109th Street
Edmonton, Alberta T5K 2J8
Tel: (403) 420-3183

Pacific Region
Director General:
N. Hoyt
1166 Alberni Street
Vancouver, British Columbia
V6E 3W5
(604) 666-2681

Defence Construction Canada (DCC)

President:
Lorne Atchison
(613) 998-9541

Administrative Services,
Manager
K. A. MacDonald
(613) 998-9518

Address:
Sir Charles Tupper Bldg.
3rd Floor, A Wing
Riverside Drive
Ottawa, Ontario K1A 0K3
(613) 998-9541

CHAPTER FOUR

The Government's Central Purchasing Agencies: A Profile

If you know the prime minister or an important cabinet minister, you probably can translate that connection into some sale to the government. And if you can start a letter to a deputy minister with "Dear Dad", you too may be well placed to get contracts out of Ottawa. Most of us don't have this sort of pull, though.

In fact, the great majority of contracts are ordered and handled by civil servants who have no connection to those with whom they are dealing. So, if you know the official or bureaucratic points of access to the federal purchasing system, you generally have as good a chance as the next person, and could be on your way to a sale.

As we discussed in the first three chapters, Supply and Services Canada (SSC) and Public Works Canada (PWC) are very big, central agencies who handle purchasing for many government organizations. So you need to know both of them well. However, they are not the only government entities who buy goods and services from the private sector. You also need to know who these other buyers are, and who sets the rules under which they all operate and who steers the course of the larger buys.

To truly cash in on federal procurement dollars, you need to know how to reach, in addition to SSC and PWC, all of the following:

a) the central control agencies like the Treasury Board, the Prime Minister's Office and others who watch over the public procurement pie, and especially the bigger buys.

b) the common-service agencies, like SSC and PWC and the Bureau of Management Consulting, who buy or commission goods or services for client departments or agencies and themselves.

c) the principle *client* departments who buy through SSC and PWC, the two big service agencies.

d) the really big buying departments and agencies who buy on their own and fund SSC or PWC acquisitions. (This will be covered in Chapter 5.)

e) the Crown corporations who are also the big buyers of goods and services through service agencies like SSC or on their own. (You will learn about these in Chapter 6.)

f) the big firms who already have or are likely to get major federal contracts, so that you can become their subcontractor. (For these, see Chapter 7.)

This chapter covers the first three of these areas in some detail. It also explains what the various SSC regional branches do and buy.

The Central Control Agencies

Any large bureaucracy, including companies like General Motors or IBM, tries to keep some overall, organization-wide control over its resources, policies, and its decisions. Governments, too, try to ensure such management co-ordination through the use of "central control agencies".

There are three of these agencies of special significance to anyone trying to sell to the federal government: the Prime Minister's Office, the Privy Council Office, and the Treasury Board.

Getting one of them on your side definitely helps your chances of getting government work, especially for larger contracts. Getting one opposed to you, or really wild about your competition, can harm you just as surely. So just as you would do with the formal board of directors and senior management structure of a regular corporate client, you need to keep these powerful agencies or their senior staff at least neutral.

The Prime Minister's Office

For the past twenty years, Canadian prime ministers have filled the Prime Minister's Office with personal and political confidants whom they personally hired or fired. In a sense, the PMO is like the office of the chairman of the board in a corporation. It usually doesn't decide who gets a contract to repair government buildings, but its staff are listened to in PWC, SSC and in the departments and agencies. They are not part of the civil service, and their concern is politics, or getting the government party and PM re-elected. Yet their access to the most powerful person in the country and their skill in using this advantage with ministers and civil servants give them considerable clout in policy and in procurement matters.

If you are interested in a senior government job too, you should note that the PMO also co-ordinates, clears, and "shortlists" patronage appointments. The PM has some 2,613 senior patronage jobs under his direct control, according to his deputy chief of staff responsible for government appointments, Marjory LeBreton—but they're not all as high-paying or high-profile as the newspapers sometimes claim.

The Privy Council Office

In addition to getting re-elected, a Prime Minister is also faced with the job of running the day-to-day operations of government and making broad policy decisions. Assisting him in this role is the Privy Council Office. The PCO is composed of public servants, and is not supposed to be directly concerned with the re-election of the government.

The PCO keeps the agenda for government and the cabinet, much as a secretary to a board of directors keeps its directors on track. The PCO also staffs powerful cabinet committees which (in theory) make most of the large decisions in procurement and other policy matters, after SSC and other officials have given them several options to examine. PCO staffers are career civil servants, and the PCO is definitely a high-status place to work. The deputy minister of this department is the top mandarin of them all.

Treasury Board

Like all federal contracts, federal procurements are also governed by the general management guidelines laid out by the federal government's central management committee, the Treasury Board (TB). This is Ottawa's general manager. The "Board", as civil servants call it, is technically a committee of the cabinet, comprised of a half-dozen or so key ministers who meet once or twice a month to make important decisions on government expenditures. These members also hold other full-time cabinet jobs. They are co-ordinated by a full-time president, who is also a cabinet minister.

Members of TB also have a full-time secretariat to handle submissions to the Board for project or funding approval. Composed of powerful career civil servants, this headquarters group controls much of the Board's agenda and its decisions. Its role is especially important on large buys like Major Crown Projects. As a rule, TB officials are middle- to senior-management level, on the fast-track to greater things in the bureaucracy.

TB also prepares and oversees the Government Contract Regulations made under the authority of the Financial Administration Act (FAA). While the FAA sets out the general framework for the management of federal money, GCRs cover contracts issued by SSC, PWC, and other departments, but do not include contracts entered into by Crown corporations listed in Schedule C of the FAA.

The Board also issues general-policy or administrative rules for hiring personnel and for contracting. One of the most important of these sets the dollar limits which can be contracted by particular government organizations or officials and the organizational levels of approval required to exceed these contracting limits. (A number of these limiting guidelines have been mentioned in previous chapters.) TB also approves expenditures above these limits or in areas where the government has some special overriding general policy or political concern.

While deputy ministers can enter into contracts as the heads of their departments, they must do so within dollar limits set out by TB. The latest limits are listed in a July 23, 1987, TB Circular 1987-36, TB Number 806000. Such a contracting authority also can sign a goods or non-consulting services contract without TB approval if the contract has been negotiated as part of a TB-approved Standing Offer. As well, Treasury Board also provides for exceptional contracting limits in certain cases.

Department of Justice

The federal Department of Justice acts like a common-service agency since it provides a pool of lawyers who handle almost all government agreements, contracts, court cases, and prosecutions as Ottawa's in-house legal counsel. Yet its real power base comes from its ability to draft and screen or vet laws and regulations. In effect, this makes it as much a control agency as the PCO or Treasury Board.

The Justice minister can give any law firm or lawyer legal work to do—plum patronage jobs for loyal firms or individuals. As well, public-service competitions are held for jobs at the Justice Department, where all of these officer jobs are filled by lawyers. Many Justice Department lawyers work full-time for a particular agency or department operating out of the client's premises; others work at the Justice Department's headquarters.

Common-Service Agencies: One-Stop Selling

Large organizations often try to spread overhead and other costs for common, in-house services (like word-processing pools, printing services, or data processing) over as wide a number of units in the firm as possible. The federal government does this too, and in many cases this practice provides you with a sort of one-stop selling situation, because if you can just sell your service to the central buyer, your service will then be used by many departments.

In fact, the departments and subdivisions who pay for the goods do not have a lot of discretion as to whether or not they want to use the central agency as their purchasing-agent: they must use it, or at least go to it before going to an outside supplier. As a result, departments annually pay Ottawa's biggest common-service agency, SSC, $600 million a year for it to do the legwork as their purchasing agent.

Formally, client departments or agencies decide the "what", "where" and "when"; common-service agencies such as SSC or PWC look after the "how" of procurements. In reality, of course, these decisions are interwoven: the service agency often has a major say in exactly when a good should be purchased, or where, and very few client departments leave the "how" entirely to an outside purchasing-agent.

To properly tap the government market, you need to be known by the common-service organizations that handle your sort of product as well as by the likely client department you expect will pay for them. If you understand and can use the psychology and the office politics at work in this sort of arrangement, you can often close a sale.

In fact, most departmental levels resent being a captive to SSC or any other common-service agency: they want to manage their departments, not pay for someone else's empire. So they develop ways to get around a service agency. Let's see how this happens.

In theory, SSC buys goods and services, but mostly it buys goods. Departments are freer to buy services than goods, essentially to "rent bodies", and many do. Thus, when a client department sees the quality or priority of work differently from the way a particular common-service agency does, or defines the nature of the work to be done differently, the department may go directly outside to the business community for the item needed, or perhaps tell the agency at a later stage that it needs the item urgently, or that there was only one supplier—the one they hired.

For example, all departments that need documents translated into French must use the centralized Secretary of State (SOS) translation process. To get around that requirement and the delays it can impose, a department might instead say it requires that a document be "adapted", or "edited", not translated, in which case they can use either avenues for procurement. In practice, bureaucrats get very good at these sorts of semantic games.

There are several other federal, common-service agencies which are not as well known as PWC or SSC, but which may be good markets for your services or goods. We'll look at them below.

Public Service Commission

The Public Service Commission (PSC) is the federal government's recruitment and staff training service: it's where you go to get hired as a public servant. It also has several branches which buy services. Its Staff Development Branch, for example, handles much of the employee training within the government. This Branch has a lot of experience and expertise in using outside teachers or trainers in human relations, management and computer skills, and the two official languages, and it hires people to teach in these and many other areas. Another innovative program run by the PSC is "Interchange Canada", which promotes the exchange of employees between businesses, universities, and governments.

Translations Operations Branch, Department of the Secretary of State

The Secretary of State's department too is a market for social-science and humanities graduates and for linguists, especially in English, French, or Romance languages, German, Russian, or Japanese. Work ranges from preparing commercial or legal documents to House of Commons or Senate documents, to simultaneous-translation assignments. Quite a lot of this work is freelanced.

The Government Telecommunications Agency

The Government Telecommunications Agency (GTA) is the federal government's own telephone company, located within the Department of Communications (DOC). It handles local and long-distance calls on lines rented from phone companies. If you manufacture goods or offer services in the telecommunications area, the GTA is a good place to look for a customer, and being hired by them is an excellent endorsement of your product.

Audit Services Bureau

The Audit Services Bureau (ASB), housed inside SSC with some 300 auditors on staff, is the largest source of auditing expertise in the government. It audits contracts for SSC, for Health and Welfare Canada, DRIE, and for many other energy or welfare expenditures. It also conducts comprehensive auditing of organizational operations and does systems audits and auditor training.

The ASB hires private-sector firms and auditing or accounting professionals when the workload warrants it. It also has regional offices outside Ottawa.

Bureau of Management Consulting

The Bureau of Management Consulting (BMC) is Ottawa's in-house management consulting firm which is also located in SSC. On a fee-for-service basis, it provides highly-trained experienced consultants to federal, provincial, and international agencies in consulting fields such as finance and management science; management-information systems; general management consulting; program operations; economics; organization and human-resources management.

If you or your firm are interested in being considered for freelance work as a management consultant, you definitely should read recent and back issues of BMC's quarterly publication, *Optimum,* mentioned in Chapter 8. (You will find the addresses and contact agents for ASB and BMC in Appendix I of Chapter 3.)

The "Supply Side"
of Supply and Services Canada

SSC's "Supply side" buys scientific, commercial, and technical goods including film and video; printing and publishing; advertising management; expositions; traffic management; industrial security; equipment maintenance and repair, and warehousing and distribution. It also disposes of surplus government material. In addition to the Supply Operations sector handling these items, SSC has some other units worth noting in a quick trip through SSC's corridors.

The Program Planning and Evaluation Sector performs SSC's quality-assurance function, provides useful statistical research, evaluates existing SSC programs and develops new ones. (A number of its internal studies are quoted in this book.) It provides personnel to staff Procurement Review Committees (PRCs), which review all purchases between $2 million and $100 million. It studies defence preparedness, looks after internal audit, and access to information and liaison with Treasury Board and Parliament. SSC's Annual Procurement Planning Strategy (APPS), a government-wide shopping-list, started here.

The department's Contract Settlements Board offers an in-house supplier/client department conciliation service for supplier contracts that have gone sour. Procurement and Acquisition Support System (PASS) is SSC's program to link user-departments and SSC through common access to source-lists and computerized contract management.

Another checkpoint on this tour of SSC is the Statistical Information and Data Management Branch which handles supplier source listing and receives bids and compiles most of the *Suppliers Guide*. As well, it develops SSC's master sourcing-list from suppliers' replies to initial sourcing-forms, edits the *Bulletin of Business Opportunities* (BBO) and keeps the central registry for the National Automated Sourcing Information System (NASIS).

Perhaps the biggest employer of security guards and firms in Canada, the Security Branch of SSC, handles industrial security among suppliers for Canadian and U.S. defence contracts, including protection of personnel, materials, or premises, and electronic data-processing areas.

SSC's supply operations are concentrated in five distinct Product Directorates. They are:

- Communications Services (CSD)
- Aerospace, Marine and Electronics Systems (AMES)
- Industrial and Commercial Products (ICPD)
- Office Automation, Services and Information Systems (OASIS)
- Science and Professional Services (SPSD), which also houses the Canadian General Standards Board (CGSB), a stand-ards-writing body

Communications Services Directorate

The Communications Services Directorate (which is Canada's "Queen's Printer") buys a great deal of outside services and products. These vary from writing and publishing to audio-visual advertising and public-relations services. This is an area in which SSC has determined to have even more work contracted out. All departments and ministries of the federal government must send their publishing work here. It is a common service within another common-service agency, SSC.

From across the country in 1985-86, 695 suppliers provided printing services to the Canadian Government Printing Services (CGPS) a division within CSD, for a total commercial-printing business volume of $107.5 million. These printing services included fine printing, pamphlets, periodicals, business forms, posters, and folders.

CGPS prints sensitive and top-secret documents, constituency newsletters for Members of Parliament, Parliamentary papers such as debates of the House of Commons and Senate, legislation, government policy documents, commission reports, and the minutes of 40 parliamentary committees.

Printers are given a special form to complete in addition to the regular NASIS application for source-listing. This provides information on the type of equipment in the plant and the kind of work that the printer is interested in and is best equipped to do. CGPS classifies print suppliers by specialties such as composition, graphic design, business forms, copying services, offset printing, etc. Each is categorized by quality level, i.e., duplicating or photocopying, information, library, and prestige. Source-lists are also maintained by city or geographical area.

ITTs, both national and regional, are posted daily on bulletin boards at regional headquarters and in Ottawa. Extra copies of the tender documents are available to take away when a printer submits a bid in the normal manner to encourage a printer to browse through the tenders and select only those which interest him or her most. This is the most efficient way for SSC to avoid sending out "many tenders for relatively low dollar value requirements, while giving you a good chance to bid on printing jobs". CSD has experimented with an electronic bulletin board as well.

The Canadian Government Publishing Centre (CGPC) turns out some 300 new, priced titles a year, making it the largest publisher in Canada. Total sales amounted to $17 million in 1985-86. CGPC operates a co-publishing fund to subsidize the production of government handbooks or manuals that would be too costly for departments to produce out of their own budgets, with private-sector publishers doing the editorial work, design, and printing.

All of this publishing, of course, requires paper, lots of it at a time. A June 1988 contract to Domtar Inc. of Montréal, for example, was for $7,623,742.

The Canadian Government Film and Video Centre provides Ottawa with consulting, production, and administrative services in the audio-visual arts. It also provides state-of-the-art photo developing, printing, and related services. Last year it spent $17 million. Its staff are experienced in video, animation, film drama, or multi-media packages, slide shows, and other types of A-V programs.

The Photo Centre has a complete range of photo services such as processing, printing, duplicating, copying, mounting, slide-tape productions, and passports, and a still library of government pictures.

The Canadian Government Exposition Centre in 1985-86 purchased or produced $24-million worth of exhibit and display products and services for various federal departments. Of this total, eighty-two per cent was contracted out to the private sector.

While public servants have been trying for decades to be objective in the selection of advertising agencies and strategies, the Cabinet still has a great deal of say over who gets such work. Frequently, contracts are awarded to public-relations or advertising agencies who have been loyal to the party in power. Advertising suppliers are listed jointly with SSC's Advertising Management Services Centre and Advertising Management Group, the operational component of the cabinet committee on communications. It advises departments on media strategy and evaluation, reviews proposed advertising plans and provides departments with a statement of "project or plan concurrence" from the chairman of the cabinet committee.

CSD's Communications Planning Services subgroup provides support to departments in marketing, implementation of communications programs, and their evaluation, for which they sometimes use private-sector consultants.

Office Automation, Services and Information Systems Directorate

Office Automation, Services and Information Systems Directorate (OASIS), notes an SSC booklet, is the procurement centre of Supply and Services Canada for all electronic data-processing systems (EDP), EDP professional services, office equipment, office furniture and supplies, micrographic and word-processing services. EDP buys include simple off-the-shelf equipment and services as well as complex, tailor-made systems which are required to meet end-user defined specifications. Its annual business volume is around $900 million.

As of May 1988, 50 companies held Standing Offers for programmers, program- and systems-analysts, and managers and project leaders worth $32.7 million. Another 178 contractors held $18.6 million Standing Offers for computer experts.

The Procurement Operations Branch deals with some 3,000 suppliers "for the purchase, rental or lease of equipment, furniture and supplies, as well as software and maintenance services". It "establishes Standing Offers worth $60 million a year for the provision of computer-related professional services." Its buys range from information systems to pens, pencils, binders, and stationery, to sophisticated printing, duplicating, photocopying, calculation and mailroom equipment; from basic typewriters, to shared-logic, shared-resource word-processors, office furniture, chairs, cabinets, shelving, and custom-designed furniture for executive use and the electronic office. Ottawa's collective buying power also is used in buying photocopier, micrographic, and facsimile paper.

For DND, OASIS now is setting up a data-processing and communications capability for intelligence and security operations; and a secure on-line communications system between several North American missions and consulates and External Affairs headquarters in Ottawa.

While the more important buys are handled out of Ottawa, some major buys are made in the regions too, using both ITT and RFP procedures. Simple off-the-shelf equipment is supported by competitive prices and/or published price lists. Requirements are generally small, less than $30,000 and have short procurement lead times. Complex requirements are supported by competitive bids and/or detailed price breakdowns. These requirements are generally large in value, normally in excess of $100,000 and may involve lease/purchase options and, in the case of data-processing services, may extend over several years.

Industrial and Commercial Products Directorate

The 350 or so staff in the Industrial and Commercial Products Directorate (ICPD) spend some $1.45 billion a year on a broad range of commercially available products ranging from textiles and uniforms to heating fuel and construction equipment.

For example, ICPD's purchases of food, cattle fertilizers, drugs, clothing textiles, and chemical protective equipment in 1985-86 totalled $350 million. ICPD also buys 500 different types of clothing, including dress, work and operational uniforms and clothing of all kinds. Recently, for example, Textiles Monterey Inc. of Montréal received a $1,501,402 contract to make cloth for the Canadian Armed Forces. This will maintain 12 jobs for more than six months. At around the same time, Empire Clothing Manufacturers Inc. of Montréal received a $343,279 contract for RCMP tunics; the contract will maintain 110 jobs. Canada Packers Inc. of Toronto won a $1,042,561 contract to provide Canola oil to CIDA. If your business operates in any of these areas, get on the bandwagon!

ICPD farms out Ottawa's Central Travel Service, worth some $100-million plus a year, and operates a Central Removal Service for household goods, and a Central Freight Service. Overseas Traffic Service also moves $160 million in goods overseas.

ICPD buys all Ottawa's petroleum products (heating oil for the government's 3,600 buildings, gasoline, diesel, marine, and aviation fuels), lubricating oils and greases, industrial chemicals, coal, compressed gases and pest-control agents as well as airport-crash trucks, tractors, snowblowers, sweepers, tires and tubes, rail-cars and locomotives—some $615 million a year, and RCMP patrol cars. In May 1988, for example, 11 Chev Olds dealers across Canada won contracts totalling $6.95 million for RCMP vehicles.

The Directorate manages the government credit-card system to let employees charge gasoline and routine maintenance; buys non-armoured military vehicles for DND including trucks, jeep-type vehicles, and tracked vehicles for all-terrain operations in the North, as well as special equipment kits, spare parts, and maintenance training. ICPD has 25 military specialists on staff, although the Aerospace, Marine and Electronics Systems (AMES) directorate is the major military purchasing agent.

ICPD spends $200 million on scientific, electrical, meteorological, test, mechanical, and construction products, and provides project management for another $170 or so million for various departments. These include scientific, photographic and meteorological equipment, electronic and testing equipment, electrical and mechanical equipment, security and safety equipment, construction equipment and tools, prefabricated buildings and building maintenance, and packaging supplies.

To qualify for approved-products listing, ICPD says, suppliers must submit samples of their products for evaluation. ICPD publishes a yearly catalogue for scientific, electrical, mechanical, and construction products totalling some 4,000 categories of goods, worth about $220 million a year. There are around 7,000 suppliers on record.

Aerospace, Marine and Electronics Systems Directorate

The AMES Directorate is largely responsible for engineering procurement which equals almost around half of all SSC buys. It covers ships and aircraft design and maintenance; electronic systems and industrial systems together with related products, services and life-cycle support for federal-government clients including CCC on behalf of foreign governments. It provides expertise and equipment and service to customer departments in all technologies involving aerospace, marine, and electronics systems and armament products. AMES is organized to parallel the operational and engineering organizations of its major customers such as DND or TC. It puts out its own excellent booklet, *Doing Business with the Aerospace, Marine and Electronics Systems Directorate*, on how to approach it for business (cited in Chapter 8).

AMES acquires both military and civil aircraft, ships, helicopters, air-cushion vehicles, and the necessary electronic communication and navigation systems including the fitting of special mission-related equipment (e.g. side-looking airborne radar, load-extraction parachutes, etc.). In addition, it contracts out for initial flight-training for aircrew and equipment operators, initial spares for the complete aircraft including electronics systems, ground handling-equipment, special tools, aircraft and electronic testing equipment, engines, airframes, avionics, and training equipment.

It also buys munitions and pyrotechnics; gun systems (small arms, guns and howitzers, fire-control instruments); armoured vehicles; rockets and missiles. It purchases mechanical, structural, and instrumentation components for the entire Canadian military air fleet (fighting, training, reconnaissance and transport aircraft and helicopters, jet aircraft engine components, propellers, aircraft instruments, gauges, air conditioning, avionic components, etc.); and repair and overhaul of components and assemblies for the land-based military fleet of armoured fighting vehicles.

AMES handled the recent federal-provincial buy of Canadair CL-215 waterbombers, and a $100-million contract for drone aircraft for West Germany. Now in construction under its auspices for the Canadian Coast Guard are eleven large new vessels, a host of small boats, and the mid-life modernization of three existing vessels, and it is developing a Polar 8 icebreaker for Transport Canada.

Electronics systems, according to an SSC brochure, which include "navigational and traffic control systems; personal and area security systems; training simulators and electro-optics systems; secure communications systems; underwater detection and weapons systems; missile control, satellite and communications systems; radar detection and control systems, and tactical computers and information processing and display systems. . . . may range from $250,000 to over $200 million." Sometimes, though, AMES jobs are larger, such as the 10-project $3.8 billion Canadian Airspace System Plan (CASP); the $810 million Radar Airport Modernization Program (RAMP); and a new international standard Microwave Landing System for 1995 to cost $300 million, for Transport Canada.

AMES procures industrial systems and contracts for the manufacture, repair, and overhaul of custom-engineered marine, electronics and industrial equipment, from designing automated mail-handling systems for Canada Post to modernizing a complete railway for a Third World country on behalf of the Canadian International Development Agency.

AMES' aerospace and marine procurement groups also operate from supply centres in Dartmouth, Montréal, Toronto, and Vancouver to provide on-site contract administration services and technical inspection. When SSC's inspection workload exceeds the regional manpower availability, contracts are placed with the private sector for aeronautical engineers or naval architects or marine engineering firms to carry out on-site technical inspections. So, if you or your firm work in engineering, drafting, or technical support in these fields, you need to prospect these groups too.

Generally, if a procurement is for a number of consignees scattered through two or more regions, the design authority is based in the national capital region. If the project is a Major Crown Project, the procurement is carried out by headquarters. When none of these factors apply and the regional aerospace or marine procurement group has the capacity to make the purchase, it will do it. At the time of writing, AMES is involved in some 30 MCPs, each worth $100 million or more.

While selling to the Industrial and Commercial Products Directorate is largely a matter of price, selling to AMES is a bit more complicated, with products usually tied to detailed military or industrial specifications. As a potential supplier, you will be asked to provide specific product or service activities in which the company is qualified and has some capability and interest in developing further; description of long-range plans; industrial security arrangements and status; qualifications of management and scientific and engineering personnel; brief historical company background; description of unusual facilities; outline of production and marketing capabilities; copies of latest financial statements.

AMES uses ITTs and RFPs very frequently. Criteria used to evaluate bids and proposals, in addition to factors already mentioned, could include the firm's comprehension of requirements; experience; record or performance; technical merit; probability of success; price, special terms and conditions; financial and technical commitments; evidence of sound managerial, financial, and organizational practices and procedures; adequacy of facilities; need for outside assistance; Canadian content; socio-economic benefits; and industrial, trade, and regional development strategies.

Factors open to later negotiation might include the perceived benefits to the government and industry; proprietary rights; source and type of materials to be used; direct and indirect costs; requirements definition; freedom in allotting subcontracts; defining of performance; division of management responsibilities between AMES and the contractor; and the use of contractor- or government-supplied equipment.

Science and Professional Services Directorate

The SPSD Directorate provides a focal point for client department needs in areas of natural and human sciences and is a centre for the receipt and processing of unsolicited proposals of a scientific nature from the private sector. It buys goods or services ranging from geodetic surveys in the high Arctic, the design of remote-sensing satellites and the management of projects in developing countries to writing/editorial services; training and technical services; and public-relations and conference services.

SPSD pioneered the use of remote-controlled submersibles to map the sea; a fiber-optic system to provide rural communities with full telecommunications services simultaneously; and a portable atomic absorption spectrophotometer to measure very low concentrations of trace elements. It also helped interest the National Research Council in funding a Spar Aerospace Limited unsolicited proposal that later came to be the Canadarm used on the U.S. space-shuttle program, muses NRC vice-president Dr. Clive Willis.

The Science Branch was created in 1973 to stimulate scientific and technological research in Canadian industry. The research for government programs in science and technology is to be contracted-out to private industry whenever feasible through this branch as part of Ottawa's contracting-out policy. In 1987, SSC contracted out some $322.4 million of science work on behalf of client departments.

SPSD also hires individuals and firms to perform other services. They include experienced pilots; aircraft fitted with remote-sensing equipment to carry out ice reconnaissance surveys; language teachers to support the government bilingualism program; air-transportation services in the high Arctic; and surveyors to carry out a topographic survey for CIDA.

The Professional Services Branch, on a contract basis, provides consultants and other professional services required by client departments and agencies. It serves 90 client departments, probably a lot more than any one of its 2,000 suppliers can ever hope to reach on his or her own, and issues some 3,000 contracts worth $300 million in any one year.

As an SSC booklet puts it, the Branch "acquires a wide range of professional, technical and special services on behalf of its client departments and agencies." These services range from general needs such as security, training and writing services, to specialty requirements like forest-fire fighting, management consulting, surveying, map production, and air charter services, including Class 4 and Class 7 air charters and related support services, and business and consulting services; and engineering/architectural services.

While the SPSD is headquartered in Ottawa, SSC's Regional Operations Sector also has some responsibility for contracting federal government R & D requirements. Of the $322 million contracted out last year for SPSD, about a third ($116.9 million) went out through regional offices. SPSD also acts as a contracting agency for foreign governments and international organizations, notably through the Canadian Commercial Corporation. SPSD and the regions keep special lists of firms and organizations capable of conducting scientific R & D activities.

Most contracting goes through SPSD Ottawa. If the requirement is complex, SPSD, or a region in some circumstances, may call a bidders' conference, chaired by the SPSD science-contracting officer. If no conference is held, the RFP will ask you to submit any questions you have in writing to the contracting officer. Written answers are then telexed to all invited bidders.

ITTs and RFPs are widely used, though two-stage bidding also is becoming more common, with the final choice made after a short-listing process. The winner is picked generally through a point system "to assess technical and managerial competence". The final choice, SPSD's booklet says, hinges on a point system which follows criteria clusters such as "lowest firm price, or ceiling price, acceptable bidder"; that is, you've won the RFP if you're okay with SSC and the client, and have the lowest bid.

Another is "best value—financial limitation," which is the most common basis of evaluation—rather like the most bang for the buck; and "best value—ceiling," used when the client has limited funds but wants to have a guaranteed work package within the budget. Finally "most meritorious," where the bidder has the highest point rating for the funds specified in the RFP.

Selling To SSC Regions

For several years, SSC has been consciously delegating contract and purchasing authority to its regional offices in order to move procurement decisions closer to the end-user departments and suppliers. This provides more opportunities for regional suppliers to participate in federal-government contracting; develops suppliers outside the Ottawa-Toronto-Montréal triangle; and provides faster service with lower operating costs through the employment of speedier, simpler, and lower-cost procurement resources and processes. In 1985-86, regional contracting operations generated $1.8 billion, compared to an SSC headquarters procurement budget of $4.9 billion.

The 4,000 individuals involved in regional operations, handle many supply activities, provide SSC acquisition and printing services; stock items; provide warehousing; provide maintenance and repair; handle assets management and disposal of surplus assets at the local level.

A director-general at each of four regional directorates in Canada, Atlantic, Québec, Ontario, and Western, can sign contracts worth up to $2 million. Using Memoranda-of-Understanding tied in to the SSC regions, provinces also have begun to share federal source-lists.

Regional Operations runs a network of offices in major cities in Canada, as detailed in Appendix III of Chapter 3. These generally are comprised of a regional office, district, and sub-purchasing offices, printing plants, copy centres and self-service stores selling to departments items like paper clips, rubber stamps, and file folders.

In addition, this sector is the source-listing arm for the Canadian Commercial Corporation (CCC) which contracts and manages contracts for Canadian goods and services with foreign governments and international agencies. The sector assists in hyping Canadian firms to these foreign powers.

The Washington, D.C., region is responsible for maintaining government-to-government contact with the United States for the purchase of specialized Canadian requirements in aerospace technology and armaments. It also handles source development, provides more efficient access to SSC sourcing-information on Canadian capabilities and assists in exports.

In 1983-84, Regional Operations handled 3,000 contracts with foreign governments worth over $600 million. Much of this was under the Defence Development Sharing Agreement (DDSA) and the Defence Production Sharing Arrangement (DPSA) which create a free-trade market in the U.S. and Canada for defence and aerospace goods. (See Chapter 5.)

The European Region, which has its headquarters in London, England, is responsible for procurement from Scandinavian countries and all of Europe, with the exceptions of Germany, France, and Belgium. These are serviced by purchasing offices in Koblenz and Lahr, West Germany.

SSC Is Several Buyers

As we've seen, you can sell to almost any agency, and SSC and other common-service agencies can be especially attractive buyers. As we've also seen now, there are a number of sub-divisions and directorates within the conglomerate Department of Supply and Services Canada. As with any marketing strategy, you should determine precisely which SSC agencies, directorates, or bureaus are most likely to buy your goods or services.

Furthermore, you can often sell the same item to several SSC product directorates, although sometimes you may have to market or configure your product a bit differently. You could, for instance, get computer-consulting assignments through BMC, ASB, OASIS, or SPSD, depending on which aspect is needed.

To take another example, you could get writing assignments directly from a department as a service; or through SSC's SPSD; or through its CSD and probably others. Or you could agree to write a book, manual, pamphlet or project report for an SSC unit or buying department or agency. Presumably, that was the case when Energy, Mines and Resources (EMR) recently had SSC issue a $42,190 contract to P. Fawkes of West Vancouver for production of a Canadian small-energy newsletter.

If you provide construction products, you certainly could market them through ICPD, but if they had military uses, AMES might be interested, and if they have scientific uses, perhaps SPSD. And don't forget PWC, and the National Capital Commission (and the larger Crown corporations which we'll look at more closely in Chapter 6). Geographically, you could chase SSC three ways: go after SPSD in Ottawa; your local SSC office; and other SSC headquarters directorates such as Aerospace or Industrial Products. And don't forget to make yourself known to possible client departments, like National Defence or Transport.

If you're serious about government business at this point, you should immediately start making a file on each possible market you can find in the government, and then begin gathering information: find out who does the buying, what similar items have been bought, what publications are available from those departments, what specific tendering or bidding regulations apply, and so on. A gradual and well informed-approach is the key to future success. To help you further with this task, Chapter 5 will look at the big federal departments, that is, the ones who consistently spend the most.

Appendix I

Contact List For Central Management Agencies

Note: All telephone numbers are area code 613 unless noted.

Prime Minister's Office (PMO)

Prime Minister
Rt. Hon. Brian Mulroney

Principal Secretary
Bernard Roy

Chief of Staff
Derek H. Burney

Address:
Langevin Block
Parliament Buildings
Ottawa, Ontario K1A 0A2
992-4211

Privy Council Office (PCO)

President and Deputy PM
Hon. Don Mazankowski
957-5657

Clerk of the Privy Council and
Secretary to the Cabinet
Paul M. Tellier
957-5400

Chief, Materiel Management
A. Quinn
957-5106

Address:
Langevin Block
Parliament Buildings
Ottawa, Ontario K1A 0A3
957-5153

Treasury Board (TB)

President
Hon. Patricia Carney
957-2666

Minister of State (TB)
Hon. Doug Lewis
995-3532

Treasury Board Secretariat
Secretary of the T. Board
Gérard Veilleux
993-5215

Materiel and Services
Contracting
Director
R. K. Campbell
957-2525

Address:
L'Esplanade Laurier
East Tower
140 O'Connor Street
Ottawa, Ontario K1A 0R5

Finance (FIN)

Minister
Hon. Michael Wilson
996-7861

Deputy Minister
Frederick W. Gorbet
992-4925

Minister of State (Finance)
Thomas Hockin
996-3170

Director, Administrative
 Services
Finance (and Treasury Board
 and Comptroller-General of
 Canada)
J. T. Eadie
992-6650

Superintendent of Financial
 Institutions
M. MacKenzie
992-0378

Materiel Management Head
M. Miron
995-8847

Address:
L'Esplanade Laurier
140 O'Connor Street
Ottawa, Ontario K1A 0G5

Justice (JUS)

Minister and Attorney General
Hon. Ray Hnatyshyn
992-4621

Deputy Minister and Deputy
 Attorney General
Frank Iacobucci
957-4997

Chief, Contracting and Materiel
 Management
M. Gagnon
957-4590

Address:
Justice Building
Kent & Wellington Streets
Ottawa, Ontario K1A 0H8
957-4222

Appendix II

Contact List for Common-Service Agencies

Note: All telephone numbers are area code 613 unless noted.

Communications (DOC)

Minister
Hon. Flora MacDonald
990-6886

Deputy Minister
Alain Gourd
996-4052

Director-General, Government
  Telecommunications Agency
  (GTA)
J. Gilbert
990-2314

Chief, Materiel Management
R. H. Sitland
990-1915

Journal North Bldg.
300 Slater Street
Ottawa, Ontario K1A 0C8

Secretary of State (SOS)

Secretary of State
Hon. Lucien Bouchard
997-7788

Under Secretary of State
Jean Fournier
(819) 994-1132

Director-General
Translation Services
G. Asselin
(819) 997-1719

Director, Security and Facilities
  Management Directorate
Jacques L. Grenier
953-2691

Address:
Department of the Secretary of State
  of Canada,
Ottawa, Ontario K1A 0M5
1-800-267-0441 or 997-0055

Public Service Commission of Canada (PSC)

Chairman
Dr. Huguette Labelle
992-2788

Chief, Materiel Management Division
R. Brunet
992-3435

Executive Director, Training,
  Programs Branch
J. Arthur St. Aubin
995-6134

Executive Director, Staffing
E. J. Baker
992-0894

Address:
L'Esplanade Laurier
300 Laurier Ave. W.
Ottawa, Ontario K1A 0M7
996-5010

Other Important Agencies

Office of the Governor General

Secretary to the Governor General
Leopold Henri Amyot
993-0259

Financial Administrator Chief
M. Brisebois
993-0252

Address:
Government House
1 Sussex Drive
Ottawa, Ontario K1A 0A1
993-8200

House of Commons

Speaker of the House
Hon. John A. Fraser
992-5042

Manager, Purchasing
E. Fournier
992-8284

Address:
House of Commons
Parliament Buildings
Wellington Street
Ottawa, Ontario K1A 0A6

Senate of Canada

Speaker
Hon. Guy Charbonneau
992-4416

Leader of the Government
Hon. Lowell Murray
995-2407

Leader of the Opposition
Hon. Allan MacEachen
992-9171

Clerk of the Senate and Clerk of
the Parliaments
Charles Lussier
992-2493

Chief, Stationery and Furniture
Y. Lorrain
996-0692

Address:
Parliament Buildings
Wellington Street
Ottawa, Ontario K1A 0A4
(613) 995-1900

Library of Parliament

Parliamentary Librarian
Erik Spicer
992-3122

Director, Administration &
Personnel
J. J. Cardinal
996-4477

Address:
Parliament Buildings
Wellington Street
Ottawa, Ontario K1A 0A9

Supreme Court of Canada

Chief Justice
Hon. Brian Dickson

Registrar
G. Y. Goulard

Assistant Administrative Officer,
S. Stewart

Address:
Supreme Court Building
Wellington Street
Ottawa, Ontario K1A 0J1
995-4330

Federal Court of Canada

Chief Justice
Hon. A. L. Thurlow

Administrator
Robert Biljan

Supervisor, Materiel
  Management
F. Simard
995-9276

Address:
Federal Court of Canada
Supreme Court Building
Wellington Street
Ottawa, Ontario K1A 0H9

Tax Court of Canada

Chief Judge
Hon. J. C. Couture

Registrar
E. M. Germain

Chief, Administrative Services
Mrs. E. Morin
992-1693

Address:
Centennial Towers
200 Kent Street
Ottawa, Ontario K1A 0M1
992-0901

CHAPTER FIVE

Hitting the Big Departmental Markets

Name a good or service, and it is almost certain that some federal entity is a potential purchaser for it. Running around the bureaucracy or Crown corporations in Ottawa or across Canada trying to find that specific department or individual who might buy your product could be a lifetime's work in itself; but it doesn't have to be, if you make a couple of strategic decisions early in the game. Let's review what we've covered so far.

You should prioritize which segments of the $30-billion Canadian federal purchasing market you want to go after, in what time frame, and how. In the most general terms, segments include:

1. The formal federal government apparatus as accessed *indirectly* through a common-service agency like SSC or PWC (Chapter 4); or as accessed *directly* through a buying-arm within the department or agency (this chapter); or both. This segment of the federal market will spend some $15 billion or so in 1988 on goods and services.

2. The 150 or so federal Crown corporations, another $15-billion-plus-a-year market for goods and services (Chapter 6).

3. Subcontracting to a prime contractor who works for or is being paid by a government entity. Frequently, this is a faster, easier and more lucrative market to penetrate than the first two (Chapter 7), and can open up the huge U.S. market to you.

Some Strategic Options

You can narrow these choices by making a couple of decisions about your direction. Each strategic choice, though, has certain dangers. There are two paths you can walk.

1. You could concentrate your effort on smaller departments or buyers who you feel are more approachable. But if you sell a small product which is not necessarily required by the big purchasers, you could spend a lot of effort going after a host of departments with relatively few resources and with too many different people already at their doors.

2. You could go after the really big buying-departments like TC or DND first, gearing your marketing and production runs to the goals and needs of these big buyers. This plan, however, could lead you to distort your output to meet the big department's overriding priorities rather than your own, or to become captive of one giant department; it's sort of like marrying someone for his or her money.

Small firms can be especially susceptible to this malady. One year a small repair shop might be able to operate at capacity relying solely on repair and overhaul work for DND which alone spends $180 million on R & O. Next year, it might get zip.

So you may want to follow the practice of a number of other successful firms in putting a ceiling on your sales to any one department. For example, you might have a "ten per cent rule", so that before sales from a single purchasing-department reach ten per cent of your annual sales over a year or two you diversify outside the department, or at least develop other products; while twenty per cent might be an alarm point.

Your best bet is to pursue both paths, going after the richest departments, and simultaneously building up lists of other likely customer departments and purchasing agents. Take a lesson from veteran suppliers to Ottawa and government consultants who develop "files" on each of their target markets, those government entities they think could be buyers for their goods or services. You can start or add to them by monitoring and clipping newspapers and business press reports on target departments, or on proposed buys. Add or delete departments or branches within departments or contact persons as you go from bureaucrat to bureaucrat, gauge your responses, or compare notes with other suppliers or industry associations. Add in official forms and agency information.

One good way to build these files or fill in missing details on what a department buys or does is to read the official bulletins of the department. Many of these are detailed in Chapter 8. You should contact each one you might target, and ask for copies of its public-information literature, and especially its annual report. All departments and Crown corporations must file an annual report with Parliament. They are public information and are free to you. They also tell you something about who runs the place, and its plans for the next year or two. You can ask for this material by writing to the public-affairs branch of the department's headquarters in Ottawa, phoning a local office, or writing to the minister.

Another ploy is to use one set of federal officials to cope with another. For example, you should look at the chances of selling to foreign governments by answering "yes" to the NASIS question which asks if you have an export interest (see Chapter 3); or by contacting a key Canadian government export agency such as External Affairs Canada (EAC) or Canadian Commercial Corporation (CCC). The prospect of foreign sales not only expands your sales horizons, but also makes available to you a great deal of useful free Canadian government assistance and informed officials from agencies like EDC or CCC. If they accept you as a supplier for a foreign market, they become, in effect, salespeople for you. And whatever you learn about writing proposals or government procedures can also be applied to Canadian government markets.

To guide you through the federal-departmental maze, this chapter will provide you with access points for the biggest federal buyers, and show you a couple of government resources you can use in your attempts to sell to the government.

The Top Spenders

Whether they buy on their own account or through SSC, a handful of federal departments or agencies regularly dominate the federal procurement process. Indeed, two —the Department of National Defence and Transport Canada—pay out more than half of the dollars Ottawa spends for goods and services. This pattern has held true over the recent Progressive Conservative and Liberal regimes.

While the totals vary annually for each department, figures assembled by Jim Bagnall for *The Financial Post* found the following ranking according to contracting dollars for 1984-87, under the current Conservative government. These numbers cover contracts going through SSC only. (See *Figure 1* below.)

Ottawa's Biggest Buyers: The Tory Years

Agency or Department	$ million (annual average)
1. Department of National Defence (DND)	4,260
2. Canadian Commercial Corporation (CCC)	743
3. Transport Canada (TC)	543
4. Department of Regional Industrial Expansion (DRIE)	218
5. Energy, Mines and Resources Canada (EMR)	170
6. Canadian International Development Agency (CIDA)	159
7. Environment Canada (EC)	151
8. Fisheries and Oceans (F & O)	143
9. Royal Canadian Mounted Police (RCMP)	118
10. Correctional Service Canada (CSC)	100

Figure 1

Under the Liberals from 1980-84, the division had been much the same. (See *Figure 2* next page.)

A more detailed breakdown of SSC contracting figures for recent years fills in the gaps showing what some other departments spent, and gives you an idea of whether most contracts for a particular department are large or small. (See *Figure 3* on page 109.)

Ottawa's Biggest Buyers: The Liberal Years

Agency or Department	$ million
	(annual average)
1. Department of National Defence (DND)	3,880
2. Canadian Commercial Corporation (CCC)	500
3. Transport Canada (TC)	410
4. Department of Regional Industrial Expansion (DRIE)	220
5. Environment Canada (EC)	140
6. Canadian International Development Agency (CIDA)	110
7. Energy, Mines and Resources Canada (EMR)	100
8. Fisheries and Oceans (F & O)	100
9. National Research Council (NRC)	90
10. Royal Canadian Mounted Police (RCMP)	80

Figure 2

As you can see, the "Top Ten" list has changed little during the decade. This means that if you are listed with SSC and PWC, the two big central purchasing-agencies, and with the largest of these departments, you've covered a good two-thirds of the government proper. It is, therefore, obvious that this handful of departments or agencies who fund SSC's procurements and also buy on their own should be the focus of much of your marketing strategy.

It bears repeating that it is imperative for you to research each separate department's purchasing needs, its formal or informal sourcing-system, and how to access it, because although SSC (with its NASIS) and CIDA (with their Consultant Selection System) have the two most formal procurement systems in the government, many other departments are less organized.

A 1983 consultant's study by the Loecus Consulting Group for SSC found that the norm was more like what happens in Health and Welfare, and Agriculture, who "spend a significant amount of money, but do not appear to have any formal sourcing systems.... Neither have any formal sourcing procedures".

SSC Contracting Figures, averaged for 1985-87 by Major Client Department

Major Customers	No. of Documents	%	$000	%
National Defence (DND)	28,149	49.1	2,245,435	45.8
CCC Pay Office	2,308	4.0	926,799	18.9
Transport Canada (TC)	2,458	4.3	383,857	7.8
SSC, Master Standing Offer	507	.9	177,842	3.6
CIDA (food and economic aid)	822	1.4	127,660	2.6
Energy, Mines and Resources (EMR)	2,432	4.2	112,996	2.3
Industry, Trade and Commerce	115	.2	74,470	1.5
Employment and Immigration Canada	1,771	3.1	74,056	1.5
RCMP	1,466	2.6	70,046	1.4
National Research Council (NRC)	1,004	1.8	64,108	1.3
Supply and Services (SSC)	2,032	3.5	55,298	1.1
Regional Industrial Expansion (DRIE)	426	.7	54,511	1.1
Indian and Northern Affairs (DINA)	378	.7	51,201	1.0
Fisheries and Oceans (F&O)	934	1.6	41,826	.9
Revenue Canada (Taxation)	1,097	1.9	39,604	.8
Other Customers	11,472	20.0	407,195	8.3
TOTAL	**57,371**	**100.0**	**4,906,904**	**100.0**

Figure 3

All told, the study found some 20 systems, mostly "bottom drawer sourcing inventories". So although the forms and procedures outlined in Chapter 3 will get you listed with SSC or PWC, if you want to go after each of the other departments individually or deal with the persons making the real purchasing decisions, you'll have to sift out and adapt to each target's peculiar system—or lack thereof!

Tactically, we can simplify your research and selling work even more by concentrating our discussion here largely on the bigger spenders among the SSC "Top Ten": the five departments and agencies referred to in the last few paragraphs and a couple of other key departments or agencies. Since these five pay three-quarters of SSC's bills, they have considerable clout in federal procurement. I'll leave you to research the role and purchasing needs of the departments purchasing less than $175 million a year each. (See Appendix II.)

As well, among the five top spenders, three (Department of National Defence, Canadian Commercial Corporation, and Department of Regional Industrial Expansion) provide access to lucrative export markets and expert staff who can give you the sort of help you need to increase your public-sector sales in Canada. There are a couple of other export-oriented agencies or departments with strong expertise in government procurement in Canada and abroad that I'll touch on along the way.

The "Big Five" Buyers

1. Department of National Defence/ U.S. Department of Defense

The Department of National Defence (DND) purchases its major defence equipment through Supply and Services Canada, and through local bases for low-dollar-value routine maintenance and acquisitions. DND pays the bills for major purchases, and is responsible for evaluating the bids from the various competitors.

The 1987 White Paper on defence policy by Defence Minister Perrin Beatty signals a new era for Canadian military procurement. It establishes two per cent annual increases as a funding floor, rather than a ceiling as in earlier years, with major buys funded above this. The forecast is for purchases totalling some $200 billion for the Canadian Armed Forces over the next fifteen years.

Beatty's policy statement calls for a three-ocean strategy; improved Canadian capacity for surveillance and defence; consolidated land and air commitments in Europe; expanded and revitalized reserve forces; and an adequate command, control, and communications infrastructure.

"Until now," argues David Silverberg in the influential U.S. publication *Defense News,* "because Canadian defense procurement was so limited, suppliers were well known to DND and SSC. Canada bought the majority of its defense equipment from the United States through the foreign military sales program. When there was direct commercial procurement, RFPs were invited from a very small number of suppliers from source lists maintained by SSC."

He goes on: "Canadian industry emphasizes subsystems and components so that new requirements do not emerge from the laboratories or the field to the same degree as in the U.S. This is what makes the White Paper so pivotal." In other words, the new policy should encourage research, development, and manufacture of entire weapons systems.

The DND procurement process seems a bit strange to the non-military mind, even to professional bureaucrats. Your best approach to this market probably is to join forces with other companies or individuals who actually understand what all the military abbreviations mean, and can get to the bodies involved. SSC and DND call these *teaming* arrangements. To point you on your way, you will find a list in the appendix at the end of Chapter 7 showing a number of the past or possible prime contractors who have, or have had, DND contracts and who may welcome you as a subcontractor. Many have ex-generals or former mandarins on staff or on retainer. The list also includes some non-DND projects like Transport Canada's Radar Airport Modernization Program.

As well, DND has an important role in selling to the huge U.S. Department of Defense (DOD) market.

Compared with some other Western countries, Canadian defence procurement is quite small. So Canadian firms look to sell their products abroad, especially to the giant U.S. defence market. While the Canadian military buys a couple of billion dollars a year, the U.S. military buys tens of billions. Each year Canadian firms capture a couple billion dollars in sales to the U.S. military—with the help of Canada's DND, EAC, and CCC.

Canadian firms are able to sell to the U.S. easily for several special reasons. For the past forty years or so, Canada and the U.S. have been part of a giant free-trade area for military procurement. This means that Canadian defence suppliers are exempt from many of the "buy American" provisions which restrict U.S. federal procurement, because the United States regards Canada as part of the North American defence "industrial base".

The Canada-United States Defence Production Sharing Agreement and Defence Development Sharing Agreement, with the waiver of the Buy America Act and the high duty imposed to enforce it, generally allow Canadian suppliers access to this market. Any company which has a high-quality product at a good price should consider this access.

For DOD contracts, DND provides sales support through the Director, Defence Sales Support (DDSS), assists with quality assurance via the Director, General Quality Assurance (DGQA), and with product qualification via the Director, Engineering and Maintenance Planning and Standardization (DEMPS). SSC handles industrial security for Canadian federal agencies, and for the U.S. military in Canada.

As External Affairs Canada publication, *Canadian Industry and the United States Defence Market*, puts it: "There are three routes into the U.S. defence market: a) as a prime contractor to the U.S. Department of Defense (currently possible only for contracts worth less than $25,000); b) as a contractor to the U.S. Department of Defense through Canadian Commercial Corporation (currently for contracts worth more than $25,000); c) as a subcontractor to a U.S. defence prime contractor (any amount)."

If the U.S. military is a potential market for you, contact: DND's Defence Sales Support, (613) 992-9605; DRIE/DIST;

your provincial department of trade/industry; or External Affairs/Defence Programs Bureau (DPB), telephone (613) 996-1836; CCC; and the U.S. Defense Department's Defense Contract Administration Service Management Area (DCAS-MA), 365 Laurier Avenue West, Ottawa K1A 0S5; telex 053370; telephone (613) 992-2687.

To research the DOD market, get highly informative U.S. government publications such as *Selling to the Military*, and *Small Business Subcontracting Directory*, a list of 1,000 U.S. defence firms in search of subcontractors, and some other useful Canadian ones, mentioned in Chapter 8, free from DPB, External Affairs.

2. Canadian Commercial Corporation

"CCC channels foreign government procurement orders to Canadian industry; evaluates Canadian suppliers; acts as prime contractor on large bids or where Canadian firms are not known to the foreign government, and facilitates sole sourcing", says CCC vice-president Paul Theberge. In other words, CCC is a procurement agency for foreign governments, and especially DOD. At any time, CCC has 2,500 to 3,000 active contracts with more than 500 Canadian suppliers, about half of those firms with less than $5-million annual sales. Most contracts are under $100,000.

Suppliers are picked from SSC's NASIS lists, or from the U.S. Defense Department's bidders lists. DCASMA and CCC will help your firm with U.S. DOD paperwork. In fact, U.S. regulations make CCC technically the prime contractor for all DOD acquisitions in Canada over $25,000, with the Canadian supplier acting as subcontractor for one hundred per cent of the requirement.

CCC also provides the mandatory certification and endorsement of DOD bidders' mailing lists (BML) and bids; sends suppliers lists of Canadian firms to U.S. DOD buying agencies; assists Canadian contractors in the preparation of bids; guarantees performance of its subcontractors; collects and disburses contract payments; manages the U.S. Industrial Preparedness

Program in Canada and conducts facility surveys of potential Canadian manufacturers.

3. Transport Canada

Transport Canada licenses planes, trains, boats, and the people who run them. It also operates a string of airports and one of the most complex air-traffic-control systems anywhere. It buys or rents computers, planes, pilots, security personnel, construction, waste disposal, and numerous other goods and services. Many of its private contracts are for air services, and it is a career destination for many pilots or sailors.

Probably two-thirds of all TC contracts are issued by regions or airports with the rest going through the Materiel and Contracting Services Branch at TC's headquarters. Thus it contracts for services and goods in the national capital region, and in regional offices. According to Pat Delabio of Materiel and Contracting Services, you should try to meet departmental contracting officers in person, not through your agent, to find out what TC is buying or thinking of buying, and to acquaint them with your firm, and the types and quality of products it offers.

That suggestion also comes from many DOD, SSC, DND and other senior procurement personnel. They want to know you and your firm first, and your agent later.

To be considered as a TC supplier, you first are asked to complete a two-page five-item source-list questionnaire, which inquires about your company's organization, officers, recent jobs, specialties, and references. Head office tries to direct you to the appropriate regional office and group within the department, that is marine, air, or surface. However, TC is a big department. So I would advise you to cover yourself and market to each group, and especially go after airport general managers. Headquarters will send you a list, or check the blue pages of your telephone directory.

At present, TC is privatizing some airports, so the procurement process may change even more in the next year or two and be even more local. However, you will note in Chapter 8 that the task force on program review saw TC as perhaps the only department that actually had developed a workable long-term procurement plan, the Canadian Airspace System Plan (CASP).

Recent or emerging big buys at TC include its Radar Airport Modernization Program (RAMP); a nuclear icebreaker; microwave landing systems for airport; and an air navigation system update.

4. Department of Industry, Science and Technology

DIST is likely to be the new name for what used to be Regional Industrial Expansion (DRIE) and the Ministry of State for Science and Technology (MOSST). DIST is to be an industry advocate in Ottawa, and leave regional economic development and equalization to the Atlantic Canada Opportunities Agency (ACOA) and the Western Diversification Office (WDO).

Several DIST institutions are worth special attention from small business. The federal Small Business Office (SBO) staff study federal procurements and purchasing policy, and, at no cost to you, will help you with SSC and other departmental paperwork. Do get in touch with the SBO. I've found this help invaluable.

As well, DIST houses a number of highly qualified industry marketing specialists who know what is going on in this sector of the business world and within the government procurement system. They often can find a path through DND or SSC for you when the trail seems blocked. They are real pros at their job and identify with industry.

In addition, you might want to list your firm with DIST's Business Opportunities Sourcing System (BOSS). This is a prerequisite to applying for a PEMD grant. BOSS feeds into the WIN Exports (World Information Network for Exports) system at External Affairs. While neither is used directly for government procurement, both can lead to sales opportunities. BOSS inventories 14,000 Canadian manufacturers and trading houses, and covers some 16,000 product codes and 32,000 product descriptions, including those military goods covered by Defence Industry Productivity Program (DIPP). It's good no-cost advertising for you. Which brings something else to mind.

Often, when some headquarters paper-shuffler at, say SSC, is overreacting to the latest scandal in Frank Howard's "Bureaucrats" column in *The Ottawa Citizen* or obfuscating on some perfectly simply issue, I find contacts at DRIE, EAC, or even DND will tell you what is really happening. So when you deal with government and get stonewalled by some department or a bureaucrat who won't tell you what he is supposed to tell you or what you need to know, don't be depressed. Develop your own personal parallel sources of information, your own contacts in the department and in competing bureaucracies who can tell you what goes on in the third department. Use one arm of the bureaucracy to get through to or to get the story on another.

Most civil servants, I find, are really unhappy at having to treat simple or routine matters as secret just to cover for some bureaucrat or politician. And when they have to cover for another department, which could be a competitor for tax dollars, they usually are even less content. I always take great care to keep my source's identity a secret and to double-check my facts, although generally few expect anonymity. I suggest you do, too.

5. Canadian International Development Agency

The Minister for External Relations also controls (theoretically) a $400-million procurement pot, which, in fact, is exercised at the advice of Canadian International Development Agency (CIDA) officials.

The Canadian government spends over $2.5 billion a year on official development assistance, mostly channelled through CIDA, notes Marcel Belanger, a director-general in CIDA's Business Co-operation Branch. These funds largely go to governmental or quasi-governmental agencies to buy Canadian products or services to help the local economy in Third World countries grow. CIDA, operating at arm's length from the cabinet, supports Canadian business initiatives aimed at transferring technology as part of an overall development program, largely through its Business Cooperation program.

Government-to-government programs are administered by the Anglophone Africa, Francophone Africa, Americas, and

Asia Branches. Special Programs Branch supports over 300 Canadian non-governmental groups (NGOs)and institutions in international development. *Multilateral programs* are the avenue through which Canada supports various United Nations and international organizations. CIDA's Industrial Co-operation Program underwrites part of the risk for Canadian companies who invest in Third World countries.

In 1984 CIDA hired some 1,500 firms from all parts of Canada to identify and gain access to new markets and opportunities in approximately 90 developing countries, and spent a little over $440 million in total funds. It also engages in joint ventures and provides financial assistance to help Canadian companies adapt. CIDA has a roster or source-list of 5,000 individuals or firms listed as professional consultants. For smaller projects, CIDA hires individuals or firms directly. In 1985-86, CIDA let out more than 1,229 contracts, for a total value of $274 million—that's $23 million a month—for professional services alone.

To get listed as a possible consultant contact, obtain the Consultant Registration Form "CIDA 432". (Again, details are in Appendix I.)

As well, the Technical Co-operation Services Directorate (Professional Services Branch) recruits a small number of Canadians with special skills to implement, follow-up, or evaluate certain projects. They are called "Co-operants". Last year, CIDA had 85 specialists working on direct contract on projects around the world. They complement the work of other overseas personnel who are hired mostly by Canadian firms, NGOs and institutions under contract to implement CIDA bilateral projects.

If you are a professional interested in working as a co-operant you should note that the roster used by Technical Co-operation Services Directorate is not the same one which forms the basis for consultant or procurement contracts.

Other Useful Allies

1. External Affairs Canada

Trade commissioners posted abroad can do preliminary market research for you; advise you on selecting suitable agents in foreign countries; recommend translators; advise you on marketing your product; arrange business meetings for you; and provide you with information on local laws and customs. They will act as liaison and market researchers —but not sales staff— for your firm or product. They will not be present at all your negotiations, serve as your translator, act as your agent, train your staff, or be your bill collector.

Because Canada imports a lot of high technology and defence materiel, EAC also has experts in these areas, and on the Canadian governmental and/or industry's needs. These experts can help you sell abroad, or in other Canadian agencies.

To contact a trade commissioner for a particular country or to get information on exporting, contact EAC headquarters or an office of the Department of Regional Industrial Expansion. There is even a toll-free number to get you started: 1-800-267-8376. External also provides grants to bring in foreign trade missions and send you on one abroad, and will help with Defence Industry Productivity Program (DIPP) applications, an R & D grant program, or other assistance schemes.

Similarly, provincial officials often are very well informed about foreign government buys. Most provinces have an agent in London and elsewhere. For example, Ontario has 18 offices abroad; Québec has 17; and Alberta and Saskatchewan have 4 each. Most provinces provide some liaison and financial assistance for exporters, whether they are selling to foreign governmental entities or to private companies.

Foreign and Canadian chambers of commerce, boards of trade or regional trade associations, and associations of manufacturers also may be of help. In particular, the Canadian Chamber of Commerce, Canadian Exporters Association, and the Canadian Manufacturers' Association are useful contacts to marketing abroad. The business or trade press in Canada and your target country also contain valuable information. Ask your local reference librarian to help you locate those most appropriate to your sales, or contact:

> Canadian Business Press Association
> 100 University Avenue, Suite 508
> Toronto, Ontario M5J 1V6
> Telephone (416) 593-5497

2. Export Development Corporation

EDC provides competitive financing, insurance, and guarantee services for sales to foreign governments and companies. Remember, CCC is a purchasing agent: EDC is a lending institution. EDC's most widely used service, export credits insurance, protects exporters against non-payment and cost-incurred losses which may occur as a result of commercial and political risks, usually for up to ninety per cent of the loss. Transactions covered range from $100,000 to as much as $1 billion.

In 1986, EDC financed $605 million in goods and services and issued 2,000 purchase contracts from 1,000 suppliers worth $831 million, with some forty-three per cent of these subcontractors being small- and medium-sized companies.

EDC lending activities include export financing support of medium- to long-term loans to foreign borrowers and for Canadian goods and services such as training and engineering consultation. It covers up to eighty-five per cent of their value. EDC tries to "optimize the Canadian content, of the export sale", says its informational material.

3. National Research Council

The National Research Council provides laboratory space and financial assistance to industry and universities. It is especially active in research on construction, biotechnology, and robotics and integrated manufacturing, and has some of the best minds in the country in these and in other areas such as aeronautics, industrial materials research, chemistry, and marine dynamics.

One of NRC's best known programs is the Industrial Research Assistance Program (IRAP) which won rave notices in the evaluation of the federal task force on program review. The key person there is Dr. William Coderre, at (613) 993-0695. He's keen on helping businesspeople who want to supply the research and development sector, or want to do R & D themselves.

Astute bidders use the services of NRC's Canadian Institute for Scientific and Technical Information (CISTI), the best high-tech library in the country, and its data base of scientific publications, *CAN-OLE*, to make state-of-the-art proposals for government scientific or engineering jobs.

Combine this with a little networking with NRC experts, and you have a good picture of who is doing what in almost *any* scientific or engineering field. NRC staff can often provide you with scientific and engineering advice or information on other departments, and on private-sector or provincial projects. Frequently they know what is coming up, who will be ordering it, and what will be the major problem to be overcome in the project or proposal.

NRC buys some goods and services though SSC, and some through its twenty-three independent supply centres. They range from test tubes and electronic instruments to computer chips. You can get a copy of the list of supply centres and officers at your nearest NRC industrial development office, or write to the procurement general manager, Dr. Gerhard Finch.

If you are in the construction field, you may be especially interested in NRC's Institute for Research in Construction. You will find other leads at NRC on your own.

The Free Trade Agreement

According to External Affairs Canada, the Canada-U.S. free trade agreement will open up an "additional CDN $4 billion in potential U.S. federal government non-defence purchases a year" from Canadian suppliers, and another CDN $665 million in Canadian federal government purchases from American suppliers.

The agreement is to cover 11 of 13 U.S. federal government departments (excluding the departments of Energy, and Transportation, and 40 governmental agencies and commissions, as well as NASA and the General Services Administration, the U.S. government's major common-purchasing agency. U.S. Department of Defense purchases are covered within certain defined product categories such as vehicles, engines, industrial equipment, and components, computer software and equipment, and commercial supplies.

For Canada, 22 government departments and 10 agencies are covered including National Defence non-military items. Excluded are Transport Canada, and the departments of Communications, and Fisheries and Oceans. Canada's access to U.S. defence procurement under the Defence Production Sharing Agreement is not affected by the agreement, which for decades has been a sectoral free trade agreement, dating well before the Auto Pact.

Goods covered by the main free trade agreement will include "vehicles, scientific apparatus, aircraft equipment, mineral products, industrial machinery, plastic, rubber and leather products, electrical machinery, chemical products, power generation machinery, and heating and lighting equipment".

The agreement increases the amount of procurement open for competition between Canadian and U.S. suppliers in each other's market and lowers the threshold on the purchase of goods covered by GATT from (U.S.) $171,000 (about CDN $238,000) to $25,000 U.S. (about CDN $33,000). All government buys are to be "open to competition unless they are reserved for small business or excluded for reasons of national security". It also provides for the regular exchange of government procurement information. "An impartial reviewing authority" will handle complaints.

There is no doubt, then, that with free trade Canadian firms could find a vast U.S. public-sector market opening up, and U.S. firms could find a huge Canadian public-sector market at their call. So start building market files, and researching the other country's agencies *now*. You can already make sales, and get a head start on the listing process that will operate under free trade. See also the section in Chapter 8 on "Selling to Uncle Sam".

Appendix I

Key Contacts in the "Top 10" Departments

(in descending order of procurements in dollars)
Note: All telephone numbers are in area code 613, unless noted.

National Defence (DND)

Minister
Hon. Perrin Beatty
996-4450

Associate Minister
Hon. Paul Dick
996-3100

Deputy Minister
Daniel Bevis Dewar
992-4258

Chief of Defence Staff
General Paul Manson
992-5054

Materiel
Assistant Deputy Minister
E. J. Healey
992-6622

Associate Assistant
Deputy Minister
Maj. Gen. G. MacFarlane
992-6622

Director
Supply Policy Control and
Administration
Mr. R. A. Butler
992-5454

Address: 101 Colonel By Drive
Ottawa, Ontario K1A 0K2

Canadian Commercial Corporation (CCC)

President
Hugh J. Mullington
996-0042

Vice-President, U.S. Group
N. McIntosh
996-1782

Vice-President,
Corporate Affairs
Paul Theberge
996-0262

U.S. Bid Sourcing and Bidders
Mailing-List Service
995-6105

Address:
50 O'Connor Street
Ottawa, Ontario K1A 0S6

Transport (TC)

Minister
Hon. Benoit Bouchard
996-7501

Deputy Minister
G. S. Shortliffe
992-5031

Minister of State (Transport)
Hon. Gerry St. Germain
996-7501

Operations Sector
  Assistant Deputy Ministers,
  Aviation Group
Claude LaFrance
992-3838
  Marine Group
R. A. Quail
998-1571
  Surface Group
V. Barbeau
998-1876
Executive Director
Airports Authority Group
D. McAree
990-3001

Director
Materiel & Contracting Services
R. Kingston
993-4007

Chief of Contracts Division
P. Brennae
995-5371

Address:
Place de Ville
330 Sparks Street
Ottawa, Ontario K1A 0N5

Department of Regional Industrial Expansion (DRIE)

DRIE or its successor is supposed to be a much stronger advocate for the business community in government than in recent years, and presumably a voice for the small business community in getting a sweeter hunk of the federal procurement pie.

Minister
Hon. Robert R. de Cotret
995-9001

Minister of State for Small
  Business and Tourism
Hon. Bernard Valcourt
995-1333

Deputy Minister (DRIE)
Harry Rogers
992-4292

Manager, Contracts and Materiel
  Administration (DRIE)
Suzanne Jacques
954-2720

Address:
235 Queen St.
Ottawa, Ontario K1A 0H5

Science and Technology Canada

Minister
Hon. F. Oberle
991-3725

Secretary B. Howe
990-1645

Address:
C. D. Howe Building
240 Sparks Street
Ottawa, Ontario K1A 1A1.

**Small Business Contacts in DRIE
Regional Offices**
  Newfoundland
  Director of Regional
    Programs
  Bruce Deacon
  (709) 772-4902

Nova Scotia
Small Business Development
  Division
Ted Withers
(902) 426-9363

New Brunswick
Agent supérieur du
  développement
Victor Landry/Mike Sheen
(506) 857-6461

P.E.I.
Stuart Sheppard
(902) 566-7409

Québec
Directeur des opérations
  régionales
Germaine Pare
(514) 283-6334 or 283-6335

Ontario
Development Officer
Ulana Weleschuck
(416) 365-3773

Manitoba
Senior Economist
Bill Cavey
(204) 949-6871

Saskatchewan
A/Director Planning & Analysis
Daryll Sewell
(306) 975-4395

Alberta
Manager, Economic Analysis,
  Planning and Evaluation
Joe Guinan
(403) 420-2944

British Columbia
Director
Tom Turner
(604) 661-2223

Canadian International Development Agency (CIDA)

Secretary of State for External
  Affairs
Rt. Hon. Joe Clark
995-1851

Minister for External Relations
Hon. Monique Landry
994-6161

President
Margaret Catley-Carlson
(819) 997-7951

**For Canadian-based
Administrative Services:**
Chief, Accommodation &
  Facilities
Roy Oxton
(819) 997-7781

Procurement, Inventory
  Control and Stores Officer
R. Letourneau
(819) 994-3897

For Goods for Other Countries:
Director, Procurement Division
L. Heuckroth
(819) 997-6630

For Consultant Services:
A/Director, Consultant
  Selection Secretariat
Donald Burke
(819) 997-7675

For Full-time Work Abroad:
A/Director
Technical Cooperation Division
Paul Hitschfeld
(819) 997-1197

Address:
200 Promenade du Portage
Hull, Québec K1A 0G4

Energy, Mines and Resources (EMR)

Minister,
Hon. Marcel Masse
996-2007

Deputy Minister
Arthur Kroeger
992-3456

Associate Deputy Minister,
  Mines,
Pierre Perron
996-4057

Assistant Director,
  Materiel Management
J. Gelinas
996-0825

Address:
580 Booth Street
Ottawa, Ontario K1A 0E4

Environment Canada (EC)

Minister
Hon. Tom McMillan
(819) 997-1441

Deputy Minister
Genevieve Ste.-Marie
(819) 997-4203

Director, Materiel Management
  & Administrative Practices
J. G. Touchette
(819) 994-1337

Address:
10 Wellington Street
Hull, Québec K1A 1C7

Royal Canadian Mounted Police (RCMP)

Commissioner
N. D. Inkster
993-0400

Address:
1200 Alta Vista Drive
Ottawa, Ontario K1A 0R2
Director "S" Directorate
Supply and Services
Chief Superintendent
J. G. A. Roy
993-0930

Address:
400 Cooper Street
Ottawa, Ontario K1A 0R2

Fisheries and Oceans (F & O)

Minister
Hon. Thomas Siddon
995-4988

Deputy Minister
Dr. Peter Meyboom
993-2200

Manager, Headquarters
  Materiel Management
R. Cyr
993-2815

Address:
200 Kent Street
Ottawa, Ontario K1A 0E6

Agriculture (AGC)

Minister
Hon. John Wise
995-9133

Minister of State
  (Grains and Oilseeds)
Hon. Charles Mayer
996-2508

Minister of State (Forestry)
Gerald Merrithew
990-6881

Deputy Minister
Jean-Jacques Noreau
995-8091

Associate Deputy Minister (Forestry)
Jean-Claude Mercier
992-1107

Director Policy Planning &
  Systems
D. J. Dobson
995-5118

Address:
Sir John Carling Bldg.
930 Carling Avenue
Ottawa, Ontario K1A 0C5

Appendix II

Key Contacts in the Other Departments

Note: All telephone numbers are in area code 613 unless noted.

Consumer and Corporate Affairs Canada (CCAC)

Minister
Hon. Harvie Andre
997-3530

Deputy Minister
Ian D. Clark
997-2683

Chief, Materiel and Forms
  Management
N. St. Laurent
994-4635

Address:
4th Floor, Trafalgar Bldg.
207 Queen St.
Ottawa, Ontario K1P 6E5

Employment and Immigration Canada (EIC)

Minister
Hon. Barbara McDougall
994-2482

Deputy Minister/Chairman
Gaetan Lussier
994-4514

A/Director,
Materiel Management
J. Mallen
994-2083

Address:
Place du Portage
Phase IV
140 Promenade du Portage
Hull, Québec K1A 0J9

External Affairs (EAC)

Secretary of State for External Affairs
Rt. Hon. Joe Clark
995-1851

Minister for External Relations
Hon. Monique Landry
992-2659

Minister for International Trade
Hon. John Crosbie
992-7332

Under-Secretary of State for
  External Affairs
James H. Taylor
993-4911

Deputy Minister for
  International Trade
Gerald E. Shannon
990-4999

Director, Materiel Procurement and
  Transportation
G. E. Saucier
995-5926

Address:
Lester B. Pearson Bldg.
125 Sussex Drive
Ottawa, Ontario K1A 0G2

Health and Welfare Canada (HWC)

Minister, Hon. Jake Epp
957-0200

Deputy Minister
Dr. Maureen Law
957-0213

Fitness and Amateur Sport
  Minister of State
Jean Charest
995-2424

Chief, Materiel Administration
N. Perry
957-8707

Address:
Brooke Claxton Bldg.
Tunney's Pasture
Ottawa, Ontario K1A 0K9

Indian and Northern Affairs (INAC)

Minister
Hon. Bill McKnight
(819) 997-0002

Deputy Minister
Harry S. Swain
(819) 997-0133

Head, Procurement & Supply
  Services Section
G. Baller
(819) 997-0303

Address:
Les Terrasses de la Chaudière
10 Wellington Street
Hull, Québec K1A 0H4

Labour (LAB)

Minister
Hon. Pierre H. Cadieux
(819) 997-0622

Deputy Minister
Jennifer McQueen
(819) 997-1482

Director, Financial and
  Administrative Services
A. C. Chu
(819) 977-3048

Address:
Labour Canada
Ottawa, Ontario K1A 0J2

National Research Council of Canada (NRC)

President
Dr. Larkin Kerwin
993-2024

General Manager
  Administrative Services
Dr. Gerhard Finch
993-0328

Address:
Montreal Road
Ottawa, Ontario K1A 0R6
993-9101

Revenue Canada, Customs and Excise (RC-CE)

Minister
Hon. Elmer MacKay
995-2960

A/Chief, Materiel Management
R. Poirier
954-0174

Address:
Connaught Bldg.
Mackenzie Avenue
Ottawa, Ontario K1A 0L5

Revenue Canada Taxation

Minister
Hon. Elmer MacKay
995-2960

Deputy Minister
Pierre Gravelle
957-3683

ADM Management Services
M. J. Cardinal
957-2257

Address:
Headquarters Bldg.
875 Heron Road
Ottawa, Ontario K1A 0L8

Solicitor General Canada (SGC)

Solicitor General
Hon. James Kelleher
991-2857

Solicitor General Canada
  Secretariat
Deputy Solicitor-General
John C. Tait
991-2895

Director, Finance and
  Administration Division
E. Plunkett
990-2615

Agencies Reporting to the
  Solicitor-General:
Commissioner of Corrections
Rheal Leblanc
996-5781

Commissioner of RCMP
Norman Inkster
993-0400

Chairman, National Parole
  Board
Ole Ingstrup
996-1308

Director, Canadian Security
  Intelligence Service
Reid Morden
782-0000

Address:
Sir Wilfrid Laurier Bldg.
340 Laurier Avenue West
Ottawa, Ontario K1A 0P8

Veterans Affairs (VA)

Minister
Hon. George Hees
(616) 996-4649

Deputy Minister
David Broadbent
(613)996-6881
(902) 566-8280

Finance, Personnel and
  Administration Branch
Assistant Deputy Minister
D. N. Rive
(902) 566-8047

Director General,
  Management Services Division
P. Sorensen
(902) 566-8236

Field Operations Branch
Assistant Deputy Minister
  (Field Operations)
D. J. Steele
(613) 995-2231

Address:
East Memorial Building
284 Wellington Street
Ottawa, Ontario
K1A 0P4

CHAPTER SIX

Ottawa's Second $15-Billion Market — The Crown Corporations

In addition to government departments which nominally come under a cabinet minister's authority, Ottawa also has a raft of other often mysterious, more or less independent agencies. It calls these boards, commissions, councils, or Crown corporations.

In theory, these entities are governed by the same hiring and contracting rules that operate throughout the departmental structure, including the need to let contracts through PWC and SSC. As a rule, though, such independent agencies are administered quite differently from departments, often outside the regular departmental structure and decision-making and ministerial control.

In almost every case, the agency is governed by a board of some sort appointed for a set number of years, unlike deputy ministers who on paper can be fired on the prime minister's whim. This arrangement gives them a degree of freedom from regular government interference, including cabinet or Treasury Board approval for all but the largest buys.

Day-to-day administration generally comes under the president or chairperson or some other designated member who is a powerful individual within his or her sphere. Some agency heads also make very frequent use of outside personal service, and goods and services contracts to make up for short staffing, huge workloads or special agency priorities. Other opportunities for contracts arise because some agencies are freed from departmental requirements to hire staff through the Public Service Commission or to let contracts through SSC. All of these can add up to big sales opportunities for you.

While there are far too many agencies to give them all individual treatment, the appendices at the end of this chapter will identify most of them for you. From these starting points, your research and files should tell you which ones have a close affinity for your type of goods or services, which are shorthanded, and which are looser with their purses. For information, ask the agencies themselves, your competition, and industry associations, and read business magazines. In making your federal target list, you really should go after one type of federal hybrid organization with a lot of dollars to spend: the Crown corporations.

The Rise – and Size – of Crown Corporations

Compared to their U.S. equivalents, governments in Canada have always had greater involvement in the economy. In the nineteenth century, this took the form of public works, notably roads and canals, and patronage or job creation. Later, it took on a more ideological focus with the protective tariff to shield Canadian industry from competition and the federal government's construction of a national railway.

Most Canadian political scientists argue that the U.S. political system came about because of colonial distrust of government, in that case the distant one in London. On the other hand, the Canadian one was set up by individuals who had supported government, that same government in London, and turned to government for aid in their new homes in British North America. At one time, this meant government jobs and land grants to those who had remained loyal to the British Crown.

Today, it means a degree of government economic activity alien to the U.S. Thus, proportionately, the Canadian public sector is much larger than its U.S. equivalent, and the federal and provincial governments not only administer and regulate the economy but also own and run a number of businesses. Canada has a large number of such government business entities or

Crown corporations (Crowns), and the federal government itself owns some very big companies in key economic sectors such
as airlines, railroads, shipping, agriculture, energy, and broadcasting. Provinces too own companies in key sectors like
electricity, insurance, and telephones.

Ottawa has found itself in these businesses for a number of
reasons. Some Crowns, like the Canadian National Railways
and VIA Rail, are heirs to losing businesses that supplied what
was considered an essential need. Their successors are still running to Ottawa for bail-outs.

Some Crowns, like the Farm Credit Corporation or Canada
Mortgage and Housing Corporation, were set up as instruments
of federal economic policy to promote distinctive Canadian
values. Others like the Canadian Broadcasting Corporation and
Téléfilm Canada were set up as federal instruments of national
cultural policy or to distance day-to-day operations from partisan interference. Still others were set up simply for
administrative convenience.

In fact, Ottawa now has so many Crowns that "not even Ottawa specialists can provide the names of all federal Crown
corporations," asserts University of British Columbia regulatory
studies professor William Stanbury in his book, *Business-
Government Relations in Canada*, published in 1986.

In 1977, for example, the Privy Council Office published a list
of 366 federally-owned and -controlled corporations. By 1980
the Comptroller-General of Canada, Ottawa's chief accountant, found 464, including 213 subsidiaries and sub-subsidiaries
and 126 "associated" corporations.

Economist Tom Kierans, writing in the journal *Policy Options*
in 1984, found that 50 federal commercial Crowns and their 129
subsidiaries employed more than 209,000 persons and controlled $47 billion in assets, while 18 provincial Crowns listed in *The
Financial Post 500* employed more than 129,000 and controlled
$77.5 billion in assets. In comparison, the 50 largest private in-
dustrial corporations employed 1,137,000 and controlled assets
of $165.3 billion.

The father of Crown corporations, according to economist
Stanbury, was Pierre Trudeau, who created a total of 541 in his
term up to July 1983. Prime Minister Brian Mulroney may have

reversed this pattern. His administration has privatized Canadair, de Havilland, Canadian Arsenals, Canada Development Corporation, Eldorado Nuclear, Téléglobe Canada, and a number of others, and began to sell off Air Canada.

However you count them, though, federal Crowns and independent agencies are big business. *The Financial Post 500* for 1988 found federal Crowns with 1988 incomes as follows:

	$ billion
Petro-Canada	5.079
Canadian National Railway	4.598
Air Canada	3.213
Canada Post	2.970
Canadian Broadcasting Corporation	1.049
Canada Mortgage and Housing Corporation	0.901
VIA Rail	0.715
Export Development Corporation	0.665

Large Crowns have large payrolls. For example, Canada Post has 61,640 staff, CN has 61,124, Air Canada has 22,134 and Petro-Canada has 10,565 employees. Crowns also buy almost anything you can think of: well over $15 billion worth a year. Indeed, a federal-provincial study, *The Canadian Public Sector Market*, released in 1988, calculated that in 1983 federal government enterprise had spent $16.2 billion for procurements, about one-fifth of all public-sector buys.

The procurement budget for the 147 federal Crowns it looked at, reported the federal task force on program review in 1985, represents two per cent of Canada's gross national product. However, ninety per cent of this was for operating supplies and maintenance, and only ten per cent for capital equipment. But these capital expenditures in some cases were massive. In 1983, for example, it found four Crowns alone spent $1.13 billion on capital expenditures. These four were: CN ($500 million); Air Canada ($350 million); Petro-Canada ($150 million); and VIA Rail ($130 million). The other 143 Crowns had capital expenditures considerably less than $100 million each annually.

If we divide these 1983 capital expenditures into sectors, we find that $386 million was spent on transportation equipment; $258 million on petroleum and coal products; $146 million on electrical products; $94 million on metal fabricating; $85 million on machinery; and $81 million on food and beverages. Spending in other sectors totalled $283 million.

Applying these percentages to a conservative 1988 figure of $15 billion for goods and services bought by Crowns would mean some $13.5 billion in operating supplies and maintenance and some $1.5 billion a year in capital expenditures. Next year Canada Post alone will spend $350 million to update postal facilities, outlets, and delivery vehicles, and Air Canada will begin replacing its fleet of aging Boeing 727 jets.

Legally or administratively, most federal Crowns come under the Financial Administration Act. Ottawa has four types of Crowns. Simply put, "departmental" Crowns advise and regulate. They include the Economic Council of Canada and the National Energy Board. In many cases, they could just as easily have been departments, except that some detachment from the partisan process was desirable. "Agency" corporations like Air Canada or the Canadian Dairy Commission handle commercial tasks for the government.

"Proprietary" corporations (Petro-Canada is one example) supply goods and services to the public. Sometimes they even pay taxes like the rest of us, though admittedly the dividing line between agency and proprietary corporations is a bit thin. "Unclassified" ones, such as the Bank of Canada, have their own charters or acts of Parliament, and serve unique, very specific purposes, sometimes as government-supervised monopolies.

Others like Telesat have mixed ownership: Ottawa has some, but not all, of the shares.

Marketing to the Crowns

Your Road to the Crowns

To sell to any federal board, commission, council, or corporation, your first and hardest job is likely to be finding it! To help you with this irksome task, I've provided you with some basic contact information on most existing Crowns and independent agencies not covered elsewhere in these pages. I've identified both the corporate heads and procurement managers for some of the larger and better known ones, and provided names, addresses, and telephone numbers. For the lesser known or smaller ones, though, I've listed only information on corporate heads and headquarters.

From these, make up your own short list of possible "target" firms. You might narrow your list to Crowns with offices nearby, or pick those you, your competitors, or your industry association report as live prospects.

Next, as with SSC, PWC, or the buying departments of government, you have to study and contact your best prospects, find out how to get listed as a supplier; who their chief purchasing officers are at headquarters, in their regions and in your locale; and who you should see to make a sales call or send an information sheet.

If you know anyone who works in or for your target, call him or her first. Then when you call procurement you can say, "Jones in accounting suggested I call. My company makes the best [cheapest, largest, etc.] widgets in Canada."

If you don't know Jones, write or call the executive assistant to the head of the corporation or agency and ask for an annual report, and the names of the individuals in the firm who purchase your type of goods or services. You should also ask for a list of the goods and services that the agency buys, and for any registration or sourcing forms. (It's also really good form to ask for these items before you call your friend Jones!)

When you do contact a warm body, you probably will be well received because Crowns always need suppliers of goods and services. For example, when I called the National Capital Commission (NCC), I learned a great deal about NCC purchasing requirements from its chief purchasing officer, Michael Taylor.

As you know, Ottawa is a green city, full of parks and canals and bike trails. Most of these are owned and operated by the NCC. Overall, around twenty per cent of the Ottawa-Hull and surrounding region comes under the control of the National Capital Commission. This independent Crown agency also manages many of the area's federal buildings and its famous special events, such as the Ottawa Winter Carnival and the Festival of Spring. To handle all this, the NCC buys a great deal from outside suppliers. As Taylor puts it, "We are looking for a wide range of goods and services, from clowns and actors to construction workers."

To become a supplier, he asks you to fill in a very straightforward half-page contractor questionnaire which asks you to check off the items you supply. Normally, the NCC uses a rotational system to invite tenders. While projects over $40,000 go to public tender, those under $40,000 go to invited tender as a rule. Quotations are called for anything under $5,000.

When you do speak with someone in charge in a target corporation, or talk with a government relations consultant, or confer with others in your industry about it, make sure to find out whether or not the agency or corporation buys through SSC or PWC; on its own; or when it can do so. This means you need to be somewhat familiar with government procurement terms and practices, as well as those used in your industry or field.

After that, to a great extent, it is a matter of making your firm and product known, through proposals, personal contacts, sales presentations, trade fairs, or media stories. A number of small high-technology firms near Ottawa have borrowed a common promotional tactic from the U.S. to help make them known to departments, Crown corporations, and major suppliers to government.

There, ambitious firms—or more correctly ambitious executives—with small budgets for advertising and promotion frequently commission professional magazine writers to prepare articles for trade magazines highlighting their product or firm or simply showing the company's existence. Sometimes the articles are in the name of the writer. Sometimes they are ghost-written for a company executive. In turn, such articles can be used as sales aids, for talks, sales presentations, or proposals. A few thousand dollars spent in this way can yield the equivalent of many more thousands of dollars in advertising space, and help a corporation's image at the same time.

This tactic works well for two reasons. First, trade magazines are chronically short of good stories and tend to want pro-business items, something that newspapers seldom run these days.

Secondly, those running individual government departments and corporations often place a great deal of stock in such trade-magazine stories. Certainly, many successful suppliers manage to use them effectively to win the right contract or grant.

As in selling to any government organization, catalogues and price lists are important, but as noted in chapters 5 and 9 and elsewhere in this book, even more important with government is personal contact. Government clients want to know "you" and your senior executives, not your agents, at least not at first. Indeed, SSC's "priority lists" referred to earlier place agents far down the list of SSC's preferred contacts. So be prepared to spend some time and effort contacting feds in departments and Crowns yourself, presumably after your promotional and selling campaigns have softened up the target agency a bit.

What Do Crowns and Other Independent Agencies Buy?

Way back in Chapter 1, we looked at the wide variety of goods and services the government itself buys for its departments. There I made the point that departments each pay for a wide variety of products and services, sometimes to support unique departmental program needs like environmental-impact assessments, but frequently of a non-departmental or housekeeping nature, such as hiring typing services.

Crown corporations, too, buy all sorts of products and services. I want to caution you, though: don't underestimate what these markets buy. Sometimes the names or purposes of a particular Crown may suggest some products it will buy, but this is almost always too narrow.

For example, looking at the largest-spending Crowns listed in Appendix I at the end of this chapter, you probably would rightly guess Air Canada might be a purchaser of airplanes and an employer of flight attendants and pilots. Yet it also buys electronic equipment, bearings, pumps, fuels, bags and wrapping supplies, tools, tires and uniforms, liquor, rubber stamps, accounting services, maps, advertising, nursery supplies, blankets, food services, soap, cologne, and thousands of other items.

Similarly, Canada Post pretty obviously is a big buyer of paper, and printing and uniforms and tires, trucks and data processing. But you might not have guessed that they also buy a great deal in terms of writing and editing services, construction work, and videotapes.

And while Petro-Canada might seem a big buyer of petroleum-engineering services, rig services or gas pumps, you would not think that it might use a lot of foreign-language services or aircraft as well. It does, and it buys thousands of other types of goods and services.

So, research the goods and services your targets buy, and start building up your lists of the important names—people in the purchasing departments—so you can conveniently drop them at the right time!

Appendix I

Contact List for the Major Crowns

(in descending order of dollars spent)
Note: All telephone numbers are in area code 613,
unless noted.

Petro-Canada (PC)

Chairman and CEO
Wilbert H. Hopper

President and Chief Operating
 Officer
Edward M. Lakusta

Petro-Canada Resources
 President
James M. Stanford

Petro-Canada Products
 President
Robert J. Mayo

Address (Head Office):
P.O. Box 2844
Calgary, Alberta T2P 3E3
(403) 296-8000

Canadian National Railways (CN)

President and CEO
Ronald E. Lawless

Address:
P.O. Box 8100
Montréal, Québec H3C 3N4
(514) 399-5430

Regional Offices:

 Atlantic Region
 CN Terminal Building
 1234 Main Street
 Moncton, N.B. E1C 1H7

Prairie Region
CN Station
123 Main Street
Winnipeg, Man. R3C 2P8

St. Lawrence Region
1060 University, Floor 6
Montréal, Québec H3B 3W6

Mountain Region
CN Tower
10004–104th Avenue
Edmonton, Alberta T5J 0K2

Great Lakes Region
277 Front Street, Floor 8
Toronto, Ontario M5V 2X7

Pacific Region
2000 – 777 Hornby St.
Vancouver, B.C. V6Z 1S4

Air Canada (AC)

President and CEO
Pierre J. Jeanniot

Address:
Place Air Canada
Montréal, Québec H2Z 1X5
(514) 879-7000

Canada Post Corporation (CPC)

President and CEO
Donald H. Lander
998-8440

Director, Materiel Management
V. McNabney
957-7926

Address:
Sir Alexander Campbell Bldg.,
Confederation Heights
Ottawa, Ontario K1A 0B1
998-8440

Canadian Broadcasting Corporation (CBC)

President
Pierre Juneau
738-6505

Headquarters, Corporate Manager
Materiel Management
J. G. Methot
727-1123

Address:
1500 Bronson Avenue
P.O. Box 8478
Ottawa, Ontario K1G 3J5
724-1200

Canada Mortgage and Housing Corporation (CMHC)

President
George D. Anderson
748-2900

Chief, Purchasing Section
J. G. Allard
748-2147

Address:
682 Montreal Rd.
Ottawa, Ontario K1A 0P7
748-2000

VIA Rail Canada Inc. (VIA)

President and CEO
Denis De Belleval

Vice-Presidents:
Executive
B. Eldon Horsman

Corporate Planning
James Roche

Development
Réjean Bechamp

Equipment Maintenance
W. C. Gelling

Finance and Administration
Nicole Beaudoin-Sauvé

Human Resources
J. R. Boivin

Marketing and Sales
Murray Jackson

Transportation
R. J. Guiney

Address:
P.O. Box 8116, Station A
Montréal, Québec H3C 3N3
(514) 871-6208

Regional Offices:

VIA Atlantic
777 Main Street
Moncton, N.B. E1C 1E9

VIA Québec
44 Elgin St., Floor E
Place Bonaventure
Montréal, Québec H5A 1H2

VIA Ontario
20 King Street West
Toronto, Ontario M5H 1C4

VIA West
191 Broadway Street
Winnipeg, Manitoba R3C 3T8

Export Development Corporation (EDC)

President and CEO
Robert L. Richardson

Senior Vice-President,
  Export Insurance Group
B. R. King

Address:
151 O'Connor Street
P.O. Box 655
Ottawa, Ontario K1P 5T9
598-2500

Farm Credit Corporation (FCC)

Chairman
James J. Hewitt

Administrative Officer
Mrs. B. McMinn
996-6606

Address:
P.O. Box 2314, Postal Station D
Ottawa, Ontario K1P 6J9
996-6606

Atomic Energy of Canada Limited (AECL)

President
James Donnelly

Address:
275 Slater Street
Ottawa, Ontario K1A 0S4
237-3270

Appendix II

The Rest of the Federal Government: Crowns, Agencies, and Commissions

Note: All telephone numbers are in area code 613, unless noted.

Agricultural Products Board
Chairman
Giles Lavoie

Secretary-Manager
A. E. Proulx

Address:
Sir John Carling Building
930 Carling Avenue
Ottawa, Ontario K1A 0C5
995-5880

Agricultural Stabilization Board
Chairman
Gilles Lavoie

Address:
930 Carling Avenue
Ottawa, Ontario K1A 0C5
995-5880

Atlantic Enterprise Board
Chairman
Gilbert Finn

Address:
Atlantic Enterprise Sec.
770 Main Street
P.O. Box 1210
Moncton, New Brunswick
E1C 8P9
(506) 857-6498
In-watts 1-800-561-7862

Atlantic Pilotage Authority
Chairman
A. D. Latter

Address:
Bank of Montreal Tower
5151 George Street, Suite 1203
Halifax, Nova Scotia B3J 1M5
(902) 426-2550

Atomic Energy Control Board (AECB)
President
René J. A. Lévèsque

Head, Materiel Management
  and Accommodation
C. H. T. Shellhorn
995-1419

Address:
270 Albert Street
P.O. Box 1046
Ottawa, Ontario K1P 5S9
992-8828

Atomic Energy of Canada Limited (AECL)
President
James Donnelly

Address:
275 Slater Street
Ottawa, Ontario K1A 0S4
237-3270

Auditor General's Office (AGO)
Auditor General of Canada
Kenneth M. Dye

Professional Services,
  Deputy Auditor General
Edward R. Rowe

Administrative Services,
  Deputy Auditor General
Ronald M. Warme

Chief, Materiel Management
P. A. Gervais
995-1925

Address:
C. D. Howe Bldg.
240 Sparks Street
Ottawa, Ontario K1A 0G6
995-3766

Bank of Canada (BC)
Governor
John W. Crow

Director of Administration
W. Albert McKay

Address:
234 Wellington Street
Ottawa, Ontario K1A 0G9
782-8111

Bureau of Pension Advocates
Chief Pensions Advocate
A. Lemieux

Address:
P.O. Box 7700
Charlottetown, P.E.I. C1A 8M9
(902) 566-8641

Canada Council (CC)
Director
Peter Roberts

Address:
99 Metcalfe Street
P.O. Box 1047
Ottawa, Ontario K1P 5V8
598-4635 or 598-4366
(may accept collect calls)

Canada Deposit Insurance Corporation (CDIC)
President and CEO
Charles C. De Léry

Office Manager
Mrs. D. Desjardins
996-2081

Canada Grains Council
President
Dr. Donald A. Dever

Address:
760 – 360 Main Street
Winnipeg, Manitoba R3C 3Z3

Canada Labour Market and Productivity Centre
Chairpersons
Shirley Carr
Rodrique J. Bilodeau

Address:
99 Bank Street, Suite 601
Ottawa, Ontario K1P 6B9
234-0505

Address:
320 Queen Street
P.O. Box 2340, Station D
Ottawa, Ontario K1P 5W5
996-2081

Canada Labour Relations Board (CLRB)
Chairman
Marc Lapointe

Materiel Management Officer
R. Boivin
996-9466

Address:
C. D. Howe Building
240 Sparks Street
Ottawa, Ontario
K1A 0X8
996-9466

Canada Pension Commission (CPC)
Chairman
John Patterson Wolfe

Executive Secretary
J. H. Eckley
Address:
Daniel J. MacDonald Bldg.
161 Grafton Street
P.O. Box 9900
Charlottetown, P.E.I.   C1A 8V6
(902) 566-8800

Canada Ports Corporation
President
Jean-Michel Tessier

Manager, Administrative Services
D. Guenette
957-5106

Address:
Ports Canada
99 Metcalfe Street
Ottawa, Ontario K1A 0N6
957-6787

**Canadian Advisory Council on the
Status of Women (CACSW)**
President
Sylvia Gold

Address:
110 O'Connor Street
P.O. Box 1541, Station B
Ottawa, Ontario K1P 5R5
992-4975

**Canadian Aviation Safety Board
(CASB)**

Chairman
Bernard M. -Deschenes
Chief Administrator
Jean Laporte
(819) 994-8004

Address:
Box 9120
Alta Vista Terminal
Ottawa, Ontario K1G 3T6
(819) 994-4317

**Canadian Centre for
Occupational Health and Safety
(CCOHS)**
President
Gordon R. C. Atherley

Address:
250 Main Street East
Hamilton, Ontario L8N 1H6
(416) 572-2981

**Canadian Dairy Commission
(CDC)**
Chairman
Roch Morin

Address:
2197 Riverside Drive
Ottawa, Ontario K1A 0Z2
998-9490

Canadian Eskimo Arts Council
Executive Secretary
Ene Schoeler

Address:
P.O. Box 2126, Station D
Ottawa, Ontario K1P 5Y1
997-0580

**Canadian Environmental
Assessment Research Council
(CEARC)**
Chairman
Dr. Fred Roots

Address:
FEARO
Fontaine Building
Hull, Québec K1A 0H3
(819) 997-1000

**Canadian General Standards Board
(CGSB)**

Address: see SPSD
Ottawa, Ontario K1A 1G6
(819) 956-0400

Canadian Grain Commission
Chief Commissioner
G. G. Leith
Address:
303 Main Street
Winnipeg, Manitoba R3C 3G8
(204) 949-2770

**Canadian Human Rights
Commission (CHRC)**
Chief Commissioner
Max Yalden

Chief, Administrative Services
A. Hopkins
995-1151, ext. 221

Address:
400 – 90 Sparks Street
Ottawa, Ontario K1A 1E1
996-0026

Canadian Import Tribunal
Chairman
Robert J. Bertrand

Address:
365 Laurier Avenue West
Journal Tower South
Ottawa, Ontario K1A 0G5
993-4601

Canadian Institute for Inter-national Peace and Security

Chairman
William Barton

Executive Director
Geoffrey Pearson

Address:
307 Gilmour Street
P.O. Box 3425, Station D
Ottawa, Ontario K1P 6L4
990-1593

Canadian Patents and Development Limited (CPDL)
President and CEO
W. D. Gordon

Treasurer
Miss L. Lipke
990-6100

Address:
275 Slater Street
Ottawa, Ontario K1A 0R3
990-6100

Canadian Radio-Television and Telecommunications Commission (CRTC)
Chairman
André Bureau

Materiel Supply and Control Officer
L. Boyer
(819) 977-4535

Address:
Central Bldg.
1 Promenade du Portage
Hull, Québec K1A 0N2
(819) 997-0313

Canadian Security Intelligence Service (CSIS)

Director
Reid Morden

Address:
P.O. Box 9732,
Ottawa Postal Terminal
Ottawa, Ontario K1G 4G4
993-9620

Canadian Saltfish Corporation
President
William R. Moyse

Addresses:
200 Kent Street, 11th Floor
Ottawa, Ontario K1A 0E6
(613) 993-2031

P.O. Box 6088
St. John's, Newfoundland
(709) 772-6080

Canadian Transport Commission (CTC)

President
Hon. Erik Nielsen

Chief, Administrative Services
J. H. Bernier
(819) 997-4290

Address:
15 Eddy Street
Hull, Québec K1A 0N9
(819) 997-6567

Cape Breton Development Corporation (DEVCO)
President and Chief Executive Officer
Derek Rance

Address:
General Mining Bldg.
Glace Bay,
P.O. Box 2500
Sydney, Nova Scotia B1P 6K9
(902) 564-2848
Telex: 019-35132

Civil Aviation Tribunal
Chairman
James Snow

Address:
Canada Bldg.
Place de Ville, Tower A
Ottawa, Ontario K1A 0N5
998-1275

**Commissioner for Federal
Judicial Affairs**
Commissioner
Pierre Garceau

Chief, Administration and
Finance
Mrs. L. St. Jacques-Ayoub
995-2310

**Commissioner of Official
Languages (COL)**
Commissioner
D'Iberville Fortier

Chief, Administrative Services
R. G. Gauthier
996-6036

Address:
110 O'Connor Street
Ottawa, Ontario K1A 0T8
996-6368

Competition Tribunal
Chairman
Madam Justice Barbara Reed

Address:
P.O. Box 1899, Station B
Ottawa, Ontario K1P 5R5
957-3172

**Construction Industry
Development Council**
Chairman
W. L. Mallory

Executive Director
John N. Dempsey

Address:
235 Queen Street
Ottawa, Ontario K1A 0H5

Correctional Investigator Canada
Commissioner
Ronald Stewart

Address:
P.O. Box 2324, Station D
Ottawa, Ontario K1P 5W5
990-2692

**Correctional Service of Canada
(CSC)**
Commissioner
Rheal Joseph Leblanc
Director General, Materiel
Management and Administration
G. Hooper
992-2871

Address:
Sir Wilfred Laurier Bldg.
340 Laurier Avenue West
Ottawa, Ontario K1A 0P9
992-5891

Economic Council of Canada (ECC)
Chairman
Judith Maxwell

Address:
P.O. Box 527, Station B
Ottawa, Ontario K1P 5V6
993-1253

**Emergency Preparedness
Canada**
Minister
Hon. Perrin Beatty

Executive Director
W. B. Snarr

Address:
Gillin Bldg.
141 Laurier Avenue West
Ottawa, Ontario K1A 0W6
992-7380

**Enterprise Cape Breton
Board**
Executive Director
L. McNeil

Address:
P.O. Box 2001
295 Charlotte Street
Sydney, Nova Scotia B1P 6K7
1-800-565-9460

Farm Credit Corporation (FCC)
Chairman
James J. Hewitt

Administrative Officer
Mrs. B. McMinn
996-6606

Address:
P.O. Box 2314, Postal Station D
Ottawa, Ontario K1P 6J9
996-6606

Freshwater Fish Marketing Corporation
Chairman
John G. McFarlane

President
Thomas Dunn (Winnipeg)

Addresses:
200 Kent Street
Centennial Towers, 11th Floor
Ottawa, Ontario K1A 0E6,

1199 Plessis Road
Winnipeg, Manitoba R2C 3L4

Grain Transportation Agency
Administrator
Hon. J. H. Horner

Address:
135 Lombard Avenue
Winnipeg, Manitoba R3B 0T4
(204) 949-3212

Grains Group
Executive Secretary
R. H. M. Cathcart

Address:
235 Queen Street
First Floor West
Ottawa, Ontario K1A 0G2
(613) 995-7127

Great Lakes Pilotage Authority Ltd.
Chairman/CEO
R. G. Armstrong

Address:
132 Second Street East
Cornwall, Ontario K6H 5R9

Historic Sites and Monuments Board of Canada
Address:
10 Wellington Street
Environment Canada
Hull, Québec K1A 0H3
(819) 994-3222

Immigration Appeal Board
Chairperson
Mrs. Michelle Falardeau-Ramsay

Materiel Management Officer
D. Idone
996-8943

116 Lisgar Street
Ottawa, Ontario K1A 0A6
995-6486

International Boundary Commission (IBC)
Canadian Commissioner
Dr. Alexander C. McEwen

Address:
615 Booth Street
Ottawa, Ontario K1A 0E9
995-4960

International Centre for Ocean Development (ICOD)
President
G. C. Vernon

Address:
5670 Spring Garden Road
Halifax, Nova Scotia B3J 1H6
(902) 426-1512
Telex: 019-21670 ICOD HFX

International Development Research Centre (IDRC)
President
Ivan L. Head

Address:
P.O. Box 8500
250 Albert Street
Ottawa, Ontario K1G 3H9
236-6163

International Joint Commission (IJC) (Canadian Section)
Chairman
Pierre-André Bissonnette

Secretary
D. G. Chance
995-2984

Address:
100 Metcalfe Street
Ottawa, Ontario K1P 5M1
995-2984

Investment Canada (IC)
President
Paul Labbé

Services Administrator
Mrs. D. Malone
995-1896
Toll-free number 1-800-267-0490

Address:
P.O. Box 2800, Postal Station D
Ottawa, Ontario K1P 6A5
995-9639

Laurentian Pilotage Authority
Chairman
Jacques Chouinard

Address:
1080 Beaver Hall Hill
Montréal, Québec H2Z 1S8
(514) 283-6320

Law Reform Commission
President
Mr. Justice Allen M. Linden

Manager, Materiel Management
G. B. McAlear
996-4086

Address:
130 Albert Street
Ottawa, Ontario K1A 0L6
996-7844

Livestock Feed Board of Canada
Chairman
Denis Ethier

Address: (Headquarters)
5180 Queen Mary Road
Montréal, Québec H3W 3E7
(514) 283-7505
Telex: 055-67137

Marine Atlantic Inc.
President and CEO
Rupert J. Tingley

Address:
100 Cameron Street
Moncton, New Brunswick
E1C 5Y6
(506) 858-3600
Telex: 014-2833

Medical Research Council of Canada (MRC)
President
Dr. Pierre Bois

Chief, Administrative Services
E. E. Wright
995-1941

Address:
Jeanne Mance Bldg., 20th Floor
Tunney's Pasture
Ottawa, Ontario K1A 0W9
954-1809

National Advisory Council on Fitness and Amateur Sport
Chairman
Dr. Bryce Taylor

Address:
Journal Tower South
365 Laurier Ave. West
Ottawa, Ontario K1A 0X6
996-4510

National Archives of Canada (NA)
National Archivist of Canada
Jean-Pierre Wallot

Address:
395 Wellington Street
Ottawa, Ontario K1A 0N3
992-9359

**National Arts Centre
Corporation (NAC)**
Chairman
J. Pierre Boutin

Director General
R. Blackburn

Manager, Supply and Services
Y. R. Dube
996-5051, ext. 253

Address:
Ottawa, Ontario K1P 5W1
996-5051

**The National Battlefields
Commission**
Chairman
F. Tremblay

Address:
390 De Bernieres Avenue
Québec, Québec G1R 2L7
(418) 648-3506

National Energy Board (NEB)
Chairman
Roland Priddle

Executive Director
R. Glass

Chief, Property and Materiel
  Management
A. Laframboise
993-5067

Address:
Trebla Bldg.
473 Albert Street
Ottawa, Ontario K1A 0E5
998-3448

National Film Board (NFB)
Government Film Commissioner and
  Chairman
François N. Macerola

Addresses:
150 Kent Street
Ottawa, Ontario K1A 0M9
992-3615

P.O. Box 6100
Montréal, Québec H3C 3H5
(514) 293-9000

National Library
National Librarian
Marianne F. Scott

Address:
395 Wellington Street
Ottawa, Ontario K1A 0N4

Information Enquiries
995-9481

Procurement Chief,
  National Library/National
  Archives
P. Mifflen
995-1036

Address:
395 Wellington Street
Ottawa, Ontario K1A 0N3
992-9359

**National Museums of Canada
(NMC)**
Chairman
Dr. Sean B. Murphy

Secretary General
John R. Edwards

Address:
200 Kent Street, 9th Floor
Ottawa, Ontario K1A 0M8
954-4331

Chief, Materiel Management
  Section & Administrative
  Services
Mr. R. F. Pilon
National Museums of Canada
8th Floor, Room 8060
Centennial Towers
200 Kent Street
Ottawa, Ontario K1A 0M8
954-4426

Procurement Officer
Mrs. P. M. Wynne
Administrative Services
  Division
Canadian Conservation
  Institute
1030 Innes Road, Room 212
Ottawa, Ontario K1A 0M8
998-3721

Chief, Materiel Management
Mr. C. Woods
National Museum of Science
  and Technology
2380 Lancaster Road
Room 118
Ottawa, Ontario K1A 0M8
991-3041

National Parole Board (NPB)
Chairman
Ole Michaelsen Ingstrup

Chief, Administrative Services
V. Nadon
995-1308, ext. 102

Address:
340 Laurier Avenue West
Ottawa, Ontario K1A 0R1
995-1308

**National Transportation Agency
(NTA)**
Chairman
Hon. Erik Nielsen

Address:
Terrace de Chaudière
Hull, Quebec K1A 0N7
(819) 997-4470

**Natural Sciences and Engineering
Research Council (NSERC)**
President
Dr. Arthur W. May

Administrative Officer
Mrs. C. Cudahy
995-6220

Address:
200 Kent Street
Ottawa, Ontario K1A 1H5
995-6295

Northern Pipeline Agency
Commissioner
Hon. Mitchell Sharp

Administrative Assistant
Miss P. Sabourin
992-9652

Address:
Station 210, Centennial Towers
200 Kent Street
Ottawa, Ontario K1A 0E6
993-7466

**Office of the Superintendent of
Financial Institutions**
Superintendent
M. A. MacKenzie

Executive Director
R. M. Emond

Chief, Office Services Division and
  Library
R. G. Sabourin
990-2141

Address:
122 Bank Street
Ottawa, Ontario K1A 0H2
995-3521

Offices of the Privacy and
**Information Commissioners of
Canada**
Privacy Commissioner
Dr. John W. Grace

Information Commissioner
Inger Hansen

Chief Administrative Services
R. Dore
995-0870

Address:
Tower B
112 Kent Street
Ottawa, Ontario K1A 1H3
(613) 995-2410
1-800-267-0441

Pacific Pilotage Authority
Address:
300 – 1199 W. Hastings Street
Vancouver, B.C. V6E 4G9

**Public Service Staff Relations Board
(PSSRB)**
Chairperson
Ian Deans

Head, Materiel Management
and Office Services
M. Wolfe
990-1750

Address:
Box 1525, Station B
Ottawa, Ontario K1P 5V2
990-1800

**Restrictive Trade Practices
Commission of Canada**
Chairman
O. G. (Gerald) Stoner

Chief, Administration and
Finance
R. Dow
996-5252

Address:
P.O. Box 336, Station A
Ottawa, Ontario K1N 8V3
992-0274

**Science Council of Canada
(SCC)**
Chairman
Dr. Geraldine Kenney-Wallace

Financial Officer
J. C. Cloutier
996-5769

Address:
100 Metcalfe Street
Ottawa, Ontario K1P 5M1
996-1729

**Security Intelligence Review
Committee**
Chairman
Hon. Ronald Atkey

Address:
365 Laurier Avenue West
Post Box 2430, Station D
Ottawa, Ontario K1P 5W5
990-8441

**Social Sciences and Humanities
Research Council (SSHRC)**
President
Dr. John Leyerele

Manager,
Materiel Management
R. Quirouette
992-4263

Address:
255 Albert Street
P.O. Box 1610
Ottawa, Ontario K1P 6G4
992-0562

St. Lawrence Seaway Authority and
**Seaway International Bridge Cor-
poration Ltd.**
President
William A. O'Neil

Address:
360 Albert Street
Ottawa, Ontario K1R 7X7
598-4600

Standards Council of Canada
President
Georges Archer

Manager, Administration
R. MacDonald
992-2943

Address:
Suite 1203
350 Sparks Street
Ottawa, Ontario K1R 7S8
238-3222

**Status of Women Canada
(SWC)**
Co-ordinator
Kay Stanley

Address:
151 Sparks Street
La Promenade Bldg.
Ottawa, Ontario K1A 1C3
995-7835

Statute Revision Commission
Chairman
Mary Dawson

Address:
West Memorial Bldg.
344 Wellington Street
Ottawa, Ontario K1A 0H8
957-0057

Tariff Board
Chairman
Donald Yoemans

Assistant Secretary
R. C. Lefebvre
990-2414

Address:
365 Laurier Avenue West
Ottawa, Ontario K1A 0G7
990-2452

Téléfilm Canada
Executive Director
Peter Pearson

Address:
Tour de la Banque Nationale
600 de la Gauchetière Street West
25th Floor
Montréal, Québec H3B 4L2
(514) 283-6363
Telex: 055-60998

CHAPTER SEVEN

Subcontracting –
The Indirect Approach to
Government Purchasing Dollars

Some businesses are too small, or the range of goods and services they offer too narrow, for them to expect to snag big government projects and major non-competitive purchases on their own. However, that need not cut them out of the picture entirely. Small or very specialized firms can still have a go at government dollars by subcontracting to the larger firms that win the overall project-management prize. Indeed, the federal government itself has recognized the value of supporting small businesses in this endeavour and has set up programs to encourage subcontracting and teaming on larger projects. This has been doubly necessary, given the fact that many major capital projects are awarded to foreign firms as prime contractors because no Canadian firms are large enough to handle the entire job.

One of these commendable initiatives illustrates just how hard a fight any minister can have to change an entrenched departmental policy or practice when some departmental bureaucrats don't really care for the change. It also gives us a unique look at the priority—or lack of priority—small business has had inside SSC in recent years.

I'm referring to the on again/off again SSC Small Business Subcontracting Opportunities Program. Since the then SSC minister introduced the measure almost a decade ago, SSC senior management largely has ignored the program, at least until Brian Mulroney appointed Otto Jelinek as Supply and Services Minister. Now the program appears to be on again, permanently, one hopes.

SSC's Canadian Business Subcontracting Program

In 1981 SSC, then under minister Charles Lapointe (a former small-business minister) created the Canadian Business Subcontracting Opportunities Program, in order to help Canadian firms get more subcontracts. His public announcement said: "It has been difficult to determine which Canadian firms were subcontracted. However, it is known that in certain cases subcontracts that were let out to foreign firms represent between thirty per cent and fifty per cent of the retail cost of products."

In total, he said, 64 prime contractors participated in the subcontracting program. "Over the two preceding fiscal years, SSC has granted these 64 companies contracts totalling $1.569 billion," noted Lapointe as the program was presented. He asked each large contractor to appoint a co-ordinator of Canadian supply, whose duties, primarily, would be to increase the overall proportion of Canadian content in the products the company sold to the public and private sectors. He or she would also be responsible for co-ordinating the activities of firms attempting to obtain subcontracts with those of purchasing officials within SSC.

Companies tendering for contracts worth more than $2 million could be required to include as part of their bid a Canadian business subcontracting opportunities plan, that is, to describe in advance the subcontracting work they intended to have done. "From now on", the program outline intoned, "the department intends to publish details of an upcoming project and invite subcontractors to send in a brief outline of their capabilities in the project."

The first major project to be published was the Department of Transport's Radar Airport Modernization Program (RAMP). It also seems to have been the last, judging from a March 1987 SSC policy study entitled "Detailed Progress Report on SSC Small Business Program". It cited several initiatives that had floundered since the grand announcement. One such initiative was the "establishment of focal responsibility points in each directorate to focus on national objectives (small business being one of these objectives)"; another was "development of a

Market Strategy and Planning Guide", and third, "development of a policy statement on post qualification of sources versus pre-solicitation qualification of sources".

"Pre-qualification" means your company has to pass all the government tests before your bid can be considered. This can cost you a lot of time, effort, and money to fill out forms, and provide samples of your goods for contracts which you have no remote chance of winning. "Post-qualification" means you go through most of the quality-assurance and other tests after your bid or proposal has made it at least to the short list stage. Over-all, business hates pre-qualification, while some public servants like it because their bureaucratic empires can be increased without adding to the number of potential contractors with whom they must negotiate.

The small-business task force found the usual size for small subcontracts was $500,000 and up. However, an accompanying Bureau of Management Consulting (BMC) study, called "Small Business Program Subcontracting Data Information System", found that SSC "is not aware of the total magnitude of their con-tracting impact on small business as no subcontracting data is currently collected." It found "somewhere between SSC management approval of the small business program and the subsequent implementation announcement by the minister, the establishment of a meaningful data base and the design of an ap-propriate costed system never happened."

In fairness to SSC, the BMC and 1987 policy study cited above were SSC initiatives, albeit with a lot of prompting from the Small Business Office at DRIE. It also is widely known in Ottawa that a number of SSC officials had long been concerned that the department had failed to attract enough small businesses as sup-pliers, and were pushing for action. SSC's two most recent deputy ministers also have wanted such a push.

Presumably, then, the Subcontracting Program simply fell be-tween the cracks in SSC for several years. The recent appointment of Otto Jelinek as Supply minister at a time when the Small Business minister Bernard Valcourt and his staff and some at SSC were looking at ways to steer more public-sector dollars to small business has rescued this useful initiative from public service purgatory, for the moment anyway.

These two gentlemen have persuaded their cabinet colleagues to adopt several key measures put forward in the
"Report on Small Business" mentioned above. Under their
program, part of a package called "Access Small Business", the
announcement says: "Prime contractors will be required to submit a Small Business Subcontracting Plan on contracts between
$10 million and $100 million where appropriate. This will ensure that smaller firms will receive a greater portion of
subcontracts on larger federal projects." Further, all industrial
benefit packages on projects over $100 million will now "include
both small business subcontracting plans and supplier development plans. These will be considered as part of the bid
evaluation criteria."

In addition, companies competing for contracts over $25,000
will be put on a rotation basis so that "other firms can have a
crack at them. SSC also will hire six small business advocates to
identify opportunities for small business suppliers and let them
take advantage" of the chances.

Other initiatives include: improved publications on how to
do business with the government, expanded use of standards and
qualified products lists and a contracts-information centre in Ottawa, and co-operative efforts with the Western Diversification
Office (WDO) and the Atlantic Canada Opportunities Agency
(ACOA).

Subcontracting –
Not Necessarily "Second Best"

Business obtained by subcontracting has built some of the most
successful firms in Canada. Indeed, Canadian federal procurement and economic development strategies are built around
subcontracting.

For example, *The Financial Post*'s defence writer Jim Bagnall
has estimated that of $4 billion going to Saint John Shipbuild-
ing Ltd. of New Brunswick to manage the Canadian Armed
Forces acquisition of six new frigates, Saint John will actually
only keep thirty per cent, while Paramax Electronics Inc., a four-
year-old Montréal firm will get forty per cent of the total for its
subcontracted role of integrating the electronic naval weapons

systems. The actual shipbuilding, Bagnall calculated, accounted for only one-quarter of the project.

Other large "subs" for Saint John in this DND project include: CAE Electronics Ltd. of Montréal; MEL Defence Systems of Stittsville, Ontario; and SED Systems Inc. of Saskatoon. Each of these firms, which provide training systems and various electronics and communications systems, has subcontracts worth $19 million to $40 million. In turn, each has supplier networks to build subcomponents for them. Other large firms—just a few of many—with active subcontracting programs include: Litton Systems Ltd., McDonnell Douglas, and Oerlikon Aerospace.

A couple of dozen high-technology firms have signed Memoranda of Understanding with DRIE and other agencies pledging to spend large amounts of federal procurement or grant money under programs like the Defence Industry Productivity Program, on small-business subcontracting.

The fact that these MOUs are confidential makes many DRIE officials unhappy. As one put it, "After all, we're trying to show small business we care, and we're trying to help them. How can we if they don't know that these opportunities are available?"

If you want the information on MOUs between businesses and DRIE revealed, write to the Prime Minister, and send a copy of your letter to the Minister of State for Small Business, and the Minister of Supply and Services at the addresses listed above. Or you could make a formal request under the federal access to information legislation. For information on how to do this, call 1-800-267-0441.

Meanwhile, though, if you go to a bit of bother, you can find out who some of these firms are, or other firms who are looking for "subs". I've had a try at this for you. In Appendix I at the end of this chapter you will find a list of some leading federal prime contractors, and how to get in touch with them. DRIE project co-ordinators who can get your firm, product, or service listed are in Appendix II. In addition, you can match up aerospace or defence products with the project co-ordinators at SSC by consulting the excellent guide put out by SSC's AMES Directorate, *Doing Business with the Aerospace, Marine and Electronics Systems Directorate.*

These could be good customers for all sorts of goods, services, and ideas. Many of the sourcing procedures and jargon that the feds use are paralleled in these companies who have success in dealing with government. Contact them, and find out how to sell to them. As a first step, you could ask their PR departments to put you on the mailing-list for their press announcements which frequently name the firms they are using as subs, or announce other big government contracts they are pursuing.

"Subcontractor Beware" –
The Ins and Outs of Working With the Primes

SSC has formulated a policy on subcontracting which is explained in publications SPM 6053, SSC General Conditions 1026, and SPM Policy 6052 entitled, "Assignment of Contracts". For instance, to legally subcontract for $10,000 or more "a contractor cannot subcontract without the prior written consent of the Minister. . . . However, a contractor may subcontract such portions as is customary in the carrying out of similar contracts if the contract of the Minister does not direct otherwise." In other words, the policy is not rigorously followed by prime contractors even though Supply Policy Manual 6053 specifically calls for the filing of SSC form 1137.

Subcontracting to U.S. Firms

You also should think of subcontracts from the big firms in the U.S., and look at what kinds of goods or services they are buying. There are 1,000 prime defence contractors in the U.S., some of whom are much bigger than any firm in Canada. Remember too that we already have a free trade agreement in defence.

In this way you can get another whack at Canadian government dollars. The Canadian feds import a lot, especially defence equipment. For example, a 1985 SSC study found foreign content of Canadian government purchases in the fiscal year for 1983-84 stood at 32 cents per dollar analyzed (or 43 cents excluding the Canadian frigate contract) and 43 cents the year before.

To access the big U.S. defence subcontracting market, look at the information sources outlined in Chapter 8 of this book, in the section "Selling to the U.S. Government", and in the portion of Chapter 5 looking at DND, EAC, DOD, and CCC. You can get a number of the key U.S. government publications from External Affairs Canada. One you will find exceptionally useful is the U.S. Defense Department's publication *Small Business Subcontracting Directory* which lists major DOD primes, products sought and lists contact persons. Unfortunately, there is no Canadian equivalent.

External also has in-house defence experts and a well-honed U.S. marketing system which can be invaluable. Contact EAC's Defence Program Bureau (DPB) in Ottawa at (613) 996-8050. I've also tested the toll-free number 1-800-267-8376, the department's Info Export Hotline. This is a different EAC branch entirely, but the individuals at this number have always had someone from the branch I was seeking return the call on a government line. I've found DPB not only helpful but almost indispensible in getting a handle on the U.S. military market. Start there. They can also advise you on paperwork, security clearance, and export permits.

Other useful allies in your search for subcontracting opportunities in the U.S. will be the Canadian Commercial Corporation, or the U.S. Defense Contract Administration Service Management Area (DCASMA), both in Ottawa; the regional office and the industry or defence-sector experts in DRIE/DIST; and your national industry associations, and industry association-sponsored defence expositions in Washington.

To effectively sell to primes in Canada or the U.S., though, you need to know the hardware that is already on the market. To help you in this, perhaps you might benefit from a visit to a defence-industry trade show. The U.S. Navy one usually takes place in March or April; Marines in July; Army in September; Air Force in October. The Armed Forces Communication and Electronics Association also holds one. In Canada, Baxter Publications, who publish the journal *Canadian Defence Quarterly,* hold a defence show in Ottawa called ARMX (for "Armed Forces Exhibition").

Just as U.S. firms trying to sell to the Canadian government face policy obstacles such as "buy Canadian" policies, there are several U.S. practices that bug Canadian firms trying to enter the U.S. defence market. One of the most annoying is the U.S. small-business "set aside" program, requiring that a significant proportion of federal contracts be given to small or minority-owned businesses. Supporting the "set aside" program, and serving as a sourcing system of subcontractors is PASS. PASS in the U.S. government stands for Procurement Automated Source System. Housed inside the U.S. Small Business Administration, PASS is a computerized directory of U.S. "small businesses" who can be sourced for federal contracts.

Canada has "PASS" too, but it's certainly not the same one the U.S. has. SSC's PASS sourcing system, that is its Procurement and Acquisition Support System, is not used to support a "set aside" program; Canada doesn't have as fully articulated a program. Nor is it exclusively a small-business system, as in the U.S. This causes a lot of confusion in the Canadian small-business community. PASS simply allows SSC client departments to access all NASIS listed firms by computer. That's it. So SSC's use of terms like PASS confuses Canadian small businesses enormously, makes them even more invisible inside SSC, and reduces their subcontracting possibilities.

Because the Canadian defence industry is relatively small, many Canadian firms are discouraged from selling to the U.S. feds. Yet since the U.S., Canadian, and NATO governments tend more and more to "sole-source" buys, it will become harder and harder for small Canadian firms to grow by using government dollars, directly. They can, however, get a fair share of the U.S. defence market by acting as subcontractors.

Appendix I

Prime Contractor Contacts and Project Managers

(DRIE / DIST)

Electronics Industrial Benefits (EIB)

Mrs. T. K. Butryn
A/Manager, Electronics
  Industrial Benefits Aerospace,
  Defence and Industrial
  Benefits (FADI)
Department of Regional
  Industrial Expansion
  (DRIE)

235 Queen Street
Ottawa, Ontario K1A 0H5
Tel: (613) 954-3425

Projects Include:

Radar Airport Modernization
Program (RAMP)
Mr. D. S. Poole
Industrial Benefits
  Manager
Electronics Industrial
  Benefits, FADI/DRIE

Mailing Address:
235 Queen Street (XRMP)
Ottawa, Ontario K1A 0H5
Office Location:
110 O'Connor Street, 8th Floor
Ottawa, Ontario
Tel: (613) 991-5673

Raytheon Company
Equipment Division
Boston Post Road
Wayland, Mass. 01778
U.S.A.

Contact:
Mr. Thomas E. Peterson, Manager,
Equipment Division Procurement
Tel: (617) 358-4570

Flight Data Systems
  Modernization Project (FDMP)

Mr. J. Bodien
Industrial Benefits Manager
Electronics Industrial Benefits,
FADI/DRIE
Mailing Address:
235 Queen Street (XRMP)
Ottawa, Ontario K1A 0H5
Office Location
110 O'Connor Street,
8th Floor
Ottawa, Ontario
Tel: (613) 990-5753

FDMP Potential Bidders and
  Industrial Benefits Contacts:

Hughes Aircraft Company
General Systems Group
P.O. Box 3310
Fullerton, California
U.S.A. 92634

Contact: W.C. (Sam) Sitland
Tel:(714) 732-7553 or
(714) 525-9550

IBM Canada Ltd.
251 Consumers Road
North York, Ontario
M2J 4R3

Contact: D. L. MacPherson
Tel: (416) 758-3361

Sanders Canada Ltd.
2421 Lancaster Road
Ottawa, Ontario K1B 4L5
Contact: M. Whalen
Tel: (613) 738-4564

Sumitomo Canada Ltd.
P.O. Box 258
1 First Canadian Place
Suite 7010
Toronto, Ontario M5X 1C8

Contact: G. Skanes
Tel: (416) 860-3816

Unisys Corporation
  Defense Systems
Custom Systems Division
P.O. Box 517
Paoli, Pennsylvania
U.S.A. 19301

Contact: P. Vandakas
Tel: (215) 648-7362

Canadian Airspace System Plan
  (CASP)/Systems Engineering &
  Integration Project (SEIP)

Mr. W. C. Edwards
Industrial Benefits Manager
Electronics Industrial Benefits,
  FADI/DRIE
Mailing Address:
235 Queen Street (XRMP)
Ottawa, Ontario K1A 0H5
Office Location:
110 O'Connor Street, 8th Floor
Ottawa, Ontario
Tel: (613) 990-5752

Microwave Landing System
  Project (MLS)

Mr. W. C. Edwards
Industrial Benefits Manager

Electronics Industrial Benefits,
  FADI/DRIE
Benefits, FADI/DRIE
Mailing Address:
235 Queen Street (XRMP)
Ottawa, Ontario K1A 0H5

Office Location:
110 O'Connor Street, 8th Floor
Tel: (613) 990-5752

Control and Performance Monitoring
  System (CPMS)/Miscellaneous
  CASP PRC Projects (CADIN/VOR/
  ATCOS/ISTN)

Mr. W. D. Evans
Industrial Benefits Manager
Electronics Industrial Benefits,
  FADI/DRIE
Mailing Address:
235 Queen Street (XRMP)
Ottawa, Ontario K1A 0H5
Office Location:
110 O'Connor Street, 8th Floor
Ottawa, Ontario
Tel: (613) 991-5672

Aeronautical Information Processing
System (AIPS)

Mr. J. Bodien
Industrial Benefits Manager
Electronics Industrial Benefits,
  FADI/DRIE
Mailing Address:
235 Queen Street (XRMP)
Ottawa, Ontario K1A 0H5
Office Location:
110 O'Connor Street, 8th Floor
Ottawa, Ontario
Tel: (613) 990-5753

North American Air Defence
  Modernization (NAADM)/ North
  Warning System (NWS)
  Communications Segment
Mr. D. B. Tod
Industrial Benefits Manager
Electronics Industrial Benefits,
  FADI/DRIE
Mailing Address:
235 Queen Street
Ottawa, Ontario K1A 0H5
Tel: (613) 954-3424
Office Location:
219 Laurier West, 2nd Floor
Ottawa, Ontario
Tel: (613) 996-6920

Canac/Microtel
North Warning System
  Communications
Suite 950
130 Slater Street
Ottawa, Ontario K1P 6E2

Contact: Mr. C. Kuspira
Contract Administration
  Engineer
Tel: (613) 232-0485

North Warning System/
  Operations and Maintenance
  (NWS/O & M)

Mr. D. B. Tod
Industrial Benefits Manager
Electronics Industrial Benefits,
  FADI/DRIE
Mailing Address:
235 Queen Street
Ottawa, Ontario K1A 0H5
Office Location:
219 Laurier West, 2nd Floor
Ottawa, Ontario
Tel: (613) 996-6920

Frontec Logistics
P.O. Box 2426
10035 – 105th Street
Edmonton, Alberta   T5J 2V6

Contact: G. H. Mead,
Vice-President
Logistics & Engineering
Tel: (403) 420-7689

Ottawa Contact:
Mr. Steven Lougheed
Director of Business
  Development
Tel: (613) 238-3217

Tactical Command Control
  and Communications Systems
  (TCCCS)

Mrs. T. K. Butryn
Industrial Benefits Manager
Electronics Industrial
  Benefits, FADI/DRIE

Mailing Address:
235 Queen Street
Ottawa, Ontario K1A 0H5
Tel: (613) 954-3425
Office Location:
222 Nepean Street, 5th Floor,
Vanier Bldg.
Ottawa, Ontario
Tel: (613) 992-7159

Mr. D. Spendlove
Industrial Benefits Manager
Electronics Industrial
  Benefits, FADI/DRIE
Mailing Address:
235 Queen Street
Ottawa, Ontario K1A 0H5
Tel: (613) 954-3421
Office Location:
222 Nepean Street, 5th Floor,
Vanier Bldg.
Ottawa, Ontario
Tel: (613) 992-3724

Intelligence and Security
  Complex (ISX)
Mr. K. Theoret
Industrial Benefits Manager
Electronics Industrial Benefits,
  FADI/DRIE
Mailing Address:
235 Queen Street
Ottawa, Ontario K1A 0H5
Tel: (613) 954-3781
Office Location:
219 Laurier Ave. West, 3rd Floor
Ottawa, Ontario
Tel: (613) 998-7267

Mr. D. Spendlove
Industrial Benefits Manager
Electronics Industrial Benefits,
  FADI/DRIE
Mailing Address:
235 Queen Street
Ottawa, Ontario K1A 0H5
Tel: (613) 954-3421
Office Location:
219 Laurier Ave. West, 3rd Floor
Ottawa, Ontario
Tel: (613) 998-7267

Canadian On-Line Secure
  Information Communications
  Systems (COSICS)
Mr. K. Theoret
Industrial Benefits Manager
Electronics Industrial Benefits,
  FADI/DRIE
Mailing Address:
236 Queen Street
Ottawa, Ontario K1A 0H5
Tel: (613) 954-3781

Office Location:
200 Blvd. Sacré-Coeur,
14th Floor
Hull, Québec
Tel: (819) 953-5092

Marine and Land Industrial Benefits

Mr. M. J. Taylor
Manager, Marine and Land
  Industrial Benefits
Aerospace, Defence and
  Industrial Benefits (FADI)

Department of Regional Industrial
Expansion (DRIE)

235 Queen Street
Ottawa, Ontario
K1A 0H5
Tel: (613) 954-3740

Projects Include:

• Canadian Patrol
  Frigate (CPF)/Ship
  Replacement Project
  Phase II (SRP II)

Mr. Jim Lovett
DRIE Manager
CPF/SRP II Project
  Management Office
190 O'Connor Street
Ottawa, Ontario K2P 1T6
Tel: (613) 995-5962

Mr. Lee Akerley
Deputy DRIE Manager
CPF/SRP II Project
  Management Office

190 O'Connor Street
Ottawa, Ontario K2P 1T6
Tel: (613) 996-0091

Saint John Shipbuilding Limited
Fifth Floor, SMT Building
300 Union Street
Saint John, New Brunswick
E2L 4Z2
Contact: Rick Hancox
Tel: (506) 632-3232

Tribal Class Update and
  Modernization Program (TRUMP)
Small Arms Replacement
Program (SARP)

Mr. Finn Johansen
DRIE Manager (TRUMP/SARP)
TRUMP Project Management
  Office
301 Elgin Street
Ottawa, Ontario K2P 2H5
Tel: (613) 996-0327

Mr. Barrie Miller
Deputy DRIE Manager
  (TRUMP/SARP)
TRUMP Project Management
  Office
301 Elgin Street
Ottawa, Ontario K2P 2H5
Tel: (613) 992-1861

• TRUMP
  Litton Systems Ltd.
  220 Laurier Avenue West
  Suite 730
  Ottawa, Ontario K1P 5Z9

  Contact: Mr. Bob Brown
  Tel: (613) 236-2358

• SARP
  Diemaco (1984) Inc.
  1036 Wilson Avenue
  Kitchener, Ontario N2C 1J3

  Contact: Mr. Peter Andrews
  Tel: (519) 893-6840

• Canadian Submarine Acquisition
  Project (CASAP)

  Mr. Richard Rantz
  DRIE Manager

CASAP Project Management
Office
270 Albert Street
Ottawa, Ontario K1P 5G8
Tel: (613) 996-7913

Mr. Andrew Morrison
DRIE Deputy Manager
CASAP Project Management
Office
270 Albert Street
Ottawa, Ontario K1P 5G8
Tel: (613) 996-7604

● Polar 8 Icebreaker
NATO Frigate Replacement
1990's (NFR-90)
Naval Reserve Modernization
Program (NRMP)

Mr. Brian Deacon
DRIE Manager (Polar 8/
NFR-90/MRMP)
235 Queen Street
Ottawa, Ontario K1A 0H5
Tel: (613) 954-3420

Ms. Margaret Lange
DRIE Deputy Manager
(Polar 8/NFR-90/MRMP)
235 Queen Street
Ottawa, Ontario K1A 0H5
Tel: (613) 954-3417

● Anti-Armour/Light Armoured
Vehicles (AA/LAV)

Mr. Ed Champagne
DRIE Manager (AA/LAV)
AA/LAV Project Management
Office
Mailing Address:
235 Queen Street
Ottawa, Ontario K1A 0H5
Tel: (613) 954-3747
Office Location:
222 Nepean Street
Ottawa, Ontario
Tel: (613) 992-4733

● Vehicle Projects
(MBT/MOST/NTV)

Main Battle Tank (MBT)
Military and Operational
Support Trucks (MOST)
Northern Terrain Vehicle (NTV)

Mr. Helmut Zankl
DRIE Manager
(MBT/MOST/NTV)
235 Queen Street
Ottawa, Ontario K1A 0H5
Tel: (613) 954-3789
(819) 956-0497 (MOST)
(613) 995-1114 (PMO Tank)

Aerospace Industrial Benefits

Mr. R. L. Hawkins
A/Manager, Aerospace
Industrial Benefits Div.
Aerospace, Defence and
Industrial Benefits (FADI)
Department of Regional
Industrial Expansion (DRIE)
235 Queen Street
Ottawa, Ontario K1A 0H5
Tel: (613) 954-3779

Projects Include:

● New Shipborne Aircraft
Project (NSA)

Mr. J. Hampton
DRIE Manager
Mailing Address:
235 Queen Street (XNSA)
Ottawa, Ontario K1A 0H5
Office Address:
255 Argyle Avenue
Ottawa, Ontario
Tel: (613) 995-4525

Mr. K. C. Birch
Deputy Project Manager
Mailing Address:
235 Queen Street (XNSA)
Ottawa, Ontario K1A 0H5
Office Address:
255 Argyle Avenue
Ottawa, Ontario
Tel: (613) 995-6595

Low Level Air Defence (LLAD)

Close Air Defence Weapon
(CADW)

Mr. A. A. Dvarionas
DRIE Manager,
 LLAD/CADW Projects
Mailing Address:
235 Queen Street
Ottawa, Ontario K1A 0H5
Office Address:
Journal South Tower
Laurier at Kent Street
15th Floor
Ottawa, Ontario
Tel: (613) 996-4058

● LLAD

Oerlikon Aerospace Inc.
225, Sud, Blvd. Du Séminaire
St. Jean-Sur-Richelieu,
 Québec J3B 8E9
Tel: (514) 358-2000
Fax: (514) 358-1744

Contact: Mr. Rolf Weyhmuller
Director of Industrial Benefits
Tel: (514) 358-2000, ext. 211

● CF-18 Project (includes CF-18 System Engineering Support and
External Fuel Tank Procurement)

Mr. J. W. Rochon
DRIE Manager, CF-18
 Industrial Benefits
Mailing Address:
235 Queen Street (XEEL)
Ottawa, Ontario K1A 0H5
Office Location:
110 O'Connor Street,
3rd Floor
Ottawa, Ontario
Tel: (613) 995-5293

McDonnell Douglas
 Corporation
P.O. Box 516
St. Louis, Missouri
U.S.A. 63166

Ottawa Contact:
Mr. R. G. Slaunwhite
Vice-President

McDonnell Douglas Canada
 Limited
50 O'Connor St., Suite 1424
Ottawa, Ontario K1P 6L9
Tel: (613) 236-0766

Contact: Manager –
 Industrial Benefits
McDonnell Aircraft Company
P.O. Box 516
St. Louis, Missouri
U.S.A 63166
Tel: (314) 233-1880

● CF-18 Peripheral
 Industrial Benefits

Mr. M. G. Dumont
DRIE Manager,
 CF-18 Peripheral Industrial
 Benefits
Mailing Address:
235 Queen Street (XEEL)
Ottawa, Ontario K1A 0H5
Office Location:
110 O'Connor Street
3rd Floor
Ottawa, Ontario
Tel: (613) 995-5522

Mr. R. E. Gingras
CF-18 Manager – Industrial
 Benefits
Electronics Warfare Division
Sanders Associates, Inc.
95 Canal Street
Nashua, New Hampshire
U.S.A. 03061-2004
Tel: (603) 885-2590

Mr. Terry O'Malley
Radar Systems Group
Hughes Aircraft Company
P.O. Box 92426
Bldg. R10, MS 1010
Los Angeles, California
U.S.A. 90009
Tel: (213) 607-1400

Mr. L. D. Horn
Program Manager
ALR-67 Program, Canadian
 Requirements
Litton Applied Technology

645 Alamanor Avenue
Sunnyvale, California
U.S.A. 94088-3478
Tel: (408) 773-7214

Mr. W. J. Finn, Jr.
Manager
Material Offset Programs
Northrop Defense Systems
  Division
600 Hicks Road
Rolling Meadows, Illinois
U.S.A. 60008
Tel: (312) 577-5105

Ms. D. Brown
Associate Contract
  Administrator
Harris Corporation/GSSD
6801 Jericho Turnpike
Syosset, New York
U.S.A. 11791
Tel: (516) 364-0400

● CP-140 and Hercules
  Industrial Benefits

Mr. Enn Norak
DRIE Manager,
CP-140 and Hercules Ind.
  Benefits
Mailing Address:
235 Queen Street (XEEL)
Ottawa, Ontario K1A 0H5
Office Location:
110 O'Connor Street
3rd Floor
Ottawa, Ontario
Tel: (613) 995-5358

Mr. R. S. Stringham
Offset Program Manager –
  Canada
International Trade
  Development
Lockheed-California Company
P.O. Box 551, B/76, A1
Burbank, California
U.S.A. 91520-9654
Tel: (818) 847-4814

Mr. J. W. Moorman
Resident Material Manager
CP-140 Industrial Benefits
Lockheed Aircraft Corpora-
  tion of Canada Ltd.
255 Albert Street, Suite 603
Ottawa, Ontario K1P 6A9
Tel: (613) 238-8141

● Electronic Support and
  Training (EST) Systems Project
  CF-5 Depot

Level Inspection and Repair &
  Avionics Update Project

Mr. M. H. Piersdorff
DRIE Manager, EST Systems &
CF-5 DLIR Projects
235 Queen Street
Ottawa, Ontario K1A 0H5
Tel: (613) 954-3379

Appendix II

Other Possible Subcontracting Sources

Since SSC seems to have silently scuttled its own Canadian Business Subcontracting Opportunity Program, here is my tabulation of some firms who have or may be getting healthy federal contracts and might be looking for subcontractors.

Bendix Avelex Inc.
200 Laurentian Blvd.
St. Laurent, Québec   H4M 2L5
Tel: (514) 744-2811
Telex: 05-826688
Fax: (514) 342-3795

The Boeing Fabrication and Services Company of Canada
Suite 1315
50 O'Connor Street
Ottawa, Ontario K1P 6L2
Tel: (613) 234-1860

Boeing Canada
De Havilland Division
Garratt Blvd.
Downsview, Ontario M3K 1Y5
Tel: (416) 633-7310
Telex: 062-2128

CAE Industries Ltd.
#3060 – P.O. Box 30
Royal Bank Plaza
Toronto, Ontario M5J 2J1
Tel: (416) 865-0070
Telex: 065-23053

Canadair Limited
P.O. Box 6087
Montréal, Québec H3C 3G9
Tel: (514) 744-1511
Telex: 05-826747
Fax: (514) 744-6586

Canadian Arsenals Limited
5 Montée des Arsenaux
Le Gardeur, Québec J5Z 2P4
Tel: (514) 581-3080
Telex: 05-24642

Canadian Astronautics Limited
1050 Morrison Drive
Ottawa, Ontario K2H 8K7
Tel: (613) 820-8280
Telex: 053-3937
Fax: (613) 820-8314

Canadian General Electric Company Ltd.
396 Attwell Drive
Rexdale, Ontario M9W 5C3
Tel: (416) 675-7500
Telex: 06-989302
Fax: (416) 674-4247

Canadian Marconi Company
2442 Trenton Avenue
Montréal, Québec H3P 1Y9
Tel: (514) 341-7630
Telex: 05-827822
Fax: (514) 340-3100

Computing Devices Company
A Division of Control Data Canada Ltd.
P.O. Box 8508
Ottawa, Ontario K1G 3M9
Tel: (613) 596-7000
Telex: 053-4139

Dowty Canada Limited
574 Monarch Avenue
Ajax, Ontario L1S 2G8
Tel: (416) 683-3100, ext. 230
Telex: 06-981295
Fax: (416) 686-3100

E. H. Industries (Canada) Inc.
275 Slater Street, Suite 801
Ottawa, Ontario K1P 5H9
Tel: (613) 563-2180

Garrett Canada
255 Attwell Drive
Rexdale, Ontario M9W 6L7
Tel: (416) 675-1411
Telex: 06-989142
Fax: (416) 675-4021

General Motors of Canada Limited
P.O. Box 5160
London, Ontario N6A 4N5
Tel: (519) 452-5184
Telex: 064-5643

Halifax-Dartmouth Industries Limited
Barrington Street North
P.O. Box 1477
Halifax, Nova Scotia B3K 5H7
Tel: (902) 423-9271
Telex: 019-22672

Hawker Siddeley Canada Inc., Orenda Division
P.O. Box 6001
Toronto AMF, Ontario L5P 1B3
Tel: (416) 677-3250
Telex: 06-968727
Fax: (416) 678-1538

Heroux Inc.
755 Thurber
Longueuil, Québec J4H 3N2
Tel: (514) 679-5450
Telex: 055-60630

Hughes Aircraft Company
P.O. Box 45066, Bldg. C1, A151
Los Angeles, California
U.S.A. 90045-0066
Tel: (213) 568-6922

IMP Aerospace Limited
2651 Dutch Village Road
Suite 400
Halifax, Nova Scotia B3L 4T1
Tel: (902) 453-2400
Telex: 019-31462
Fax: (902) 826-2125

Indal Technologies Inc.
3570 Hawkestone Road
Mississauga, Ontario L5C 2V8
Tel: (416) 275-5300
Telex: 06-961482

Leigh Industries Limited
2680 Queensview Drive
Ottawa, Ontario K2B 8J9
Tel: (613) 820-9720
Telex: 053-4129
Fax: (613) 820-2730

Litton Systems Canada Limited
25 Cityview Drive
Rexdale, Ontario M9W 5A7
Tel: (416) 249-1231
Telex: 06-989406
Fax: (416) 245-0324

Martin Marietta Canada Ltd.
#1500, 50 O'Connor Street
Ottawa, Ontario K1P 6L2
Tel: (613) 232-6430
Telex: 053-3399

MBB Helicopter Canada Ltd.
Box 250
Fort Erie, Ontario L2A 5M9
Tel: (416) 871-7772
Telex: 061-5250
Fax: (416) 871-3320

McDonnell Douglas Canada Ltd.
P.O.Box 6013
6976 Airport Road
Toronto AMF, Ontario L5P 1B7
Tel: (416) 677-4341
Telex: 06-968825
Fax: (416) 677-4341

Microtel Limited
151 Queen Street, Suite 1106
Ottawa, Ontario K1P 6L1
Tel: (613) 238-7365
Telex: 053-3799

Paramax Electronics Inc.
6111 Royalmount Avenue
Montréal, Québec H4P 1K6
Tel: (514) 340-8310
Telex: 05-824142

Pratt & Whitney Canada, Inc.
1000 Marie Victorin Blvd.
P.O. Box 10
Longueuil, Québec J4K 4X9
Tel: (514) 677-9411
Telex: 05-267509
Fax: (514) 647-3620

Raytheon Canada Limited
400 Phillip Street
P.O. Box 1619
Waterloo, Ontario N2J 4K6
Tel: (519) 885-0110
Telex: 069-55431
Fax: (519) 885-8620

Spar Aerospace Limited
Executive Office
#3690, Royal Bank Plaza
South Tower, P.O. Box 83
Toronto, Ontario M5J 2J2
Tel: (416) 865-0480
Telex: 065-24240
Fax: (416) 865-0489 (p.m.)

**Sperry Inc. Aerospace &
Marine Group**
Hwy. 17
P.O. Box 1300
Rockland, Ontario K0A 3AO
Tel: (613) 446-6011
Telex: 053-4806

**Telemus Electronic Systems
Inc.**
310 Moodie Drive
Nepean, Ontario K2H 8G3
Tel: (613) 726-1102
Telex: 053-4981
Fax: (613) 726-1114

Thomson-CSF Systems Canada Inc.
#406, 350 Sparks Street
Ottawa, Ontario K1R 7S8
Tel: (613) 594-8820
Telex: 053-3796
Fax: 236-5212

CHAPTER EIGHT

Getting Help to Sell to the Government – Key Information Sources

Elsewhere in this book you have been given a great many contact points in provincial and federal agencies who are potential markets for your goods and services. You have also been given a number of suggestions on marketing strategy and how best to approach government buyers. Yet some of your most useful allies in selling to or dealing with government can be the government itself, if you know how to use it. That is, at the federal level some government agencies or departments are gold mines of information on what other government departments need or want and how they operate. That's what we'll cover in this chapter.

STUDIES OF GOVERNMENT PROCUREMENT

Surprisingly, there are only a very few privately published studies or descriptions of the Canadian federal procurement system. Among the most useful are the following:

Government Procurement: Spending Smarter. *A study team report to the task force on program review. Eric Shelton. Task Force on Program Review, 1985* (also available in French as *Mieux Depenser*).

Doing Business with Government: Procurement Policy and Practices. Osler, Hoskin and Harcourt, 1987.

Government/Industry Procurement Information Exchange Process. Goss, Gilroy and Associates. Department of Regional Industrial Expansion, 1987.

Feasibility Study on Government-Wide Sourcing System. Loecus Consulting Group Inc., 1983.

Implementation Plan for the National Technology Marketing Network. Nordicity Group Ltd., Ministry of State for Science and Technology, March 1987.

Report on the Pilot Study of Potential Source Development and Industrial Expansion Opportunities in Federal Procurement. Electrical and Electronic Manufacturers Association of Canada. Departments of Supply and Services Canada/Regional Industrial Expansion / Transport Canada, April 1987.

Incentives in Government Contracting. R. Preston McAffe and John McMillan. University of Toronto Press, 1987.

Federal Government Procurement. Canadian Manufacturers, Association. CMA Reference Paper, No. 39.

How to Sell to Governments in Canada 1984. Debra E. Douglas. Corpus Information Services, 1984.

Canadian Government Purchasing Policies: An Introductory Bibliography. Eric Swanick. Public Administration Series, Vance Bibliographies, 1980.

Selling to Public Authorities in Canada. British Overseas Trade Board, 1979.

The Government as Publisher

Probably the most effective way to learn about government procurement is to read the publications that the various government bodies themselves issue. At the most general level, official reports of the Canadian federal Parliament and provincial legislatures, including debates, journals, statutes, and gazettes, contain references to matters of large-scale procurement or regional development. Unfortunately, many of these works are dull, verbose, and very often hard to obtain.

One exception to this has been the Special Committee of the Senate on National Defence, which has served as a long-term critic and watchdog over defence activities in Canada. Frequently, it has unearthed DND wish-lists for equipment, and weaknesses in the CAF long before most MPs or the media learned of them. Their study on Maritime Command, for example, did a lot to raise the profile of the navy and Canada's need for modern ships.

You also could monitor administrative reports and especially annual reports to Parliament which summarize each department's or agency's activities, its achievements for the fiscal year, and make recommendations for the future. These are yours free from the department or agency concerned.

Another good source of material on what the government is buying is the annual report from the federal Auditor General's Office (AGO). This office reports to Parliament on many administrative matters including procurements. While much of the AGO's work is "after the fact", the Office has zeroed in on departmental cost overruns, questionable accounting and failure to buy spare parts. Each province, too, has an Auditor General reporting to its legislature on its government's spending.

An even more specific source of intelligence is statistical reports which frequently assemble, compare, and analyze data collected by various departments. As you get to know public servants, you also begin to learn of "inside" policy studies or evaluations. These can be invaluable in helping target your proposals or in identifying market opportunities. While some are confidential, probably in ninety-five per cent of the cases you could get an official copy from someone in the system.

The procedure is straightforward. Find out who issued the paper, contact him or her, and ask for a copy. Some departments seem better than others in their openness. If this doesn't work, try another department with an interest in the same field. For example, if you find SSC reluctant to give you a list of federal projects, try DND, DRIE (DIST), TC, or even Treasury Board.

If you're still stymied, you can file a formal request under the Access to Information Act. For information on it call 1-800-267-0441, or buy a copy of *Using the Access to Information Act* by lawyers Heather Mitchell and Murray Rankin, available from International Self-Counsel Press.

Some government departments actually publish regular periodicals of use to business. We'll focus on SSC's *R & D Bulletin* in the next section, however, another good freebie is DRIE's *Canada Commerce*, which sometimes contains primary data or official statements of government policies, programs, and market opportunities. Write to:

> Canada Commerce
> Department of Regional Industrial Expansion
> 235 Queen Street
> Ottawa, Ontario K1A 0H5

External Affairs also distributes a free weekly newsletter called *Info Export* which covers many export opportunities to foreign countries. Call 1-800-267-8376.

Special reports done by outside consultants, royal commissions, or task forces can be invaluable. These often carry out extensive research and survey activities and produce a group of experts outside the federal bureaucracy itself who know what government does or buys.

You also need to examine all the publications coming from your target department, and those which deal with categories of products you sell, such as aircraft, ships, or consulting services. You can look these up through various sources in your local library. If the library doesn't have one, you can ask it to borrow a copy from another library on an inter-library loan. Don't forget about university libraries and other special reference facilities.

A data-base search through the NRC's CAN-OLE system can unearth a lot of information for you in a hurry, at a very low cost. Just contact the Canadian Institute for Scientific and Technical Information (CISTI) at NRC. It covers provincial, U.S., and some foreign sources as well.

The nice thing about these government publications is that many of them are free. Even those that do have a cover price can often be obtained free of charge. Whenever SSC (in its role as Queen's Printer) prints up a booklet for someone in the government, the client agency which pays the bill gets a large number of free copies. These go to the media, top bureaucrats, or inquiring citizens like you.

The Ottawa media know this. So when they want a key departmental publication with a price tag, they go to the agency that paid for it first. Usually, the authors or the public affairs people give them a free copy. So you may want to try this stratagem too.

There are a couple of other reference tools you can use. Bibliographies and catalogues also can provide you with information about the government's own publications. SSC's Publishing Centre issues a free booklet, *Where and How to Obtain Canadian Government Publications*, listing depository libraries and authorized bookstore agents. It also issues a weekly and other checklists of Canadian Government publications. The Publishing Centre also indexes selected titles, and subjects.

Canadiana is Canada's national bibliography, issued monthly. It is cumulated annually by the National Library of Canada. *Microlog Index*, published monthly by Micromedia Limited, could be useful too. They list federal, provincial and municipal publications.

Into the Inner Sanctum – The Key Publications

As you may have noticed, SSC produces a lot of books and reports, some for itself, but most as the official publishing arm of the government, i.e. to meet the needs of all the other departments. Unfortunately, you cannot one-stop shop for SSC publications in Ottawa or your local SSC office or a government bookstore. For some unfathomable reason, regional and local SSC offices apparently receive only single copies from headquarters of key publications for suppliers. This also means you likely will have to write to Ottawa to get a copy of the *Suppliers Guide*, although this is the backbone of the entire SSC communication effort for suppliers.

SSC also throws up another barrier to any ordinary mortal getting a copy of some departmental publication: sometimes the department does not identify which branch or directorate authored or stocked it. In theory, though, you should be able to write or call the Public Affairs Directorate for any of SSC's publications. Try it first anyway. Write to:

> Public Affairs Directorate
> Supply and Services Canada
> Ottawa, Ontario K1A 0S5

Here is a look at some of SSC publications that may be useful to you, starting with those produced by Public Affairs.

- Indexes
  Most of the publications mentioned so far tell you what the government is planning on buying, building, or spending, though you may have to search a bit, like a detective going from one clue to the next, before you find exactly what it is you want to know. However, you should know about several narrowly specialized SSC-released publications that can help direct you to the federal public servant or program appropriate for what you have to offer.

  The federal *Access Register*, prepared annually by the Treasury Board and published by the Minister of Supply and Services, tells you about the government's filing system and what it is prepared to let you see and describes some programs.

  Index to Federal Programs and Services, published annually by the Minister of Supply and Services, also outlines federal programs and services.

- SSC *Annual Report*
  Read the SSC *Annual Report* either for the current year or past years. It contains a lot of useful information on major contractors, projects in progress, and the organization of the department. You do not have to pay for it, although I've noticed some SSC employees seem anxious to have you buy one at a government-licensed bookstore, who in turn, I assume, pay SSC. Presumably they are simply misinformed.

- *The Supplier* newsletter
  Until recently called *Update*, *The Supplier* is supposed to be a monthly report on SSC activities to suppliers already on SSC source lists. While SSC appears to be a bit uncertain

about the role of this periodical, or the frequency of its publication, copies I've seen have carried useful information on departmental happenings, including RFPs (Requests for Proposals), studies, policies, and administrative changes.

Unfortunately, however, companies who might want to become source-listed and would like to get it frequently complain SSC does not seem to have any way to add them to the circulation list. Write to the department or your local MP to be added, before it occurs to the federal paper engineers to cut it out entirely.

- Leaflets
  Other material from the Public Affairs Directorate that you should ask for include a series of leaflets called *You asked us about*. ... These look at tendering, marketing to SSC, selecting potential suppliers, late and delayed bids, complaints, thirty-day payment policy, GATT, unsolicited proposals, standing offers, and contracts settlement.

- Booklets
  You also may want to request booklets describing each of the product directorates. Publications produced by other directorates which are available through Public Affairs include *Suppliers Guide* and *List of Departmental Materiel Managers*, from the Statistical Information and Data Management Branch. The latter is a list of department purchasing agents. Unfortunately, this list is dated—1987—and essentially covers only the Ottawa-Hull area.

  If you can't get either of these key documents write to: O. Simard, Supervisor, Supplier Registration Services, Supply and Services Canada, 11 Laurier Avenue, Hull, Québec, K1A 0S5, or call (819) 956-3444.

  I asked several individuals in Public Affairs for the next publication, by title. They came up with zip. A quick call to Aerospace, Marine and Electronics Systems (AMES) Directorate brought forth a copy, though. It was worth the bother. It's called *Doing Business with the Aerospace, Marine and Electronics Systems Directorate*. This is a very useful description of what AMES staff buy, and who does the buying. As a bonus, it includes organization charts for the department and for AMES, something that the Public Affairs material does not cover.

Science and Professional Services Directorate produces guides on unsolicited proposals, and public awareness of science and technology.

The Research and Analysis Branch produces a number of useful studies. These include: SSC's *Annual Procurement Plan and Strategy* (APPS), a catalogue of government-wide purchasing opportunities for years ahead; *Contracting Statistics*, an annual publication that looks at SSC buys in Canada and in each province; procurement opportunities for electronics and electrical manufacturers; and a study of the *Canadian Public Sector Market*, 1983. This material can be useful to you in identifying major buying agencies and opportunities for subcontracting. Write to: Sami Sourani, Chief Economic and Statistical Analysis, Research and Analysis Branch, Supply and Services Canada, Ottawa, Ontario K1A 0S5 (telephone: (819) 956-0808).

OASIS Requirements Forecast, is like APPS but centred on data processing and computers. The Security Branch produces *Questions and Answers About Government Industrial Security*.

- *The Research and Development Bulletin*
Produced by a freelancer for the Science and Professional Services Directorate, the *R & D Bulletin* is a handy free supplier tool. It carries current information on science and technology requirements to be contracted out, winning bidders, contracts awarded, contact names, case histories, contracting statistics, recent policy changes, and provides information on unsolicited proposals.

To be added to the mailing list, contact:

The Editor
Research and Development Bulletin
Science and Professional Services Directorate
Supply and Services Canada
Ottawa, Ontario K1A 0S5

- *The Federal Telephone Directory*
  But for some publications you've gotta pay! Number One on your list of SSC paid publications should be the *Government of Canada Telephone Directory* available through the Canadian Government Publishing Centre, Supply and Services Canada, Ottawa, Ontario K1A 0S9 (telephone: (819) 997-2560). The directory costs $13.95 per issue or $31.20 for two, and you can order it using this number—CO 35-1-1987-2—for the December 1987 issue. It appears twice a year. There also are regional editions once a year.

  A private-sector version with fewer federal names and some provincial ones included comes from Southam Communications Limited, Toronto. It's called *The Corpus Administrative Index*, is updated four times a year, and costs a couple of hundred dollars. Most large libraries carry it. Or write:

  > Corpus Administrative Index
  > 1450 Don Mills Road
  > Don Mills, Ontario, M3B 2X7

- *Supply Policy Manual*
  For an initial cost of $250 in Canada or $300 outside Canada, (and $100/$120 annually for updates), you can read the twelve volumes of the *Supply Policy Manual,* which sets out contracting procedures. It isn't light reading, but if you are serious about the SSC, this is the rule book. Local and regional offices of SSC should have a reference copy. Write to:

  > Canadian Government Publishing Centre
  > Ottawa, Ontario, K1A 0S9

- *Optimum*
  Optimum is a journal published by the Bureau of Management Consulting (BMC), Ottawa's in-house management-consulting operations. It may not interest you if you're not a management consultant, but if you are, it's a good read.

- *Bulletin of Business Opportunities*
The BBO is supposed to be Canada's version of the *Commerce Business Daily*. It isn't. It used to be free, but now every week, for $153 a year, BBO will tell you about contracts awarded the previous week across the country, and to whom, give some supplier profiles and some subcontracting opportunities, mention new government publications, and news items for the business sector, and provide information on some contracts to be let. BBO generally lists awards of contracts rather than calls for bidders for new ones.

An Updated Report on Government/Industry Procurement Information Exchange Process by Goss Gilroy Associates (GGA), February 1987, commissioned by DRIE and involving a survey of suppliers was critical of BBO. So are many suppliers.

GGA bluntly concluded that BBO "is somewhat of a problem for SSC. First, it is realized that BBO is not satisfactory to assist businessmen to identify future opportunities. BBO also covers only SSC contract opportunities, thereby leaving many departments such as CIDA, TC, EAC, PWC and CCC without a formal bulletin to announce either past or future opportunities. . . . The problems with the BBO have also been complicated by a reduction in circulation from 6,000 to 1,500 with the advent of a $153 annual charge. This is well below the 26,000 circulation required for financial break-even."

The prospect of free trade has put BBO under ever greater pressure than GGA found when it wrote that BBO "appears to be in need of a major overhaul". SSC would seem to have three options for BBO: abolish it entirely; upgrade it into an early-warning system for all federal procurement, like the U.S. government *Commerce Business Daily*, possibly using an on-line computer system or privatization.

To enrol, contact:

The Editor,
Bulletin of Business Opportunities
Supply and Services Canada

Place du Portage Phase III
11 Laurier Street
Hull, Québec K1A 0S5
Telephone: (819) 994-0690

SSC Supplier Seminars – "SSC Tells All"

The Goss Gilroy and Associates study also looked at SSC's other major information tools: its general "How to Do Business with SSC" or Supplier Awareness Briefings and its sectoral Procurement Outlook Conferences (POC). In their initial year, 1985-86, SSC ran 70 awareness seminars and 14 POCs. By 1988, SSC had cut the number of seminars in half. As a rule, the awareness seminars tend to be run through SSC Regional Operations, and the POCs through product directorates.

Thus, the POCs are sector-based, centering around sectors such as R & D, office automation, armaments and vehicles, or electronics. "The average attendance at POCs has been 200 to 400 people," reports GGA. Frequently a level of sophistication is assumed at POC seminars that could intimidate the person who simply wants to know how to get on the list.

Awareness seminars are community- rather than sector-based. For example, in Calgary they might be run by the Chamber of Commerce; in Toronto, by the Board of Trade.

Called and co-ordinated by SSC, GGA reports POCs "comprise material and content put together by individual line departments. The quality of POCs have therefore been variable, depending on the particular line department involved.... POCs have not provided sufficiently detailed information to industry." It found "conference participants have generally requested more published information on upcoming requirements. . . priorization of major acquisitions according to the level of expectation for funding approval, and an overview of industrial and regional policy."

"One directorate within SSC that has taken an aggressive approach to providing information to industry is the Office Automation, Services and Information Systems Directorate

(OASIS)." They have produced two-year requirement forecasts, productivity-enhancement seminars, and trade shows. I also have attended some useful seminars organized by SPSD and AMES.

While other departments frequently participate at these seminars or conferences, most of the communication comes downward from SSC, with the event choreographed around SSC's structure.

Some seminars do a poor job of tying federal procurement together across the government, of presenting the "big picture". The instructors who generally are senior officials, not professional communicators, tend to emphasize what their directorate is buying, rather than give the businessperson concrete assistance in approaching government. And much of the patter is laced with specialized bureaucratic buzzwords that could leave the beginner lost.

Two major POC and seminar contributors have been TC and DND. Goss, Gilroy Associates also commented on how these departments informed suppliers. "The Air Administration is probably the most advanced of all federal government line departments with respect to the provision of information to industry. Anticipated major programs to upgrade the Canadian airspace navigation, communications and traffic control systems are described in a document known as the Canadian Airspace System Plan (CASP), an overview of systems development to the year 2000 likely worth a total of at least $1 billion". CASP involves briefing 2,000 firms.

This involves, first, making a list of potential prime contractors. The potential primes are asked to provide a preliminary letter of interest. "This is used to solicit interest and to provide some advance notification about two years ahead of the actual procurement."

About a year prior to the tender, the CASP office intends to issue a price and availability (P & A) request. Finally, about three months prior to the contract, a final RFP will be issued to companies that respond to the first two stages. TC wants to update CASP every two years. "TC has made a good effort to produce longer-term plans, however, dissemination of short-term information—especially to subcontractors—appears to be weak," concluded the researchers.

With regard to DND, GGA found efforts to provide advance notification to industry "are severely handicapped by the fact that formal documented plans are not available from DND." There is a "general lack of formal long-term procurement plans to assist strategic planning or long-term pre-positioning. . . lack of integration of R & D programming with the major capital procurement process. . . unwillingness on the part of DND to release formal information on long-term procurements because of possible policy changes or changed internal priorities. . . . A number of highly regarded Canadian firms suggested that they have an easier time selling into the U.S. than to the Canadian government.

"In general, respondents stated that information at the RFP stage of the procurement process is not a serious problem," said GGA, presumably because respondents already were on the lists. All of this study may pay off. The federal, provincial, and territorial procurement ministers have proposed a book called *Practical Guide for Government Procurement in Canada* in their November 1987 *Report on Public Sector Procurement Initiatives*. I will bless the day it appears.

And a Little Help From the Private Sector – Useful Business Publications

If all of that information isn't enough, you can find similar resources coming off the presses of private firms, which will be especially useful for businesses seeking subcontracts. Start by choosing a few companies and developing files on them. Their PR departments will give you plenty of material. So will the industry associations, a number of which are listed at the end of this chapter. A really useful starting place is a book called *Sources of Information for Canadian Business* by Brian Land, now in its fourth edition, published by the Canadian Chamber of Commerce.

Make sure you keep up-to-date with the Canadian business or trade publications in your sphere of activity. Business magazines in particular provide a lot of information on government buys, and on subcontracting opportunities. Often they will be mailed for free to any firm wanting them.

There are several major publishers of business publications in Canada. The largest of these is Maclean Hunter Business Publications. For information, contact:

Charles E. Wilson
Vice-President, Business Publications Division
Maclean Hunter Limited
777 Bay Street
Toronto, Ontario M5W 1A7

Other major publishers include:

Sanford Evans Publishing Ltd.
1077 St. James Street
P.O. Box 6900
Winnipeg, Manitoba R3C 3B1

Southam Business Publications Ltd.
1450 Don Mills Road
Don Mills, Ontario M3B 2X7

Wadham Publications Ltd.
109 Vanderhoof Avenue, Suite 101
Toronto, Ontario M4G 2J2

You can get an exhaustive list of all Canadian media, including the business magazines, by sector, from the monthly publication

Canadian Advertising Rates & Data (CARD)
Maclean Hunter Limited
777 Bay Street
Toronto, Ontario M5W 1A7
Tel. (416) 596-5000

Private-industry sources your library likely will have include *Canadian Government Programs and Services* from CCH Canadian Ltd., Corpus Information Services' *Corpus Ad-*

ministrative Index, and *Canadian Almanac & Directory,* an annual from Copp Clark Pitman.

Corpus, a division of Southam Communication Limited, also publishes a weekly newsletter from Ottawa called *The Public Sector* and Informetric Co. Limited publishes *Ottawa Weekly Update.* Some consulting firms issue them too. For example, I've found the free Touche Ross *Ottawa Quarterly* useful in the past. There also are newsletters operating in various provincial capitals.

Ottawa's Senior Executives Guide, published by Communications Nova Plus, Ottawa, provides biographical sketches of some 500 of Canada's senior public servants. Also, you might like to examine a copy of Informetric's *Canadian Capital Projects,* which surveys major public and private projects.

If you have an export interest, you might like to look at *The Canadian Exporters Handbook 1987-88,* available from Samara Publications in Renfrew, Ontario; or *Export Canada* which comes out of Surrey, B.C., annually from Continental Export Promotions.

I want to say a special word about national business and trade directories. To sell your goods or services you have to know who your friends and enemies are: something the military call "intelligence gathering". Government publications and books like this one can give you some valuable intelligence to help you sell to the federal bureaucracy. However, with the government increasingly pushing joint ventures, and tending to award a few, very large contracts, you need to stay on top of what these important customers are doing.

This means you need to know who else is operating in your sector of business. They might be your competitors today, but your allies or partners tomorrow. Industry directories are invaluable to you in this study. Often they are put out by government or industry associations, although many are commercial operations.

Name an industry, and you can find an association of firms or individuals in it and a directory. Using your local library and as many industry associations as you can tap into, locate directories and the names of others who supply the same or related products. Develop alliances, where possible, to go after large, often uncompetitive, government jobs or merely to compare notes on who the good and the bad guys in government are.

In the aerospace industry, I easily found a half-dozen good industry directories including a couple of free ones. These were:

> Canadian Advanced Technology Association, *The CATAlog*,
>
> Maclean Hunter Business Publications, *Canada's Aerospace Industry: A Capability Guide*, or *Aerospace and Defence Technology* magazine,
>
> External Affairs Canada, *Canadian Defence Products Guide*,
>
> The United States Air Force, *Guide to Canadian Aerospace Related Industries*,
>
> The Ontario Ministry of Industry, Trade and Technology, *Ontario/Canada Aerospace and Defence Directory*,
>
> Alberta Economic Development and Trade, *Alberta Aerospace*.

Start to develop your own lists of allies, friends, and enemies in government and in industry. To be forewarned is to be forearmed.

Provincial Government Publications

Many provinces issue publications which describe their own procurement systems and how to access them. Examples include:

> *Directory of Public Buying Agencies in B.C., 1981*, B.C. Ministry of Industry and Small Business Development, 1981,
>
> *Purchasing Guide: Ontario's Public Sector Market Purchasing Directory*, Ontario Ministry of Industry and Trade,
>
> *Selling to the Government of Alberta*, Alberta Public Works, Supply and Services, 1984,

Doing Business with the Alberta Public Sector, Alberta
Economic Development and Trade, 1987, which is an
update of: *Alberta on Line: Purchasing Directory,*
1984/85, Alberta Economic Development, 1985,
Rapport Pomaninville: Rosalie et les fournisseurs,
Québec, 1986,

*Guide du fournisseur: Service des achats du gouverne-
ment,* Québec, 1983.

Like Ottawa, provincial governments also issue their own
departmental telephone directories.

The provinces also will provide you with details of their operations and agencies. For example, you could consult:

Organization of the Government of Alberta and *Inventory of Agencies, Boards and Commissions*, available
from Alberta Government Publication Services,

A Guide to the Nova Scotia Government, published by
the Department of Government Services,

KWIC Index to Your Ontario Government Services,
published annually by the Ministry of Government
Services, describes all provincial programs,

Répertoire de l'administration québecoise, published by
Ministère des Communications.

At present, most provinces, departments or agencies, issue
regular checklists of their government publications.

As well, many foreign governments and international organizations have their own listings of publications. You should
be aware of the other English-language government publications. *HMSO Books Catalogue* lists U.K. ones; *ILO Catalogue of
Publications* comes from the International Labor Organization;
UNDOC is a UN publication; and Current Index, *OECD Catalog
of Publications,* refers to the Organization for Economic
Cooperation and Development.

Selling to Uncle Sam

My favourite store for government-procurement publications is a mail-order establishment in Washington, D.C., run by the U.S. government. For some reason many Canadian suppliers find U.S. government information on procurements and the procurement process much clearer, better or more professionally written, and more readily available than much of the Canadian government procurement information. Furthermore, while there is a lot of U.S. material directed at small suppliers, there is almost nothing from that angle available in Canada.

For example, while suppliers to the Canadian government largely are expected to become well informed on purchasing by reading the SSC's *Suppliers Guide* (which reads like a bad research paper by a postgraduate university student) suppliers wanting to sell to the U.S. government will find that almost every U.S. agency publishes a handbook or booklet to show suppliers how to sell to it. Whether you want to sell to Uncle Sam or not, such U.S. material can improve your own selling and proposal writing capabilities enormously, and give you leads in the U.S. and Canada.

Interestingly, you can get some of the best of this U.S. stuff free from one Canadian government agency: not Supply and Services, but External Affairs Canada. As a rule, External will provide you with copies of the U.S. Defense Department's *Small Business Subcontracting Directory* and *Selling to the Military*. Or you can get a *Guide to Canadian Aerospace Related Industries* from USAF Systems, Command Liaison Office, Ottawa, Ontario   K1P 5M9. It's free, too. You also may want *Market Research Plan for Industry*.

External itself also produces a lot of good material for suppliers, which is useful for both domestic and foreign marketing. Among them are *Electronic Products for World Markets, Computer and Software Products for World Markets, Canadian Defence Products Guide,* and *Communications Products for World Markets.*

As a rule, you can get most U.S. Government publications from the Superintendent of Documents, United States Government Printing Office (USGPO), Washington, D.C. 20402 (telephone: (202) 783-3238). They welcome VISA or Master-Card.

To get an early warning of coming U.S. procurements, you might like to get the *Commerce Business Daily.* This comes out every day in print, from Monday to Friday. You also can access it on-line. To order, call (202) 783-3238 or write the USGPO.

Serious suppliers to the U.S. government should be familiar with "FARs". These are *Federal Acquisition Regulations,* Uncle Sam's version of *Government Contract Regulations.* Among the most important of these are *Air Force Federal Acquisition Regulation Supplement, DOD FAR Supplement, Acquisition Regulations Digest and Cross Indexes,* 1983, and *NASA FAR Supplement,* April 1984.

Alternatively, you could ask the Canadian Commercial Corporation or DCASMA in Ottawa to send you copies of the appropriate sections of the pertinent regulations. Frequently they will do this without charge.

U.S. government publications with more of a how-to slant include *Doing Business with the Federal Government,* a general explanation of government procurement programs in U.S. executive branch agencies. Topics discussed range over principles and procedures of government procurement; government procurement programs; government sales of surplus property; and the specifications, standards, and commercial item descriptions. Procurement programs of the Department of Defense, each of the Armed Forces Services, the General Services Administration, and 20 other civilian agencies are described in detail. It also includes a business-services directory.

Other similar publications you can order from the US GPO or the agency concerned include:

Contracting with the U.S. Department of Transportation,

Guide to Doing Business With the Department of State, 1987,

Guide to Specifications, Standards and Commercial Item Descriptions of the Federal Government, February 1984, General Services Administration 1984,

Guide to the Preparation of Offers for Selling to the Military, a 1985 DOD publication,

Guidelines for Preparation of Unsolicited Proposals, National Science Foundation,

How to Buy Surplus Personal Property from the United States Department of Defense, January 1986,

How to Do Business with HEW, the Department of Health, Education and Welfare,

How to Do Business with the Government Printing Office,

How to Sell to the United States Department of Commerce, 1984,

NIH Guide for Grants and Contracts, from the National Institute for Health,

Proposal Preparation Manual, Department of Transportation,

Selling to NASA, 1986,

Selling to the USAF,

Small Business Guide to Federal R & D, for the National Science Foundation.

Other useful titles, most of which are self-explanatory, include:

Armed Services Pricing Manual, Volume 1, 1986,

Background Notes, Canada, 1985, State Dept., 1987,

Companies Participating in the Department of Defense Subcontracting Program (quarterly),

GSA Subcontracting Directory, issued by the General Services Administration,

Library of Congress Publications in Print,

Marketing in Canada, 1985,

Militarily Critical Technologies List, 1984,

Prime Contract Awards (semi-annual),

Prime Contract Awards by State (semi-annual),

United States Government Manual,

United States Government Periodicals Index,

United States Government Purchasing and Sales Directory, 1984,

United States Government's Preferred Products List (quarterly),

United States Government Monthly Catalog, Washington: GPO Monthly with annual cumulations,

U.S. Government Procurement Offices (GSA)

Private-sector publications about the U.S. Government market include:

Sources of Information for Selling to the Federal Government, Washington Researchers, 1977,

Consulting to Government, Ottawa: Infoscan, 1979,

Congressional Information Service Index, Baltimore: C.I.S. (monthly with annual cumulations and periodic multi-year cumulations),

The $100 Billion Market, Herman Holtz, AMACOM, 1980.

Appendix I

Contacts in Federal Business Development Bank (FBDB)

FBDB has offices in many communities across Canada. It also has a toll-free number listed in the blue pages of your local telephone directory. Or you may call (613) 995-0234 in Ottawa, collect.

Guy Lavigueur
President
(514) 283-3124

Michel Azam
Vice-President of Government
 Relations
(613) 995-5225

Rupert Williams
Vice-President, Principal
 Services,
Management Committee
(514) 283-4118

René Leduc
Vice-President adjoint
 Service de gestion-conseil
(514) 283-3165

Kenneth Cavanagh
Director, Communications,
 Public Affairs
(514) 283-7515

Pat Hayes
Assistant Vice-President,
 Designated Groups
(514) 283-5904

Joe Miller,
 Vice-President &
 Regional General Manager,
 Ontario
(416) 973-0012

CHAPTER NINE

The Beginning and the End – A Smart Marketing Strategy

By now you know that selling to the government is not merely a matter of getting on someone's source-list or filling out a form or two. The bureaucratic structure is labyrinthine, the people often close-mouthed, the language jargon-filled. But if you didn't go to high school with the Governor General, or play pick-up hockey with the PM's brother, and you can't afford to keep an Ottawa staff, what *can* you do to get your share of federal purchasing dollars?

On your behalf I asked a blue-ribbon panel of experts for some guidelines on how you can develop an effective marketing strategy for selling to Ottawa, without having a full-time specialist or consultant in Ottawa to babysit the officials and politicians.

The Experts Talk

Develop Patience

Before starting your campaign, they all advise, psyche yourself up: be mentally prepared for the political and bureaucratic way of doing things. Like all large-scale bureaucracies, Ottawa relies heavily on paper and written documentation. The bureaucracy's size and its elaborate systems of committees set up to clear or vet proposals prevents speedy answers from Ottawa, says Colin Potts, a management consultant with the Ottawa office of

Deloitte, Haskins and Sells. So be prepared to wait. "You need perseverance and patience," says Potts.

Leonard L. Knott, a Toronto-based public-relations consultant, adds that "you have to remember that governmental decisions in the last analysis are political ones, and the best political compromise for the bureaucrats and the politicians usually prevails." But compromises can take a long, long time to work out, with each side giving an inch at a time.

So, as Attorney Allan O'Brien of Gowling and Henderson, one of Canada's major legal firms specializing in government relations, cautions: "Do not expect miracles. There is no one agency or official who will solve your problem."

Develop Familiarity

"You really need to know who are all the players," counsels O'-Brien, and which particular bureaucratic networks or interests they play for. And you need to know with whom they are playing. This book gives you a good start on your competition and a fair chance at the federal purse.

Sometimes, paradoxically, the fuzzy lines separating different federal policies and organizations can be really useful to you, suggests David Eisenstadt, president of the Toronto-based consulting firm, The Communications Group. Quite often you can find ambitious civil servants or politicians who want to share (or show off) their expertise, he says. They also want to tap *your* expertise, information, and community base. The sad fact is that the civil service has relatively few individuals on staff who have ever met a company payroll or know much about small business.

Andrew Kniewasser, a former top public servant in Ottawa and now president of the Investment Dealers' Association of Canada, puts it this way: "When I was in government, what I needed most was accurate information, and good constructive advice directed at the national interest rather than advice that was self-serving. I especially welcomed innovative and practical-thoughts on how to achieve goals at lower costs, with less direct government intervention." In other words, look for people who need your knowledge, to do some modern-day bartering.

You should try to build contacts with public servants, rather than politicians, all the experts advise, although they concede that having the politicians on your side can be profitable, too. This should not really be that difficult since, as O'Brien puts it: "Public servants are just like you or me. They're not out to get you. And they're often very, very bright individuals." You can usually assume that they want to do a good job. If you can show that you can help them in their performance, they'll talk to you.

Says Knott, "Of course, it is important to realize where an individual fits into the bureaucratic hierarchy. If possible, see him or her outside his office, maybe socially, and preferably outside the capital." This can mean on your turf, or somewhere neutral such as at a speaking engagement, conference, or seminar.

Certainly, it would be advantageous to know Brian or Mila, or maybe some deputy minister, assistant deputy minister or director-general from an important department or Crown corporation. However, since the federal government balances or trades off decisions or policies between its agencies to a sort of lowest common denominator, remember the heads of comparatively small agencies like the National Energy Board or Medical Research Council also are very much part of the Ottawa establishment. If individuals in smaller agencies like these know your work, they can be informed and friendly starting points for your efforts in approaching the biggies. Any degree of familiarity is better than a cold call.

Tactics

Bill Lee, a former aide to ex-Prime Minister Pierre Trudeau and now president of Ottawa-based Executive Consultants Ltd., observes that the type of government relations or marketing strategy you embark on depends on your own personal or business concerns.

"First, you need to make an inventory of your own personal resources and contacts, and those persons you can call upon", including those in Ottawa, in local federal offices, in provincial capitals, or elsewhere, and their families and friends. In other words, take stock of your current "assets" in this area.

Next, develop a "target" list of agencies or departments, and individuals in them. Select likely targets after gauging the political importance and size of the various empires. Divide these individuals or agencies up with your friends, colleagues, or subordinates for further research. Start with individuals you know and ask for referrals.

From this starting point, you should develop your government relations or marketing objectives. Evaluate alternative strategies in light of your time and resource limitations, and short-term and long-term plans. Set goals that are specific, measurable, and realistic. Then begin the task of developing specific strategies. Will you phone, write, or visit Ottawa personally? Will you concentrate on selling just a couple of your products at first or sell the whole range? Put your strategy in writing so you have something concrete to check back on in six months or a year.

Monitor government trends and media reports on relevant matters so that you can revise your strategy and react quickly to new opportunities. Co-ordinate your overall public relations and marketing plans with your advertising aimed specifically at government buyers. Share information and contacts and dovetail your efforts with other pertinent umbrella organizations like your industry association, or key experts and government insiders.

Give particular attention, Lee urges, to assessing and upgrading your own staff and those of your allies in government relations and marketing tactics. Is it worth hiring someone, full- or part-time, with previous Ottawa experience; or sponsoring employees to special seminars? Make sure that your front-line people are clued in to useful items such as statistical reports, new buzzwords in government, and departmental re-organizations. (As you will discover, shuffling people around in the government's version of musical chairs is the one thing it can be relied upon to do regularly!)

You may decide to get involved in politics financially or through volunteer work. Personal contributions to a political party in Canada, up to certain limits, may earn credits against income tax owed, or be regarded as normal marketing or promotional expenses.

As in any communications strategy, once you have decided to field some sort of political or communications effort, you should aim it well. Make sure that it is carefully thought-out, written and delivered using appropriate wording, data and examples for the officials or politicians you are trying to cultivate. "Make really sure you are talking to the right individuals, at the right time", stresses Eisenstadt.

Try always to be positive. Writing to an official's superior to praise something the subordinate has done well is likely to please the individual's boss. It also can come to the attention of the person mentioned and create a positive atmosphere. Even when the person is incompetent or absolutely wrong, blasting him likely will hurt you a lot more than it will him as I have learned the hard way.

There is an old journalism expression that applies at all times in government marketing : "KISS—Keep It Simple, Stupid." That's especially good advice the higher up the organizational structure you are trying to reach. "Avoid excessive length or technical detail in initial presentations," advises Dr. Melvin Pasternak, who teaches business communications at Calgary's Mount Royal College. Keep any technical explanations clear and brief. Make sure that any document going to a senior public servant or a minister is "two or three pages in length, or preferably shorter".

You may, of course, need to submit long detailed technical proposals, but make sure you have a capsulized version for the higher-ups. Technical proposals usually are decided well below that level, but the bosses need executive summaries because they will make the big decisions, advises George Linder, Calgary-based partner in charge of Alberta consulting for Deloitte, Haskins and Sells.

Press the Right Buttons

When pleading your case with government, "always use hard, defensible facts and analyses to win your point" or sell your product or service, advises Bill Lee. "Never say you will lose money or have to leave the country or province if you lose the contract. Instead, provide acceptable alternatives," and couch your appeal in terms of current popular governmental issues, like jobs created, R & D initiatives established, technology enhancement, Canadian content, or maybe even affirmative action or employment equity, bilingualism, national unity or multiculturalism, or whatever causes the system is endorsing these days.

A welding company owned by Native Canadians that produces on time and on budget, and "on spec" may not get a defence contract first time out, but it sure will show its flag in Ottawa. Next time, it may get the DND work, or inspire Indian and Northern Affairs or DRIE to use its services or steer outside business to it.

Since the federal bureaucracy provides "decisions by exception", you always should try to plug into or target the department as far down the structure as you can. This also allows ample room for appealing a matter to the senior levels, and for gaining supporters inside the federal system who may carry your cause upward. If you do this right, you may find yourself allied with your bureaucratic contact in going "upstairs" for more money or access to a greater chunk of the agency's work.

Keith Glegg, now vice-president of the National Research Council in Ottawa and formerly with Canadian Marconi Company, puts it this way: "You need some early contact with a middle-level civil servant to plant the seminal idea. As the buy gets bigger, more and more of what will be bought will originate with you. Many requirements are traceable to someone from a supplier who went into the agency to sell it a product" or point out a need that they could fill. "That's what we did with Doppler navigation systems at Marconi. DND didn't want it at all, but we sold it to the U.S. military, and soon they began to think they needed it here, and we had lots of Canadian sales."

Pressing the *Wrong* Buttons . . .

Like you, I've sometimes been really ticked off at some stupid government action, or inaction, or at some super-twit bureaucrat.

If you want to, you can complain, or take it to the press. But our experts don't advise it. In practice, argues Carleton University public administration professor Sharon Sutherland, when you appeal a decision or complain to politicians or mandarins, invariably these individuals go back to the same person you have been dealing with or complaining about for *their* answer.

It's sort of like a game of marbles. They've got all the marbles. So if you want to play, you play by their rules or you don't play at all!

This also applies to those who use political influence in Canada. You may get one or two contracts entirely through political pull, but ten or twenty is another matter. To last over the long haul, you must meet minimum quality-assurance specifications and price requirements, and keep the civil servants convinced that you can deliver what *they* want.

So keep your political powder dry. Save the MPs or senators for the crunch, or keep them in the background. Target the bureaucrats first, and concentrate your efforts on developing expertise and information to make your products and proposals acceptable on merit to the bureaucrats who make most of the buying decisions.

The Art of Selling to Government

Much of the trick in selling to government is just learning and understanding how government buys. As NRC's Glegg puts it: "You have to bring to the attention of government something that should cause it to buy. Selling always involves finding a sponsor, an individual who understands your product, and develops an attachment to it to carry it through the system."

When Glegg was with Canadian Marconi trying to sell Doppler navigation systems to the U.S. military, he practically sat on the doorstep of Wright Patterson Air Force Base until he managed to make a contact. Now every U.S. and Canadian C-130 government aircraft has one.

You sell to a person, not an agency, he stresses. That individual is staking a good piece of his reputation on you. "If you let your advocate down, you are dead"; he will become a deadly enemy. Your product must be something that fills his need. "If you do a good job, he will become a hero and you will become rich."

The Political Element

Obviously, you can sell to government at any time of the year, and should carefully cultivate civil servants and ministers on a day-to-day basis. Yet you can greatly improve your batting average by concentrating your effort at certain times of special importance to the key purchasers.

Sometimes the political nature of government puts a high value on certain programs or agencies. While these political goals can open up opportunities, usually this political interest or visibility does not affect day-to-day government operations or purchasing, although backing a loser might, in some circumstances, hurt your chances. Other political or bureaucratic events, however, are worth watching.

Budgets

One important political event astute suppliers follow is the budget which frequently announces new programs or initiatives. Since it can takes months before legislation creates new departments or programs like the Western Diversification Office or Atlantic Canada Opportunities Agency, suppliers who can provide a good or service *now*, rather than *after* the department is approved, can make inroads. That early period is often a boom time for personal service contracts, since after all, the new departments don't have any staff yet.

Budget time is also a good chance to propose a new product or service or persuade a department to include you in its plans. It also provides a chance to resubmit a project for new funding or to offer a new product to the government. Under the Tories, budget time is February of each year.

The three or four months preceding this event can be especially useful for you to voice your concerns and to make your case for expenditures or taxes that might benefit your business.

March Buys

"March Buys" provide an ideal opportunity to sell to the government. This term is used in Ottawa to include purchases made during the last few months of the government's fiscal year. The fiscal year for 1988, for example, runs until March 31,1989, and monies allocated for 1988 expenditures can be committed to buy goods and services until that final date. In addition, the month of April is regarded as a grace period, to permit Ottawa to pay for contracts negotiated during the preceding fiscal year.

As a rule, government departments or agencies who have failed to spend their allocated or estimated funds during the fiscal year will see these funds "lapse" or be lost to the agency. Since civil servants and ministers as a rule are very anxious to get at least the same level of funding for the next and later fiscal years, fiscal year-end often sees the departments go on shopping sprees. The astute seller will be ready to lend a "helping hand" to the ambitious bureaucrat with money to get rid of in a hurry.

Shuffles in the Corridor of Power

When a new department is created or a couple of old ones merged, or a more friendly minister moves in, you may improve your sales prospects. However, since in the Canadian political system the real power is held by a level of powerful permanent public servants, probably even more important than cabinet changes, the arrival or departure of mandarins in key departments or agencies can open new doors. These deputy ministers, assistant deputy ministers and directors-general, or agency or Crown corporation heads control much of the promotions, plans, decisions and budgets of their organizations.

Thus, when a department finds that it is going to spend millions of dollars on some new program or project, it can be payday for firms who helped or worked for such an individual along the way.

New Purchasing Agents

Government supply systems now show maturity, says Keith Glegg. That is, there is a relatively solid core of professional purchasing managers who stay in place over a long period of time.

Sometimes, though, they do move on. If you have been dealing with a good one, probably you can deal with him in his new job. And if you have not had a good experience with one, this may be your chance to try again with the department. Use the publications mentioned in Chapter 8 to monitor changes in departments in your area of interest.

The Cost of Selling to Ottawa

It costs money to market to Ottawa. The study by Goss, Gilroy and Associates referred to earlier, found "the more aggressive firms (generally subsidiaries of U.S. multinationals or large Canadian firms) indicated possible investments of up to seven to eight per cent of program value. However, the more frequent response was about one to three per cent of project value." That's money that you can't directly recover in most cases.

The president of one medium-sized firm told me that his company's unsuccessful bid for a $100-million federal contract cost $5 million. Soon after, though, the firm won a different contract of roughly the same size.

One of the frustrations of selling to big government is that no one is ever really, incontestably, in charge. No one person can buy your products. If no one is running the store, it's hard to show your products. Thus, GGA observes, "despite significant efforts by SSC to improve the supplier data bases (NASIS), many firms still complain that they have difficulty disseminating information concerning their products and capabilities to government departments."

It can be equally hard to find out what the feds are doing or buying: "A number of firms expressed a need for a detailed industry briefing at least one to two years prior to the procurement target date." Overall, GGA found, "heavy reliance on internal marketing/selling and the lack of reliance on formal information sources from government is perhaps one of the most surprising findings of the study."

Moreover, "firms with no representation in Ottawa" (for marketing or liaisons) "are at a very strong disadvantage." That's why you need a marketing and a bid strategy. You want to hit the right officials in the right departments at the right times.

Using Somebody Else's Experts

The federal procurement system and major suppliers to it both use retired military and ex-public servants, "ex-users who think like users", says NRC's Keith Glegg. Legally, there is nothing wrong with firms who win defence contracts hiring from their customer, the government, whatever experts they need. For a highly technical area like defence, there really are not too many places you can get a job outside the armed forces. That's also true for other areas of the government.

Ex-military and senior bureaucrats working in industry reject suggestions that members of government evaluation teams favour firms employing their former colleagues. "They help the government to form requirements," says Glegg. "Big Business knows government is a Big Business." You should, too. But how can you play in the big leagues without spending big dollars?

There are two way to access such experts, if you do not have them on staff: team up with firms who do have them, or hire consultants.

Teaming Up With Other Firms

As explained in Chapter 7, the federal procurement system really encourages you to team up with specialists or other companies to get at large dollar procurements or at subcontracts for them. Frequently departmental needs or wish-lists are identified months, even years, before the calling of tenders. Larger firms with Ottawa contacts or with a continuing government-relations research and monitoring commitment pick up these warning signals early and go to work selling their services or products or shaping the need.

Says the Osler, Hoskin and Harcourt *Commentary,* there is "no substitute for having marketing or procurement specialists in discussion with the procurement officials that will be acquiring and using the equipment." So, if at all possible, you should "retain an Ottawa-based firm of consultants. . . experienced in dealing with SSC or DND. . . who have spent many years working inside government in the procurement process." That's the ideal. It would include programs like research and development, contracting-out and related procurement opportunities. Where MCPs are involved you should "retain a firm engaged in government relations."

You should consult your lawyer or accountant too about teaming and joint venture arrangements. In some cases, you might ask them for help with proposal preparation and contract negotiation. Other items on which they can advise you are access to government information and disclosure; patents; technology transfer; contract disputes; bid protests; security clearances or offsets.

Cautions the Osler, Hoskins and Harcourt *Commentary*, though, "few suppliers and no single firm of government affairs specialists, communication specialists, accountants or lawyers will possess all of the skills necessary to successfully [look after all aspects of your] procurement contract."

Hiring Consultants

Consultants who operate at the federal or provincial level come in many forms. In general, government-relations specialists or lobbyists might diagnose your government markets, strategies, and tactics in advance, prepare booklets, proposals, articles, or talks for you or even have their personnel put your case across to the government. Usually they are ex-journalists or political staff. Procurement consultants might help you with the procurement process, including RFPs, budgets, subcontracting possibilities or outside experts, and who to go after in your particular case. As a rule, these are ex-public servants from DND, SSC, or maybe DRIE or TC. Lawyers, accountants, and public relations folk can help too.

One company's brochure says its "special services" to customers include "interpretation of Canadian national defence equipment requirements including associated budgetary considerations" and "analysis of industrial benefit requirements, technology transfer, offset considerations, intellectual property rights, trade imbalances, etc."

In fact, this year alone more than 2,000 employees working for 300 national associations in Ottawa will spend several hundreds of millions of dollars getting the views and interests of their members across to federal politicians, bureaucrats, and the media. In addition, hundreds of Ottawa-based policy consultants, lawyers, public relations people, and local officers of national firms will seek to cultivate the federal government.

Some consulting firms like Lee's Executive Consultants Limited or big CA firms like Deloitte, Haskin and Sells essentially sell information and expertise, but not influence or specific products, leaving these to you. That's the choice I've made, too.

While these firms have a stringent code of ethics which bars conflicts of interest between clients or any attempt to sell access to ministers and bureaucrats, many other consultants are less picky. Many do lobby government. In practice, too, you could find you are using a consultant who also is, has been, or soon will be, flogging your competitor's products. Sometimes it can be hard to tell the "good guys" from the "bad guys".

While lawyers, accountants, engineers, and some other professionals are licensed provincially, such professional designations in themselves do not guarantee competence in government relations.

Some consulting firms also operate on a contingency-fee basis, taking a percentage of the procurement if they land the jobs for you. Generally these should be avoided. Expect to pay for such service. Typically government-relations consultants based in Ottawa charge $5,000 or so a month as a retainer to represent you.

To choose one, check with your industry association, your big clients, other consultants with a good reputation, and read the press (see Appendix I). The Canadian Bar Association (CBA), the Canadian Institute of Chartered Accountants (CICA), the Canadian Public Relations Society (CPRS), and International Association of Business Communicators (IABC) also can provide lists of their members. So can the Ottawa telephone directory. It has a dozen pages listing management, public relations, government-relations, and other consultants.

Without endorsing any one firm, Appendix II lists a dozen consulting firms known to me, in alphabetic order. Call the better prospects, ask for brochures and lists of clients and check with them. If they won't tell you who their clients are, or at least whether or not they represent a competitor, you'd best forget them.

There is one more way of getting someone in Ottawa to keep you up-to-date on the bureaucracy and do your research. You might join—or more correctly, have an industry association join—the "Ottawa Watch" program of the Canadian Chamber of Commerce. The Chamber describes the program as a package of "custom-tailored intelligence monitoring services" which rents out several staff members to a dozen vertical industry associations, at an annual cost of about what you might pay a consultant in Ottawa per month. Ottawa Watch is headed by Sharon Irven.

Your retainer buys you advice on your government relations needs; a weekly telephone call or letter advising you of developments in your sector; a quarterly and an annual briefing by Chamber staff; a guaranteed place at the Chamber's "Ottawa Forum" breakfasts to discuss government relations with other experts; use of Chamber offices in Ottawa; and involvement in common-cause efforts in matters such as federal sales tax, and Royal Commissions. You also get an 800 telephone number to let you call in to Irven without paying for the call, and up-to-date lists of ministers and their staffs. Call her at (613) 238-4000.

Appendix I

Contact List
for National Associations

**Aerospace Industries
Association of Canada**
116 Albert Street, Suite 601
Ottawa, Ontario K1P 5G3
(613) 232-4297

Ken E. Lewis
President

William H. Reil
Chairman of the Small Business
  Committee
(416) 672-1070

**Association des commissaires
industriels du Québec**
261 rue St.-Jacques, 5è étage
Montréal, Québec H2Y 1M6
(514) 845-8275

Réal Patry
President
Sherbrooke, Québec
(819) 821-5577

Francine Lamarche
Secrétaire générale

**Canadian Advanced Technology
  Association Ottawa**
Roy Woodbridge
President
275 Slater Street
Suite 803
Ottawa, Ontario K1P 5H9
(613) 236-6550

**Canadian Association of Family
Enterprise**
10 Price Street
Toronto, Ontario M4W 1Z4
(416) 961-1673

David I. Gallagher
Managing Director
(416) 961-1673

**Canadian Association of Women
Business Owners**
69 Sherbourne St., Suite 315
Toronto, Ontario M5A 3X7
(416) 364-1223

Susan Cooke, Chairperson

**Canadian Association of Women
Executives and Entrepreneurs**
60 Dixon Avenue
Mississauga, Ontario M4L 1N6
(416) 690-5142

Sarmite D. Bulte
President

Canadian Bankers' Association
2 First Canadian Place
Exchange Tower, Suite 600
King & York Street
Toronto, Ontario M5X 1E1
(416) 362-6092

Robert M. MacIntosh
President

Joanne De Laurentiis
Vice-President, Public Affairs

Canadian Chamber of Commerce
200 Elgin Street
Ottawa, Ontario K2P 2J7
(613) 238-4000

Roger Hamel
President

Sharon Irven
Manager, Ottawa Watch Program

Roger Stanion
Senior Vice-President

David Gibson
Senior Vice-President
  Government Relations

Canadian Export Association
99 Bank Street, Suite 250
Ottawa, Ontario K1P 6B9
(613) 238-8888

Frank Petrie
President

Robert Noble
Government Relations

**Canadian Federation of
Independent Business (CFIB)**
4141 Yonge Street
Willowdale, Ontario M2P 2A6
(416) 222-8022

John Bulloch
President

Brian Gray
Vice-President and Executive
  Director

Jim Bennett
Vice-President, Legislative
  Affairs

Bill Parsons
Director, National Affairs

Richard Graham
National Affairs Officer

Oksana Exell
Director, Provincial Affairs
  British Columbia/Yukon
(604) 684-5325

Doug Wright
Director, Provincial Affairs
  Alberta
(403) 421-4253

Garth Whyte
Director, Provincial Affairs
  Saskatchewan/Manitoba
(306) 757-0000

Judith André
Director, Provincial Affairs
  Ontario
(416) 222-8022

Pierre Lauzier
Executive Director, Québec
(514) 842-4321

Peter O'Brien
Director, Provincial Affairs
  Atlantic Canada
(902) 423-7813

**Canadian Federation of
Labour**
107 Sparks St., Suite 300
Ottawa, Ontario K1P 5B5
(613) 234-4141

Jim McCambly
President

Austin Thorne
Secretary-Treasurer

**Canadian Industrial Benefits
Association**
c/o Litton Systems
730—220 Laurier Avenue W.
Ottawa, Ontario K1P 5Z9

Bob Brown

**Canadian Manufacturers'
Association**
One Yonge Street
Toronto, Ontario M5E 1J9
(416) 363-7261

Laurence Thibault
President & Executive Director

Eric G. Owen
Manager, Taxation & Financial Policy

**Canadian Organization of
Small Business (COSB)**
Roy Shannon
Chairman of the Board
2725—12th Street N.E.
Suite 201
Calgary, Alberta T2E 7J2
(403) 250-7144

Dan L. Horigan
President
(403) 423-2672

Don Eastcott
Managing Director & Corporate
  Secretary
10301—108th Street
Suite 103
Edmonton, Alberta T5J 1L7
(403) 423-2672

Geoffrey Hale
Vice-President
150 Consumers Road, Suite 501
Willowdale, Ontario M2J 1P9
(416) 492-3223

**Canadian Venture Capital
Association**
Archie MacKinnon
(403) 231-8535

**Commercial Travellers'
Association of Canada**
365 Bloor Street E., Suite 1002
Toronto, Ontario M4W 3L4
(416) 924-7724

Terry Ruffell
General Manager

**Conseil économique du
Nouveau-Brunswick**
236, rue St. George, Suite 314
Moncton, N.B. E1C 1W1

Rino Volpe
President

**Federation of Canadian
Municipalities**
John Hastings
(613) 237-5221

**Groupement québecois
d'Entreprises**
99 rue Cormie
Drummondville, Québec
J2C 2M5
(819) 477-7535

Paul-Henri Fillion
Président (Chairman)

Jacques Gauvin
Président
Sherbrooke, Québec
(819) 562-3803

Henri Bouchard
Vice-Président

Marcel Patenaud
Vice-Président

François Vachon
Vice-Président

René Bellegarde
Treasurer

Jean-Marie Gagnon
Secretary

Benoit Pare
Director of Communications

**Industrial Developers
Association of Canada**
1645 Pierre Place
Mississauga, Ontario L5J 3G8
(416) 822-8771

Marilyn Austin
Executive Director

Garry Gregory
President (Winnipeg)

Paul Diagle
First Vice-President (Moncton)

**International Council for Small
Business (Canada)**
c/o Ryerson Polytechnical Institute
350 Victoria Street, Suite 725
Toronto, Ontario M5B 2K3

Prof. Raymond Kao
(416) 979-5000

Prof. Randy Vandermark
British Columbia
Institute of Technology
(604) 434-5734

Douglas Lajeunesse
President of ICSB (Canada)

Robert Wyckham
Chairman of the 1987 ICSB World
   Conference
(604) 291-4186

Retail Council of Canada
210 Dundas St. West, Suite 600
Toronto, Ontario M5G 2E8
(416) 598-4684

Alasdair J. McKichan
President

Gerald Doucet
Senior Vice-President

Pat Porth
Director/Specialist,
   Divisions and Projects

Appendix II

Ottawa Consulting Firms

Arthur Anderson and Co.
155 Queen Street
Ottawa, Ontario K1P 6E5
(613) 238-8917

CFN Consultants
100 Sparks Street, Suite 400
Ottawa, Ontario K1P 5B7
(613) 238-2385

**Coopers and Lybrand
Consulting Group**
55 Metcalfe Street, 12th Floor
Ottawa, Ontario K1P 6N4
(613) 237-3702

Deloitte, Haskins and Sells
99 Bank Street, Suite 630
Ottawa, Ontario K1P 6B9
(613) 563-0321

Executive Consultants Limited
155 Queen Street
Ottawa, Ontario K1P 6L1
(613) 237-7455

Foottit-Mitchell & Associates
77 Metcalfe Street
Suite 900
Ottawa, Ontario K1P 5L6
(613) 563-0236

**Government Consultants
International**
50 O'Connor Street
Ottawa, Ontario K1P 6L2
(613) 236-7001

Public Affairs International
55 Metcalfe Street
Ottawa, Ontario K1P 6N4
(613) 238-4371

Thom, Malcolm & Associates Inc.
77 Metcalfe Street, Suite 504
Ottawa, Ontario K2P 5L6
(613) 594-3469

Price Waterhouse
180 Elgin Street
Ottawa, Ontario K2P 2J4
(613) 238-8200

**Touche Ross Management
Consultants**
90 Sparks Street
Ottawa, Ontario K1A 1E1
(613) 236-2442

Price Waterhouse
180 Elgin Street
Ottawa, Ontario K2P 2J4
(613) 238-8200

**Stevenson Kellogg Ernst and
Whinney**
90 Sparks Street
Ottawa, Ontario K1P 5T8
(613) 238-6512

List of Acronyms

A & E	Architectural and Engineering
ACCORD	Administration and Control of Contracts and Regional Data
ACOA	Atlantic Canada Opportunities Agency
AGC	Agriculture Canada
AGO	Auditor General's Office
AMES	Aerospace, Marine and Electronics Systems Directorate
APPS	Annual Procurement Planning Strategy
AQUAP	Allied Quality Assurance Publications
ASB	Audit Services Bureau
BMC	Bureau of Management Consulting
BML	Bidders Mailing List (U.S.)
BOSS	Business Opportunities Sourcing System
CAF	Canadian Armed Forces
CAN-OLE	Canadian On-Line Enquiry System
CASP	Canadian Air System Plan
CBA	Canadian Bar Association
CCC	Canadian Commercial Corporation
CGPC	Canadian Government Publishing Centre
CGPS	Canadian Government Printing Services
CGSB	Canadian General Standards Board
CICA	Canadian Institute of Chartered Accountants
CIDA	Canadian International Development Agency
CISTI	Canadian Institute for Scientific and Technical Information
CPRS	Canadian Public Relations Society
CSA	Canadian Standards Association
CSC	Correctional Service Canada
CSD	Communications Services Directorate
CVA	Canadian Value Added
DCASMA	Defense Contract Administration Service Management Area (U.S.)
DDSA	Canada-U.S. Defence Development Sharing Agreement
DDSS	Director, Defence Sales Support
DEMPS	Director, Engineering and Maintenance Planning and Standardization
DGQA	Director, General Quality Assurance

DINA	Department of Indian and Northern Affairs
DIPP	Defence Industry Productivity Program
DIST	Department of Industry, Science and Technology (formerly DRIE and MOSST)
DND	Department of National Defence
DOC	Department of Communications
DOD	Department of Defense (U.S.)
DPB	Defence Programs Bureau (External Affairs)
DPSA	Canada-U.S. Defence Production Sharing Agreement
DRIE	Department of Regional Industrial Expansion
EAC	External Affairs Canada
EC	Environment Canada
EDC	Export Development Corporation
EDP	Electronic Data Processing
EIB	Electronics Industrial Benefits
EMR	Department of Energy, Mines and Resources
F & O	Fisheries and Oceans
FAA	Financial Administration Act
FARS	Federal Acquisition Regulations (U.S.)
FBDB	Federal Business Development Bank
G & A	General and Administrative
GATT	General Agreement on Trade and Tariffs
GCR	Government Contract Regulations
GPO	Government Printing Office (U.S.)
GSIN	Goods and Services Identification Number
GTA	Government Telecommunications Agency
IABC	International Association of Business Communicators
ICPD	Industrial and Commercial Products Directorate
IRAP	Industrial Research Assistance Program
ITT	Invitation to Tender
LDV	Lower Dollar Value
MCP	Major Crown Projects
MOSST	Ministry of State for Science and Technology
MOU	Memorandum of Understanding
NASIS	National Automated Sourcing Information System
NCC	National Capital Commission
NGO	Non-Governmental Organization
NISO	National Individual Standing Offer
NMSO	National Master Standing
NRC	National Research Council

OASIS	Office Automation, Services and Systems
P & A	Price and Availability
PASS	Procurement and Acquisition Support System Canada
PASS	Procurement Automated Source System (U.S.)
PCO	Privy Council Office
PEMD	Program for Export Market Development
PMO	Prime Minister's Office
PO	Purchase Order
POC	Procurement Outlook Conferences
PRC	Procurement Review Committee
PSC	Public Service Commission
PWC	Public Works Canada
R & O	Repair and Overhaul
R & D	Research and Development
RAMP	Radar Airport Modernization Program
RCMP	Royal Canadian Mounted Police
RFP	Request for Proposals
RFQ	Request for Quotation
RISO	Regional Individual Standing Offer
RMSO	Regional Master Standing Offer
SBO	Small Business Office (DIST)
SO	Standing Offer
SOS	Secretary of State
SOW	Statement of Work
SPSD	Science and Professional Services Directorate
SSC	Supply and Services Canada
T-Buy	Telephone-Buy
TB	Treasury Board
TC	Transport Canada
UP	Unsolicited Proposal
USGPO	United States Government Printing Office
WDO	Western Diversification Office
WIN	World Information Network (EAC)

Sample Government Forms

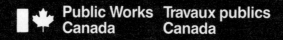

INVITATION TO TENDER

SEALED TENDERS for the projects or services listed below, addressed to the Regional Manager, Contract Policy and Administration, Public Works Canada, National Capital Region, 140 Promenade du portage, Phase IV, Hull, Quebec (mailing address) Ottawa, Ontario, K1A 0M3, will be received until 15:00 on the specified closing date. Tender documents can be obtained through the Plan Distribution Office, same address as above, at telephone number 997-5667, on payment of the applicable deposit.

No. 702761 — Fire Alarm Replacement, Brooke Claxton Building, Tunney's Pasture, Ottawa, Ontario.

Tender documents may also be seen at the Construction Association offices in Ottawa, Hull, Montreal and Toronto.

Closing Date: **Tuesday, 6 September 1988**
Deposit: **$50.00**

INSTRUCTIONS

Deposits for plans and specifications must be made to the order of the Receiver General for Canada and will be released on return of the documents in good condition within one month from the date of tender opening.

The lowest or any tender not necessarily accepted.

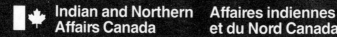

INVITATION TO TENDER

SEALED TENDERS for the project or service listed below, addressed to:
Department of Indian & Northern Affairs Canada
25 St. Clair Ave. East
5th floor
Toronto, Ontario
M4T 1M2

will be received until 14:00 hours local time on the specified closing date.
Tender documents can be obtained from the Ontario Regional Office, same address as above.

Displayed at Toronto Construction Association & Townend, Stefura, Baleshta and Nicholls, 255 Larch Street, Sudbury, Ontario Contact No. 1631-21-88/89 OR — 42774

Minor renovations to St. Anne's School, Fort Albany Indian Reserve No. 67 James Bay District.

Closing Date: Thursday, September 1, 1988, 14:00 local time

Deposit: $50.00

The lowest or any tender not necessarily accepted.

Technical enquiries: (705) 675-3383 Russell Price

General enquiries: (416) 973-1418 Gall Lee

Canadä

Supply and Services   Approvisionnements et Services
Canada   Canada

Atlantic Region Supply Centre
2 Morris Drive
Burnside Industrial Park
Dartmouth, Nova Scotia
B3B 1S6

REQUEST FOR PROPOSAL
DEMANDE DE PROPOSITION

Proposal to: Supply and Services Canada

We hereby offer to sell to Her Majesty the Queen in right of Canada, in accordance with the terms and conditions set out herein, referred to herein or attached hereto, the service(s) referred to herein and on any attached sheets at the price(s) set out therefor.

Proposition aux: Approvisionnements et Services Canada

Nous offrons par la présente de vendre à Sa Majesté la Reine du chef du Canada, aux conditions énoncées ou incluses par référence dans la présente et aux annexes ci-jointes, les services énumérés ici et sur toute feuille ci-annexée, au(x) prix indiqué(s).

Country of Foreign Content Pays d'origine des éléments étrangers	Value of Foreign Content Valeur des éléments étrangers	
	$	CDN

Solicitation closes - L'invitation prend fin

at-à 1400 AST

on-le 08 Jan 1988

SSC file No. - N° de référence d'ASC

USC87-U0392-(-12) /a

Please ensure this area appears in window of return envelope
S'assurer que cette partie figure dans la fenêtre de l'enveloppe-réponse

Canada

	Page 1 of 9 de

Date of Solicitation - Date de l'invitation

09 Dec 1987

Address enquiries to: - Adresser toute demande de renseignements à:

Boris Tsinman

Area code code régional	Telephone No. N° de téléphone	Extension Poste	Telex No. N° de télex
902	426-8550		01931554

Destination
ENERGY MINES & RESOURCES
BEDFORD INSTITUTE OF OCEANOGRAPHY
P.O. BOX 1006
DARTMOUTH, N.S.
ATTN: M.E. BEST

Instructions: (Additional instructions appear on reverse side).

Municipal taxes are not applicable, for provincial taxes, see reverse.

Unless otherwise specified herein by the Crown, all prices quoted are to be net prices in Canadian funds including Canadian customs duties and excise taxes, federal sales tax and are to be F.O.B. including all delivery charges to the destination(s) as indicated.

Instructions: (On trouvera de plus amples instructions au verso).

Les taxes municipales ne s'appliquent pas, voir au verso pour les taxes provinciales.

Sauf indication contraire, énoncée par la Couronne, dans les présentes, tous les prix indiqués sont des prix nets, en dollars canadiens, comprenant les droits de douane canadiens, la taxe d'accise, la taxe fédérale de vente et doivent être F.A.B., y compris tous frais de livraison à la (aux) destination(e) indiqué(s).

Delivery required - Livraison exigée	Delivery offered - Livraison proposée

Vendor Name and Address - Raison sociale et adresse du fournisseur

Name and title of person authorized to sign on behalf of vendor(type or print)
Nom et titre de la personne autorisée à signer au nom du fournisseur
(caractère d'impression)

Signature   Date

Supply and Services   Approvisionnements et Services
Canada   Canada

CONTINUATION - SUITE

Contract No. - N° du contract	SSC file No. - N° de référence d'ASC
	OSC87-U03y2-(012) /A

Biostratigraphic (palynological) studies of the
Scotian Shelf and Grand Banks - 2.

TITLE: BIOSTRATIGRAPHIC (PALYNOLOGICAL)
STUDIES OF THE SCOTIAN SHELF AND GRAND BANKS
-2

As opposed to an Invitation to Tender, this is a
request (commonly referred to as a Request for
Proposal (RFP)) that proposals be developed and
submitted to the Minister of Supply and Services
setting out the alternative means by which
several technical, performance, time and other
goals and objectives may be best met, having
regard to stated mandatory requirements. The
Minister will consider entering into a contract
for the implementation of the most acceptable
proposal which will be determined having regard
to the evaluation factors set out in this RFP.
In addition, the acceptability of the contract
terms and conditions upon which the respondent
would be prepared to undertake the implementation
of the proposal will be measured against the
contract terms and conditions set forth in this
RFP.

STATEMENT OF REQUIREMENT:
The Work shall be performed in accordance with
Appendix "A" attached.

DELIVERY SCHEDULE:
(SEE APPENDIX "A" REPORTS)

CONFIRMATION OF TELEGRAPHIC BIDS AND/OR DESCRIPTIVE
LITERATURE MUST BE RECEIVED WITHIN 5 DAYS OF BID
CLOSING DATE.

CORPORATE NAME:

The proposal shall contain a statement of the name
and laws under which the company was legally
incorporated and the percentage of Canadian
Ownership.

GENERAL CONDITIONS:
In lieu of the General Conditions mentioned on the
reverse side of page 1, DSS General Conditions 9224,
a copy of which the proposer hereby acknowledges to
have received and read, shall form part of and be
incorporated into the proposed contract as set out
in full herein, and the rights and obligations of
the Parties shall be interpreted in accordance with
and governed by the said General Conditions.

TERMS AND CONDITIONS:
Note regarding acceptance of electronically transmitted proposals:

In order to avoid costly misunderstandings, the
following information from the back of page 1 is
repeated:

Canada

Supply and Services   Approvisionnements et Services
Canada   Canada

Contract No. - N° du contrat

SSC file No. - N° de référence d'ASC
0SC87-00392-(012) /A

Page 3 of 9
de

CONTINUATION - SUITE

"Proposals submitted by electronic means are acceptable provided that they are received prior to the time specified for closing of proposals and contain a proposal reference number and closing date. Electronically transmitted proposals will constitute your formal proposal. Such proposals must be comprehensive and in sufficient detail so as to permit complete evaluation in accordance with the criteria set out herein. The Minister may consider entering into contract without negotiation on the basis of such electronically transmitted proposal."

ADDITIONAL TERMS AND CONDITIONS:
In case of conflict between Additional Terms and Conditions and Instructions on the reverse of Page 1, these Additional Terms and Conditions take precedence.

i) There will be no direct payment by the Crown for preparation and submission of proposals in response to this Request for Proposal.

ii) If a contract is awarded as a result of this request, the Crown reserves the right to:

a. Accept a proposal without discussion; therefore proposals should be submitted on the most favourable terms from a price and technical standpoint which the Offerer can submit to the government.

b) Negotiate changes in the technical content of the most satisfactory proposal, and,

c) Negotiate the costs of the most satisfactory proposal to determine fair and reasonable costs to the Crown generally in accordance with Contract Cost Principles DSS 1031-1.

d) Reject any or all proposals received in response to this RFP,

e) Cancel and or re-issue this requirement at any time,

f) Award one or more contracts, and

g) Verify any or all information provided by the bidder with respect to this requirement.

iii) Follow-on work might result from this requirement on a sole source basis.

iv) Any proposal must remain open for acceptance for a period of not less than 90 calendar days. An expiry date, prior to which the government must accept your proposal is only to be stipulated where the offerer has valid reasons for doing so.

v) In accordance with the Contracting Out Policy of Treasury Board, in the event that suitable industrial sources are acceptable, they will be given preference over universities and non-profit insitutions.

vi) Capability Survey - If any offer submitted in response to this solicitation is favourably considered, a survey team may

Canada

DSS-MAS 9400-22 (10/86)

Supply and Services Approvisionnements et Services
Canada Canada

CONTINUATION - SUITE

Contract No. - N° du contrat

SSC file No. - N° de référence d'ASC
OSC87-00392-(012) /A

Page 4 of 9
de

contact your facility to determine your technical and financial ability to perform. If so, current financial statements and other pertinent data should be available at that time, if not already on file with Supply and Services Canada.

vii) Inspection and Acceptance: The work performed under any contract(s) resulting from this RFP shall be subject to inspection and acceptance by the Project/ Scientific Authority to be designated in such contract.

Please note clause entitled "Special Conditions" which sets out conditions relating to:

i) Validation of Respondent Proposal
ii) Time Extension to Closing Date

PROPOSAL REQUIREMENTS:

You are invited to submit proposals on the work specified under "TERMS OF REFERENCE". Please submit TWO(2) copies of a Technical, Managerial and Financial Proposal to Supply and Services Canada, Regional Supply Office, 2 Morris Drive, Dartmouth, Nova Scotia, B3B 1S6.

NOTE: If your proposal is too large to return in the bid return envelope enclosed, you "MUST" ensure that the solicitation closing date and time, and the Supply and Services File Number is clearly marked on the outside of your envelope.

SPECIAL CONDITIONS:
i) VALIDATION OF RESPONDENT PROPOSALS:

The following is to read as an addition to Section 3 on the reverse of Page 1.

In instances where Cancellation Time Stamps or receipts show only the date and not both date and time, the bid shall be assessed as having been mailed on the date shown at the same time of day and time zone as that designated for the closing of bids for the solicitation. Canada Post Corporation Cancellation Time Stamps or official receipts showing only a time but no date will not constitute acceptable evidence.

Certificates of mailing, affidavits and other such statements, whether sworn to or not, shall not constitute acceptable evidence of timely mailing.

Bidders are cautioned that the use of private couriers for timely delivery of bids is entirely at their own risk.

Bidders may wish to advise the Contracting Officer (designated herein) of timely mailing prior to closing time and date, to ensure consideration in the event their proposal is delayed by mail.

ii) TIME EXTENSIONS:

A request for Time extension to the closing date will be considered provided it is received in writing by the Contracting Officer (designated herein) at least five

CONTINUATION - SUITE

working days before closing date shown herein. The request, if granted, will be communicated to all invited bidders at least three working days before closing, by telex, showing revised closing date.

The request, if rejected, will be directed to the originator, also by telex, at least three working days before closing.

EVALUATION CRITERIA AND RELATIVE WEIGHTS:
Proposals will be evaluated using "best value" (scientific merit, price and possible socio-economic factors) criteria rather than "scientific merit" or "price" only. The "best value" selection will be assessed utilizing the following criteria. Bidders are advised to address each of these criteria:

1. TECHNICAL PROPOSAL (40 POINTS)
2. MANAGERIAL (30 POINTS)
3. COMPANY EXPERIENCE (28 POINTS)
4. FINANCIAL (NO POINT ALLOCATION)

NOTE TO BIDDERS:

Proposals shall be signed.

Bidders are advised to address the proposal in sufficient depth to provide a "Cross Reference" index, identifying paragraphs and page numbers corresponding to each of the Evaluation Criteria.

In order to be considered technically acceptable, a proposal must score at least

70% of the total points of each of the evaluation criteria. Where two or more acceptable proposals are received, socio-economic factors may be used to make the final decision.

Neither the qualifying proposal which scores the highest number of rating points nor the one which contains the lowest cost estimate will necessarily be accepted. The selection of the Contractor will be made on the basis of the best overall value to the Crown in terms of technical merit and cost. Therefore, particular attention will be paid to determine whether the acceptance of a proposal merits the payment of a premium. This determination will be based on a "dollar per point evaluation" (bid price divided by rating points).

After the proposal closing date, no amendment to the proposal will be accepted. However, during the evaluation, representatives of ENERGY MINES & RESOURCES and Supply and Services Canada may, at their discretion, conduct interviews with bidders to obtain clarification.

For the prupose of evaluating your proposal, you agree that representatives of the Crown may interview key personnel and conduct a survey of your facilities, your technical abilities and your financial status, to determine if they would be adequate for the proper performance of the proposed contract. You agree to make your facilities available for this purpose.

(This document continues for four more pages.)

Canada

INDEX